EPIDURAL AND SPINAL
BLOCKADE
IN
OBSTETRICS

*This book is dedicated to the memory of
Josephine Ward
a superlative midwife who made epidural analgesia for normal
labour entirely superfluous.*

EPIDURAL AND SPINAL BLOCKADE IN OBSTETRICS

edited by

Felicity Reynolds

Baillière Tindall
London Philadelphia Toronto
Sydney Tokyo

Baillière Tindall
W. B. Saunders

24–28 Oval Road
London NW1 7DX

The Curtis Center
Independence Square West
Philadelphia, PA 19106–3399, USA

1 Goldthorne Avenue
Toronto, Ontario M8Z 5T9, Canada

Harcourt Brace Jovanovich (Australia) Pty Limited
32 35 Smidmore Street
Marrickville, NSW 2204, Australia

Harcourt Brace Jovanovich Japan Inc.
Ichibancho Central Building, 22–1 Ichibancho
Chiyoda-ku, Tokyo 102, Japan

First published 1990

British Library Cataloguing in Publication Data is available

ISBN 0–7020–1401–X

Typeset by Photo·graphics, Honiton, Devon
and printed in Great Britain at the University Press, Cambridge.

Contents

Contributors

P. W. Bailey, Consultant Anaesthetist, Doncaster Royal Infirmary, Thorne Road, Doncaster, DN2 5LT.

L. E. S. Carrie, Consultant Anaesthetist, John Radcliffe Maternity Hospital, Headington, Oxford, OX3 9DU.

D. W. L. Davies, Senior Registrar, University College Hospital, London.

N. J. Dennis, Registrar, Liverpool Maternity Hospital, Oxford Street, Liverpool 3.

A. Doughty, Avondale, 10 River Avenue, Thames Ditton, Surrey, KT7 0RS.

D. A. Dutton, Consultant Anaesthetist, Victoria Infirmary, Langside Road, Glasgow, G42 9TY.

D. G. Gaylard, Consultant Anaesthetist, Royal Devon and Exeter Hospital, Barrack Road, Exeter, EX2 5DW.

P. A. Gaynor, Consultant Anaesthetist, Thornthrift, Clay Lane, South Nutfield, Surrey, RH1 4EG.

N. C. Gleeson, Assistant Master, Rotunda Hospital, Parnell Street, Dublin 1, Ireland.

A. P. Griffith, Senior Registrar in Anaesthetics, Rotunda Hospital, Parnell Street, Dublin 1, Ireland.

B. B. Gutsche, Professor of Anaesthesia, Obstetrics and Gynecology, University Pennsylvania Hospital, 3400 Spruce Street, Philadelphia, Pennsylvania, 19104 USA.

S. Harris, Consultant Anaesthetist, Queen Elizabeth Hospital, Gayton Road, Kings Lynn, Norfolk, PE30 4ET.

P. Howell, Senior Registrar, Charing Cross Hospital, Fulham Palace Road, London, W6.

J. E. Howie, Consultant Anaesthetist, Victoria Infirmary, Langside Road, Glasgow, G42 9TY.

K. Jani, Consultant Anaesthetist, The Lister Hospital, Stevenage, Hertfordshire.

M. J. Jordan, Consultant Anaesthetist, St Bartholomew's Hospital, West Smithfield, London, EC1.

R. S. Laishley, Senior Registrar, St Thomas' Hospital, Lambeth Palace Road, London, SE1 7EH.

G. Lyons, Consultant Anaesthetist, St James' Hospital, Becket Street, Leeds, LS9 7TF.

R. Macdonald, Consultant Anaesthetist, St James's University Hospital, Beckett Street, Leeds, LS9 7TF.

B. McEvedy, Consultant Anaesthetist, Raigmore Hospital, Inverness.

E. M. McGrady, Consultant Anaesthetist, Monklands District General Hospital, Lanarkshire.

C. S. Martin, Registrar, Western Infirmary, Dumbarton Road, Glasgow, G11 6NT.

S. Miller, *Formerly* Paediatric S.H.O., Queen Elizabeth Hospital, Gayton Road, Kings Lynn, Norfolk, PE30 4ET.

J. K. Moore, Consultant Anaesthetist, Arrowe Park Hospital, Wirral, Merseyside, L49 5LN.

B. M. Morgan, Senior Lecturer in Obstetrics, Queen Charlotte's Hospital, Goldhawk Road, London, W6 0XG.

J. S. Naulty, Director, Obstetric Anaesthesia, George Washington University Hospital, Washington DC, USA.

G. O'Sullivan, Consultant Anaesthetist, St Thomas' Hospital, Lambeth Palace Road, London SE1 7EH.

J. A. Patrick, Senior Registrar, St Thomas' Hospital, Lambeth Palace Road, London, SE1 7EH.

F. Reynolds, Reader in Pharmacology Applied to Anaesthetics, Honorary Consultant Anaesthetist, St Thomas' Hospital, Lambeth Palace Road, London, SE1 7EH.

I. F. Russell, Consultant Anaesthetist, Hull Royal Infirmary, Anlaby Road, Hull, HU3 2JZ.

P. Tan, Charing Cross Hospital, Fulham Palace Road, London, W6.

J. Thorburn, Consultant Anaesthetist, The Queen Mother's Hospital, Yorkhill, Glasgow, G3 8SH.

M. Wrigley, Senior Registrar, The Middlesex Hospital, Mortimer Street, London, W6.

Y. S. L. Yoon, *Formerly* Obstetric S.H.O., St Thomas' Hospital, Lambeth Palace Road, London, SE1 7EH.

Preface

In 1975 Andrew Doughty wrote of the pursuit of perfection in lumbar epidural analgesia (Anaesthesia, 30, 741). This book attempts to document the efforts that have been made in the past 10 years in pursuit of that elusive goal and to acknowledge also the expanding use of spinal anaesthesia in obstetrics.

In the years 1971 and 1979, two symposia on epidural analgesia in obstetrics were held. Following each, the proceedings were published under the editorship of Andrew Doughty. It was thought that the most recent decade had also yielded its share of advances and in September 1989 at a meeting of the Obstetric Anaesthetists' Association at the University of Warwick a third symposium on epidural and spinal blockade in obstetrics was held. Dr Doughty suggested I might take on the editorship of the proceedings and I am grateful to the Obstetric Anaesthetists' Association for their support in this venture.

In planning the symposium we aimed to include subjects of topical interest and areas of research particular to the past decade. We were pleased that two distinguished American colleagues agreed to contribute a transatlantic element to the proceedings. Contributors were invited not only to speak but also to provide a chapter reviewing their subject and prepared explicitly for the written word. The content is therefore I hope, of more value to the reader than would be a simple verbatim publication of the proceedings. We also felt that a sprinkling of free papers would be welcome, so abstracts were invited to fit in with the planned programme. I was pleased to receive some for every topic selected and these have been included as "Current Research". I therefore hope the reader will forgive a modicum of heterogeneity among the chapters.

Discussion periods can enliven meetings and reveal fascinating insights into clinical practice of a character not usually mentioned in formal texts. They can also bring light relief to a book of this kind. To this end a professional audio technician was employed to record the proceedings but regrettably much of the discussion was inaudible when the tapes came to be transcribed. If any readers find that their contributions to the discussion do not appear in print, I can only apologize.

I hope this book will be of value to anaesthetists in training and to obstetric anaesthetists, to midwives and to obstetricians, because it combines within a small compass both reviews and discussions of areas that are of particular concern to all those involved with regional analgesia in obstetrics. The introductory section shows how our understanding of anatomy can be improved, for example, by modern imaging techniques and how indications and contra-indications have evolved in recent years. The section on management discusses the ever controversial subjects of test doses and the second stage, and also reflects the increasing use of infusions for pain relief in labour. Section III is devoted to risks and how to avoid them and Section IV to Caesarean section, a field that has seen a big expansion in regional anaesthesia in the last decade. The next section is devoted to another growth subject – the use of spinal opioids, while the final section addresses the concerns of the recipients, both mother and baby, the former being vocal and the latter as the object of research.

Finally I would like to thank my colleagues in the working group who helped to plan the programme (Rosemary Macdonald, Len Carrie and Ajeet Singh, who also ably organized the administrative and social side of the meeting), Margaret Macdonald of Baillière Tindall for accepting the task of publishing the text, Claire Millard for skillfully extricating most of the discussion from the tapes, Andrew Doughty for helping edit them, all the contributors for producing their chapters efficiently and promptly and my husband Geoffrey Spencer for waiting for his supper until after 9 pm on countless evenings.

Felicity Reynolds

SECTION I

Introduction

1

The lumbar epidural region: anatomy and approach

ALICE GAYNOR

HISTORICAL PERSPECTIVE

The development of epidural analgesia in the early part of this century resulted from the need to relieve the pain of labour. Kreis (1900), an obstetrician in Basel, was the first to report the use of cocaine in the subarachnoid space for the relief of labour pain. Sicard (1901) and Cathelin (1901) working independently in Paris popularized caudal epidural blockade for surgery. Stoeckel (1909), a German gynaecologist, adapted the technique for relief of labour pain. A few years later the neuroradiologist Sicard developed a safe technique for lumbar epidurography, and first described identification of the epidural space by loss of resistance to fluid injection (Sicard and Forestier, 1921). Pagés (1921) discerned the possibility of producing anaesthesia by this approach, and demonstrated that it had greater application than the caudal route. Janzen (1926), a German neurologist, accidentally discovered that there was a negative pressure in the epidural space while trying to measure the pressure in the subarachnoid space. This inspired the development and use of a variety of indicators using this apparent negative pressure. Aburel, a Rumanian obstetrician working in Paris between 1927 and 1933, postulated that continuous local anaesthesia in labour could only be achieved via the lumbar and sacral routes to the epidural space, because of the dual pathways by which labour pain is transmitted (Aburel, 1931). Dogliotti (1933) popularized the technique of loss of resistance to continued pressure applied while the needle passed through the ligaments and also described both midline and paramedian approaches.

The early workers in North America were ignorant of the research and progress in regional analgesia in Europe. In 1927 Cleland, a Canadian obstetrician, observed that a caudal block only produced perineal anaesthesia. Six years later he reported relieving uterine pain by a series of lower thoracic paravertebral injections (Cleland, 1933). During the Second World War, Hingson (an anaesthesiologist) and Edwards (an obstetrician) were stationed at a naval hospital in New York. They needed a method of analgesia that would quieten the mothers in labour, who were disturbing the adjacent wards full of badly burnt seamen. They described a technique of continuous caudal analgesia through a malleable needle (Hingson and Edwards, 1942), a method which they popularized throughout North America. Manalan developed the concept of inserting a ureteric silk catheter through the needle into the caudal epidural space, after which the needle could safely be removed (Manalan, 1942). Not only did Tuohy (1945) extend this technique by using it for continuous spinal anaesthesia, but he also invented a special needle with a curved tip for easier passage of the catheter.

Flowers et al (1949) and Curbelo (1949) adapted this technique for the passage of a ureteric catheter into the lumbar epidural space, although unsatisfactory perineal analgesia was frequently reported. Cleland (1952) suggested placing one catheter at the thoracolumbar level for first-stage pain, and a second through the sacral hiatus for second-stage pain. In this way, he was able to use the minimum dosage of local anaesthetic to maximum effect.

To many anaesthetists, however, this technique seemed unacceptably complicated, and caudal analgesia remained the method of choice until continuous lumbar epidural block with a single catheter gradually became established as the standard method of obstetric analgesia.

ANATOMY OF THE EPIDURAL REGION

Controversy still remains over the anatomy of the epidural region, despite the growing practice of lumbar epidural analgesia over the last thirty years. The many recent anaesthetic texts fail to describe adequately the topography of the epidural region, although this has long been available in standard anatomy publications.

In the living subject, the dural sac is apposed to the walls of the vertebral canal or the contents of the epidural region, being supported by the pressure of the cerebrospinal fluid within. A space can only be created by pushing the dura mater away from the vertebral canal or the contents of the epidural region by the injection of liquid or air; thus, the epidural space is a *potential* space (Bromage, 1978).

The *vertebral canal* varies in shape, being oval in the cervical and thoracic regions, becoming triangular in the lumbar region (Elsenstein, 1980) with the apex forming a posterior midline sulcus between two separate ligamenta flava. It is bordered posteriorly by the laminae and the ligamenta flava, laterally by the pedicles and the intervertebral foramina and anteriorly by the posterior longitudinal ligament.

The *ligamentum flavum* is seldom a continuous tissue spanning the interlaminar space. In most cases the two bands of ligamenta flava lie at an angle of less than 90° to each other with a discrete gap between the medial borders (Figures 1, 2) which allows the passage of small veins, but is otherwise filled with fat (Zarzur, 1984; Parkin and Harrison, 1985; Gaynor, 1986). Computerized tomography (Harrison, 1984, 1986) has shown that the ligamenta flava are 3 mm thick, which is in accord with other anatomical studies, where the thickness varied from 2 mm to 5 mm. This differs markedly from texts of obstetric anaesthesia, where the ligamenta flava have been described as up to 10 mm thick (Crawford, 1978; Moir, 1980).

The fibres of the ligamenta flava, almost vertical in direction, are attached to the lower half of the anterior surface of the lamina above, and to the posterior surface and upper margin of the lamina below. The lateral border extends as far as the intervertebral foramen, where it joins the capsule of the articular processes (Zarzur, 1984).

The *interspinous ligament* runs obliquely between adjoining spinous processes and is continuous posteriorly with the tough supraspinous ligament (Harrison, 1984; Gaynor, 1986). Examination of a transverse section from the mid-lumbar region shows that it is narrow posteriorly and appears to splay out anteriorly from the sagittal plane to become continuous with the posterior fibres of the ligamenta flava, forming the vertex of a midline sulcus (Figure 2).

The *dural sac* is cylindrical throughout its length with slight lower cervical and lower thoracic enlargements. It is formed of fibrous tissue of varying thickness, and is lined within by the thin arachnoid mater. The tip of the spinal cord, the conus medullaris, usually lies at the level of the first lumbar interspace, whereas the dural sac terminates in adult life at the lower border of the second sacral vertebra.

The *subarachnoid space* lies between the pia mater and the arachnoid mater. Between the first lumbar and second sacral vertebrae the spinal nerve roots lie closely packed within the dural sac (Figure 2), bathed in cerebrospinal fluid.

The *subdural space* between the dura and arachnoid mater is a potential space containing a film of serous fluid between the surfaces of the opposed membranes. It does not communicate directly with the subarachnoid space, but continues a short distance along the nerve roots, possibly communicating with lymph spaces and venous channels (Williams and Warwick, 1989).

Contents of the epidural region

The *internal vertebral venous plexus* drains the vertebrae, the spinal cord and meninges. This valveless plexus (Batson, 1957) is a double anterior system of longitudinal veins, the antero-internal and antero-external veins, which run together at the anterolateral border of the vertebral canal, except at the intervertebral foramen where they divide to allow the nerve root to pass through (Renard et al, 1980). The veins are connected to the systemic circulation through the internal iliac veins, the intercostal and azygos veins and through the vertebral veins to the cerebral sinuses (Domisse, 1975). These form important alternate routes of venous drainage in late pregnancy when the inferior vena cava is compressed by the gravid uterus. The engorged veins displace the dura mater locally away from the walls of the vertebral canal (Gershater and St Louis, 1979; Meijenhorst, 1982).

The *arteries* that supply the spinal cord are small branches of the segmental arteries which enter through the intervertebral foramina. They divide into small anterior and posterior radicular arteries which travel along the spinal nerve roots; some anastomose with the large anterior spinal artery and smaller posterior spinal arteries. Frequently the main blood supply to the lower section of the anterior spinal artery comes from a single large anterior radicular artery, the artery of Adamkiewicz, which usually arises from one of the lower intercostal arteries on the left side (Domisse, 1980). Occasionally this artery may arise at the upper lumbar level, and theoretically there is a risk of trauma to this large vessel during epidural cannulation.

The *lumbar anterior and posterior spinal nerve roots* cross the subarachnoid space and perforate the dura independently. Invested by a cuff of meninges, the posterior root with the spinal ganglion unites with the anterior root to form the spinal nerve at the intervertebral foramen. The lower lumbar and sacral nerve roots, forming the cauda equina, have a longer and more vertical passage.

The *epidural fat* is mainly localized in the posterior sulcus between the ligamenta flava and in the intervertebral foramina (Figure 2). It has been described as semifluid, lobulated fat (Bromage, 1978), and is variable in quantity. Observations during laminectomy show the fat to be enclosed within areolar tissue, which varies in appearance from a diaphanous layer to a pseudomembrane (Parkin and Harrison, 1985). The fat itself does not appear to hinder the identification of the epidural space or the spread of local anaesthetic solution or contrast medium.

The dura mater is connected to the walls of the vertebral canal by *fibrous connective tissue strands*, which are stronger anteriorly but weaker and longer posteriorly. The occasional presence of a

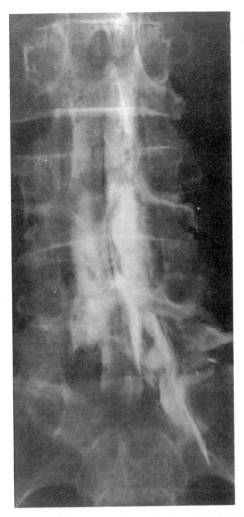

Figure 3. Lumbar epidurogram demonstrating plica dorsalis medialis durae matris (black line) which may be complete, incomplete or absent. It rarely causes a complete barrier to flow of contract medium (180 Omnipaque). (By courtesy of Dr G. Hamilton, Department of Radiology, Royal Lancaster Infirmary.)

midline translucency in epidurography (Figure 3) has led to the concept of a midline fold of dura mater, the plica dorsalis medialis durae matris. Various methods have been used to identify this anatomical feature, including cadaveric studies where ink or resin was injected into the epidural space (Lewit and Sereghy, 1975; Luyendijk, 1976; Husemeyer and White, 1980; Harrison et al, 1985), epiduroscopy, when a 2.2 mm diameter epiduroscope was inserted into the epidural region (Blomberg, 1986, 1989) and computerized tomography after epidural injection of contrast medium (Savolaine et al, 1988). All of these techniques have succeeded in demonstrating the presence of a structure variously described as a fold of dura mater or posterior midline fibrous band. However, all these techniques require the distortion of the anatomy by the insertion of a substance into the epidural region, be it dye, resin or epiduroscope. It is notable that there has been no description of this finding in anatomical studies (Figure 2), unenhanced computerized tomography (Figure 4) or magnetic resonance scanning (Figure 5); thus it is impossible to form a definitive conclusion. A posterior midline connective tissue band or a dural fold (Blomberg, 1986, 1989), if present, would influence the introduction of the needle and catheter and narrow the posterior epidural region in the midline.

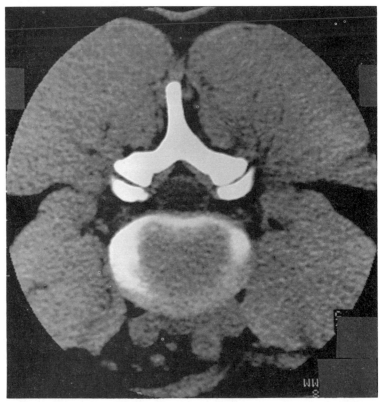

Figure 4. Computerized tomography of lower lumbar interspace, demonstrating the posterior deposit of epidural fat (black triangle) between the ligamenta flava. A posterior fold of dura mater or midline fibrous band is not visualized. (By courtesy of Dr P. Gishin, Department of Radiology, King's College Hospital, London.)

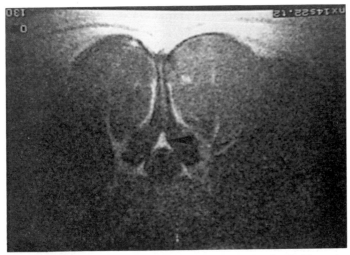

Figure 5. Transverse spin-echo (SES 44/44) image at L3-4 level. The posterior epidural fat appears as a light triangle between the ligamenta flava. Fibrous bands would probably need to be 2–3 mm thick to be apparent. (By courtesy of Dr G. Bydder, NMR Unit, Hammersmith Hospital, London.)

CLINICAL IMPLICATIONS

Position of the patient

Good flexion of the spine is possible with the patient in the lateral or sitting position. However, in the sitting position the cerebrospinal fluid pressure at the lumbar level will be up to six times greater than in the lateral position, due to hydrostatic pressure. This increases the risk of rupture of the dura mater by the needle tip. The epidural veins will also be less distended in the lateral position as the inferior vena cava is not compressed by the gravid uterus.

Distance from skin to epidural space

Studies by Palmer and colleagues (1983) and Harrison and Clowes (1985) demonstrate that the epidural region was most commonly found between 40 mm and 50 mm from the skin. In 60% of the population this distance is less than 50 mm and in only 10% is it greater than 60 mm. Clinical studies suggest that inadequate analgesia will result when the epidural space is located deeper than 60 mm, as any deviation from the midline by the needle will be magnified at greater depths (Narang and Linter, 1988; Wood et al, 1989).

Variations in reported figures may occur due to different angles of approach and interspace chosen. In the lateral position the skin may sag over the midline, and dimpling around the shaft of the needle may affect the distance measured. These findings have been confirmed with measurements from computerized tomography scans (Harrison, 1986).

Distance from posteromedial border of the ligamentum flavum to the dura mater

This depth is greatest in the second lumbar interspace and most studies demonstrate a range of 4–8 mm (Bromage, 1978; Zarzur, 1984) which concurs with measurements by Harrison (1984) using computerized tomography. At the level of the lamina the dural sac is closely applied to the periosteum. This explains the 'saw tooth' shape of the posterior epidural region seen in magnetic resonance scans (Figure 6). The needle should aim to enter the epidural space

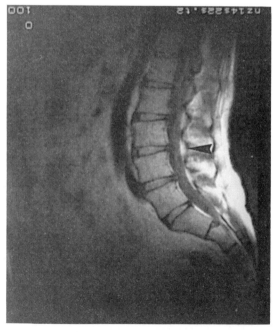

Figure 6. Sagittal spin-echo (SES 44/44) image of lumbosacral spine. The posterior epidural fat (arrowed light area) has a 'sawtooth' appearance, and the dural sac is closely applied to the laminae. (By couresty of Dr G. Bydder, NMR Unit, Hammersmith Hospital, London.)

at a point near the vertex of the posterior sulcus and midway between the adjacent laminae, to maximize the distance of the needle point from the dura and reduce the risk of dural puncture.

The ligamenta flava do not form a continuous ligament spanning the interlaminar space. There is often a gap between their posteromedial borders. If a needle is truly in the midline it would reach the epidural space by penetrating the interspinous ligament at the vertex of the posterior sulcus between the ligamenta flava (see Figure 1). Thus the expected resistance of the ligamentum flavum would not be encountered. In practice the posterior part of the interspinous ligament offers resistance to the needle which is lost on emerging from it, or it may deflect the needle slightly to one side of the midline, so that it traverses its anterior fibres, and then passes through the posteromedial border of the ligamentum flavum. In the paramedian approach, the needle always traverses the fibres of the ligamentum flavum towards the midline sulcus, giving a definite loss of resistance as the needle enters the epidural space.

Fibrous attachments of the dural sac to the vertebral canal

These fibres are usually of no clinical significance to the insertion of the catheter, or the diffusion of local anaesthetic solutions. Occasionally the posterior deposit of fat, or stronger posterior fibrous connections, may hinder threading the catheter or may deflect it laterally towards the intervertebral foramen, causing patchy analgesia. Unilateral block (Nunn and MacKinnon, 1986) may be attributed to a posterior fibrous septum, although Figures 2, 4 and 5 belie this.

APPROACHES TO THE LUMBAR EPIDURAL REGION

The approach adopted normally depends on the experience of the operator. However, there are times when the midline approach is difficult and the paramedian approach may be easier.

Successful identification of the epidural space by either approach depends on loss of resistance to saline or air injection, and apparent negative pressure of the epidural space.

Loss of resistance to saline or air injection

The advocates of the use of saline emphasize that saline pushes away the dura mater and opens up the epidural space for easier introduction of the catheter. Those who use this technique claim a reduced accidental dural puncture rate (Doughty, 1979; Macdonald, 1983; Galea, 1988; Reynolds, 1988) though a drip back of saline may be confused with cerebrospinal fluid. Testing with air may result in the formation of air bubbles, with irregular spread of local anaesthetic solution, subsequent uneven analgesia (Dalens et al, 1987) and pain in the neck and shoulders (Heggie, 1984). There is a risk of venous air embolism with this technique (Naulty et al, 1982), but a reduced incidence of paraesthesia and trauma to epidural veins when introducing the catheter after injection of air has been reported (Philip, 1985).

Apparent negative pressure of the epidural space

An artefactual negative pressure may be observed by tenting of the dura mater with the tip of the Tuohy needle (Bromage, 1953; Aitkenhead et al, 1979; Harrison, 1984), but this is unreliable and may be followed by dural puncture. However, some operators claim greater control by using both hands on a winged Tuohy needle, to which a negative pressure indicator is attached.

EPIDURAL TECHNIQUE

With the patient lying on her left side, with her neck flexed and her legs drawn up as far as possible, the line of the lumbar spines is identified. Anatomical studies suggest the second or third interspaces are most suitable. A meticulous aseptic technique must be used.

Midline approach

(Reynolds, 1984, 1988; Galea, 1988). After infiltration of skin and underlying tissues with local anaesthetic the Tuohy needle is introduced in the midline and mid-interspace, and in the sagittal plane. A recent *in vitro* study (Meiklejohn, 1987) recommends that modern disposable needles should not be rotated within the epidural space for fear of damaging the dura. For ease of introduction the bevel should face cephalad from the start of the procedure. The supraspinous ligament is difficult to penetrate, but only when the needle is firmly held by the interspinous ligament or close to it is the stylet removed and the syringe containing saline or air attached. The Tuohy needle is advanced slowly, with a slight cephalad angulation, maintaining pressure on the plunger of the syringe. A change in resistance will be appreciated as the needle enters the

Figure 1. Dissection of the posterior aspect of the vertebral canal reveals two bands of ligamenta flava lying at an angle to each other with a discrete gap between their medial borders. The posterior epidural fat that lies in the sulcus has been removed.

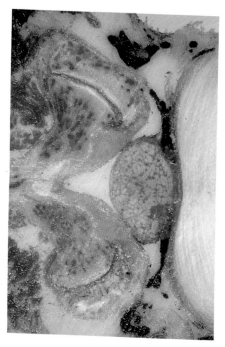

Figure 2 (a). Transverse section through second lumbar interspace, revealing cauda equina within dural sac and posterior and anterolateral deposits of fat. Note the deep posterior sulcus between the ligamenta flava, with no evidence of posterior fold of dura mater or midline fibrous band. The posterior longitudinal ligament with the longitudinal veins of the anterolateral venous plexus are clearly defined. (By courtesy of Dr J. Salisbury, Department of Morbid Anatomy, King's College Hospital, London.)

Figure 2 (b). (*Facing page*) Diagrammatic representation of transverse section through second lumbar interspace.

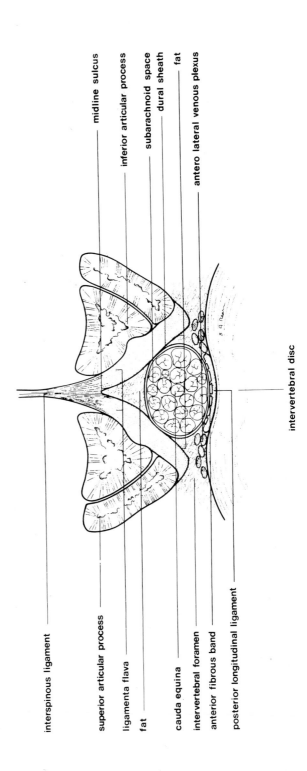

midline sulcus

inferior articular process

subarachnoid space

dural sheath

fat

antero lateral venous plexus

intervertebral disc

interspinous ligament

superior articular process

ligamenta flava

fat

cauda equina

intervertebral foramen

anterior fibrous band

posterior longitudinal ligament

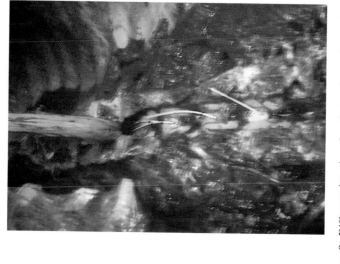

Figure 8. Different lengths of catheter (2, 4, 6 and 8 cm) were introduced by the paramedian approach at different interspaces. Dissection and removal of dural sac revealed the end position of the catheters. The catheters appeared to travel in a straight cephalad direction in the posterior epidural space.

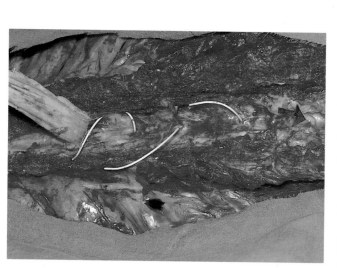

Figure 7. Different lengths of catheter (2, 4, 6 and 8 cm) were introduced by the midline approach at different interspaces. Dissection and removal of dural sac revealed the end position of the catheters. A diverse and unpredictable course was seen in all catheters where more than 2 cm (arrowed) was left in the epidural space.

ligamentum flavum. If it is truly in the midline this may not be so obvious as the needle only traverses the anterior fibres of the tough interspinous ligament. The end point is reached with loss of resistance to the pressure on the plunger of the syringe.

Paramedian approach

(Bonica, 1956; Carrie, 1971, 1977.) Local anaesthetic is infiltrated in the skin and tissues 15 mm lateral to the cephalad end of the lumbar spine below the chosen interspace, and the Tuohy needle is introduced at right angles to all skin planes. It traverses the paravertebral muscles until it touches the lamina. The depth of the needle is noted, the stylet removed and a further small amount of local anaesthetic may be injected (Carrie, 1977). The needle is partially withdrawn, redirected towards the midline in a more cephalad direction and inserted to the previous depth. In this way the blunt end of the needle will step off the lamina into the fibres of the ligamentum flavum. Because of the inferior attachment of the ligamentum flavum to the upper part of the posterior surface of the lamina, the needle may again make contact with bone. Further cephalad angulation may be necessary before the needle leaves the lamina and penetrates the ligamentum flavum. Using pressure on the plunger of the syringe, the needle is slowly advanced through the ligamentum flavum until loss of resistance is felt. When the needle enters the epidural space the smooth, convex part of the Huber tip should lie adjacent to the dura mater, and push it away rather than perforate it (Jaucot, 1986).

Introduction of the catheter

Once the flushed catheter is introduced through the Tuohy needle it should not be withdrawn until the needle has been safely removed. A final adjustment to its length is calculated and the catheter is withdrawn, leaving 20–40 mm in the epidural space (Doughty, 1974). It is important to avoid threading an excessive length of catheter in the epidural space. A transparent adhesive dressing should be used to fix the looped catheter in position on the skin, in order that inward or outward migration of the catheter can be observed (Phillips and Macdonald, 1987).

Comparison between the midline and paramedian approach

The midline approach still seems to be the most popular technique in the lumbar region, despite vigorous acclaim (Carrie, 1971, 1977; Armitage, 1976, 1977) and clinical evidence of the advantages of the paramedian route (Jaucot, 1986; Blomberg, 1988b; Blomberg et al, 1989). In a small prospective study by Griffin and Scott (1984) little difference was found between the two approaches, except that there was a higher incidence of initial failure with the midline route, whereas the paramedian route seemed more painful. They did not comment on the incidence of paraesthesia. There is a paucity of information comparing the two approaches.

It is claimed that the paramedian route is easier to teach (Carrie, 1971, 1977) because of the definite bony landmark afforded by the lamina, which gives a depth to the ligamentum flavum from the skin. If the lumbar spinous processes are difficult to identify, the position of the needle can be confirmed by acutely angling the needle medially. If correctly placed, the spinous process will prevent the passage of the needle across the midline. Good flexion of the back is important to open up the interlaminar space for the midline approach. This is not essential in the paramedian route. In the older patient, trauma to the ligaments during the passage of the needle can create local backache after the midline approach, though no evidence of this was found in parturients (Griffin and Scott, 1984). Degenerative cavities in the interspinous ligament can give rise to a false loss of resistance.

The course of an epidural catheter introduced by the midline route is diverse and unpredictable. Though a catheter cannot penetrate intact dura mater (Hardy, 1986) it is more likely to impinge directly on it and may penetrate it if the dura is already damaged by the needle, resulting in a subdural puncture (Blomberg, 1987). This is a complication that is not always recognized, and it should be suspected in a slowly developing block with a wider spread than anticipated.

The catheter frequently appears to be deflected anterolaterally, often forming a loop or a knot (Sidhu et al, 1983). This has been confirmed radiologically (Sanchez et al, 1967; Bridenbaugh et al, 1968; Muneyuki et al, 1970), by epiduroscopy examination (Blomberg, 1988a) and in an anatomical study (Gaynor, 1986) (Figure 7). This would explain the higher incidence of paraesthesia reported using the midline approach.

The cephalad angulation of the needle explains the extreme ease with which a catheter is introduced using the paramedian technique. It does not cause tenting of the dura and appears to travel in a straight cephalad direction posterior to the dural sac (Blomberg, 1988b) (Figure 8). Jaucot (1986), in his retrospective study of over a thousand cases comparing the two routes, found the incidence of paraesthesiae of 48% for the midline approach was halved using the paramedian approach. This finding is supported by Blomberg and colleagues (Blomberg et al, 1989). Fortunately, more serious neurological sequelae are rare.

An increased risk of trauma or cannulation of the epidural veins with the midline approach was found by Jaucot (1986) but not by Blomberg et al (1989). Bleeding was observed from needle or catheter in 18% of parturients where the midline approach was used (McNeill and Thorburn, 1988). An epidural haematoma is a rare but serious complication which may follow damage to an epidural vessel, compressing the spinal cord and requiring immediate evacuation.

There appears to be no direct comparison of the incidence of dural puncture between the two approaches, possibly because this is fortunately low (0.5%) in experienced hands (Bromage, 1978).

It would appear that the paramedian approach is associated with a reduced incidence of technical and catheter-related problems (Blomberg et al, 1989), especially in the parturient, and thus deserves wider application in obstetric practice.

REFERENCES

Aburel E (1931) L'anesthésie locale continue (prolongé) en obstétrique. *Bulletin de la Société d'Obstétrique et Gynécologie de Paris* **20**: 35.

Aitkenhead AR, Hothersall AP, Gilmour DG & Ledingham IMA (1979) Dural dimpling in the dog. *Anaesthesia* **34**: 14–19.

Armitage EN (1976) The paramedian approach to lumbar epidural analgesia. *Anaesthesia* **31**: 1287–1288.

Armitage EN (1977) The paramedian approach to the epidural space – a reply. *Anaesthesia* **32**: 672–673.

Batson OV (1957) The vertebral vein system. *American Journal of Roentgenology* **128**: 195.

Blomberg RG (1986) The dorsomedian connective tissue band in the lumbar epidural space of humans. An anatomical study using epiduroscopy in autopsy cases. *Anesthesia and Analgesia* **65**: 747–752.

Blomberg RG (1987) The lumbar subdural extra-arachnoid space of humans. Anatomical study using spinaloscopy in autopsy cases. *Anesthesia and Analgesia* **66**: 177–180.

Blomberg RG (1988a) Anatomy of the epidural space. *Anesthesiology* **69**: 797.

Blomberg RG (1988b) Technical advantages of the paramedian approach for lumbar epidural puncture and catheter introduction. A study using epiduroscopy in autopsy subjects. *Anaesthesia* **43**: 837–843.

Blomberg RG (1989) The lumbar epidural space in patients examined with epiduroscopy. *Anesthesia and Analgesia* **68**: 157–160.

Blomberg RG, Jaanivald A & Walther S (1989) Advantages of the paramedian approach for lumbar epidural analgesia with catheter technique. A clinical comparison of midline and paramedian approaches. *Anaesthesia* **44**: 742–746.

Bonica JJ (1956) Continuous peridural block. *Anesthesiology* **17**: 626–630.

Bridenbaugh LD, Moore DC, Bagdi P & Bridenbaugh PO (1968) The positioning of plastic tubing in continuous-block techniques: an X-ray study of 552 patients. *Anesthesiology* **29**: 1047–1049.

Bromage PR (1953) The 'hanging drop' sign. *Anaesthesia* **8**: 237–241.

Bromage PR (1978) *Epidural Analgesia*. Philadelphia: W.B. Saunders.

Carrie LES (1971) The approach to the extradural space (letter). *Anaesthesia* **26**: 252–253.

Carrie LES (1977) The paramedian approach to the epidural space (letter). *Anaesthesia* **32**: 670–671.

Cathelin F (1901) Une nouvelle voie d'injection rachidienne. Méthode des injections épidurales par le procédé du canal sacré. Applications à l'homme. *Comptes Rendus des Séances et Mémoires de la Société de Biologie* **53**: 45.

Cleland JGP (1933) Paravertebral anesthesia in obstetrics: experimental and clinical basis. *Surgery, Gynecology and Obstetrics* **57**: 51.

Cleland JGP (1952) Continuous peridural and caudal analgesia in obstetrics. *Anesthesia and Analgesia* **28**: 61.

Crawford JS (1978) *Principles and Practice of Obstetric Anaesthesia*, 4th edn. Oxford: Blackwell Scientific Publications.

Curbelo MM (1949) Continuous peridural segmental anesthesia by means of a ureteral catheter. *Anesthesia and Analgesia* **28**: 13.

Dalens B, Bazin JE & Harberer JP (1987) Epidural bubbles as a cause of incomplete analgesia during epidural anesthesia. *Anesthesia and Analgesia* **66**: 679–683.

Dogliotti AM (1933) Segmental peridural anesthesia. *American Journal of Surgery* **20**: 107.

Domisse GF (1975) *The Arteries and Veins of the Human Spinal Cord from Birth*. Edinburgh: Churchill Livingstone.

Domisse GF (1980) The arteries, arterioles and capillaries of the spinal cord: surgical guidelines in the prevention of post-operative paraplegia. *Annals of the Royal College of Surgeons of England* **62**: 369–376.

Doughty A (1974) A precise method of cannulating the lumbar epidural space. *Anaesthesia* **29**: 63–65.

Doughty A (1979) Inadvertent dural puncture – an avoidable accident. *Anaesthesia* **34**: 116.

Elsenstein S (1980) The trefoil configuration of the lumbar vertebral canal. *Journal of Bone and Joint Surgery* **62B**: 73–77.

Flowers CE, Hellman LM & Hingson RA (1949) Continuous peridural anesthesia for labour, delivery and Cesarean section. *Anesthesia and Analgesia* **28**: 181–189.

Galea PJ (1988) Avoiding accidental dural puncture (letter). *British Journal of Anaesthesia* **60**: 347.

Gaynor PA (1986) The applied anatomy of lumbar epidural anaesthesia. May & Baker Prize Essay, Royal Society of Medicine.

Gershater R & St Louis EL (1979) Lumbar epidural venography. Review of 1200 cases. *Radiology* **131**: 409–421.

Griffin RM & Scott RPF (1984) A comparison between the midline and paramedian approach to the extradural space. *Anaesthesia* **39**: 584–586.

Hardy PAJ (1986) Can epidural catheters penetrate dura mater? An anatomical study. *Anaesthesia* **41**: 1146–47.

Harrison GR (1984) The anatomy of the epidural space. Jacksonian Prize Essay, Royal College of Surgeons.

Harrison GR (1986) The topographical anatomy of the lumbar epidural region: a study using computerised tomography. *Annals of the Royal College of Surgeons of England* **68**: 110.

Harrison GR & Clowes NWB (1985) The depth of the lumbar epidural space from the skin. *Anaesthesia* **40**: 685–687.

Harrison GR, Parkin IG & Shah JL (1985) Resin injection studies of the lumbar extradural space. *British Journal of Anaesthesia* **57**: 333–336.

Heggie NM (1984) Unexplained pain during epidural anaesthesia (letter). *Anaesthesia* **39**: 609–10.

Hingson RA & Edwards WB (1942) Continuous caudal anesthesia during labor and delivery. *Anesthesia and Analgesia* **21**: 301.

Husemeyer RP & White DC (1980) Topography of the lumbar epidural space. *Anaesthesia* **35**: 7–11.

Janzen E (1926) Der negative Vorschlag bei Lumbalpunktion. *Deutsche Zeitschrift für Nervenheilkunde* **94**: 280.

Jaucot J (1986) Paramedian approach of the peridural space in obstetrics. *Acta Anaesthesiologica Belgica* **37**: 187–192.

Kreis O (1900) Über medullarnarkosen bei Gebärenden. *Zentralblatt für Gynakologie* **28**: 724.

Lewit K & Sereghy T (1975) Lumbar peridurography with special regard to the anatomy of the lumbar peridural space. *Neuroradiology* **8**: 233–240.

Luyendijk W (1976) The plica mediana dorsalis of the dura mater and its relation to lumbar peridurography (canalography). *Neuroradiology* **11**: 147–149.

Macdonald R (1983) Dr Doughty's technique for the location of the epidural space. *Anaesthesia* **38**: 71–72.

McNeill MJ & Thorburn J (1988) Cannulation of the epidural space. A comparison of 18- and 16-gauge needles. *Anaesthesia* **43**: 154–155.

Manalan SA (1942) Caudal block anesthesia in obstetrics. *Journal of the Indiana Medical Association* **35**: 564.

Meijenhorst GHC (1982) Computed tomography of the lumbar epidural veins. *Radiology* **145**: 687–691.

Meiklejohn BH (1987) The effect of rotation of an epidural needle. *Anaesthesia* **42**: 1180–1182.

Moir DD (1980) *Obstetric Anaesthesia and Analgesia*, 2nd edn. London: Baillière Tindall.

Muneyuki M, Shirai K & Inamoto A (1970) Roentgenographic analysis of the positions of catheters in the epidural space. *Anesthesiology* **33**: 19–24.

Narang VPS & Linter SPK (1988) Failure of epidural blockade in obstetrics. A new hypothesis. *British Journal of Anaesthesia* **60**: 402–404.

Naulty JS, Ostheimer GW, Datta S, Knapp R & Weiss JB (1982) Incidence of venous air embolism during epidural catheter insertion. *Anesthesiology* **57**: 410–412.

Nunn G & MacKinnon RPG (1986) Two unilateral epidural blocks. *Anaesthesia* **41**: 439–440.

Pagés R (1921) Anesthesia metamerica. *Revista de Sanidad Militar* **11**: 351–365.

Palmer SK, Abram SE, Maitra AM & von Colditz JH (1983) Distance from the skin to the lumbar epidural space in an obstetric population. *Anesthesia and Analgesia* **62**: 944–946.

Parkin IG & Harrison GR (1985) The topographical anatomy of the lumbar epidural space. *Journal of Anatomy* **141**: 211–217.

Philip BK (1985) Effect of epidural air injection on catheter complications. *Regional Anesthesia* **10**: 21–23.

Phillips DC & Macdonald R (1987) Epidural catheter migration during labour. *Anaesthesia* **42**: 661–663.

Renard M, Larde D, Masson JP & Roland J (1980) Anatomical and radio-anatomical study of the lumbo-sacral intervertebral venous plexuses. *Anatomica Clinica* **2**: 21–28.

Reynolds F (1984) Spinal and epidural block. In Churchill Davidson HC (ed.) *Wylie and Churchill Davidson's A Practice of Anaesthesia*, 5th edn, pp 856–892. London: Lloyd Luke.

Reynolds F (1988) Avoiding accidental dural puncture (letter). *British Journal of Anaesthesia* **61**: 515–16.

Sanchez R, Acuna L & Rocha F (1967) An analysis of the radiological visualization of the catheters placed in the epidural space. *British Journal of Anaesthesia* **39**: 485–489.

Savolaine ER, Pandya JB, Greenblatt SH & Conover SR (1988) Anatomy of the human lumbar epidural space: new insights using CT-epidurography. *Anesthesiology* **68**: 217–220.

Sicard JA (1901) Les injections medicamenteuses extradurales par voie sacro-coccygienne. *Comptes Rendus des Séances et Mémoires de la Société de Biologie* **53**: 396.

Sicard JA & Forestier J (1921) Radiographic method for exploration of the extradural space. *Revue Neurologique* **28**: 1264–1266.

Sidhu MS, Asrani RV & Bassell GM (1983) An unusual complication of extradural catheterization in obstetric anaesthesia. *British Journal of Anaesthesia* **55**: 473–475.

Stoeckel W (1909) Uber sakrale Anasthesie. *Zentralblatt für Gynakologie* **33**: 1.

Tuohy EB (1945) Continuous spinal anesthesia: a new method of utilising a ureteral catheter. *Surg. Clin. N. Amer.* 834.

Williams PL & Warwick R (eds) (1989) *Gray's Anatomy*, 37th edn. Edinburgh: Churchill Livingstone.

Wood CE, Shelley MP & Linter SPK (1989) The adequacy of epidural analgesia with increased distance of the epidural space from the skin. *Today's Anaesthetist* **4**: 143–144.

Zarzur E (1984) Anatomic studies of the human ligamentum flavum. *Anesthesia and Analgesia* **63**: 499–502.

ACKNOWLEDGEMENTS

I would like to thank the following colleagues for their help in the preparation of this chapter: Dr. G. Bydder, NMR Unit, Hammersmith Hospital, London; Dr. P. Gishen, Department of Radiology, King's College Hospital, London; Dr. G. Hamilton, Department of Radiology, The Royal Lancaster Infirmary, Lancaster; Dr. G. R. Harrison, Department of Anaesthesia, Queen Elizabeth Hospital, Birmingham; Dr. J. R. Salisbury, Department of Morbid Anatomy, King's College Hospital, London. I would also like to thank the staff of the Departments of Medical Illustration at King's College Hospital, Queen Victoria Hospital, East Grinstead, and Miss S. Reason and Miss K. J. Graham for their help in the preparation of photographs and illustrations. Finally, I would like to thank Mrs. V. Jones for her endless patience and professional secretarial assistance.

2

Indications and contraindications for epidural blockade in obstetrics

ROSEMARY MACDONALD

The indications and contraindications to epidural blockade in obstetrics have evolved over the last twenty years. Increasing use of epidural blockade has widened our knowledge and increased our confidence so that many medical and obstetric conditions that formerly constituted contraindications are now positive indications.

The increasing use of epidural blockade has paralleled advances in the medical and surgical management of many diseases. More women reach childbearing years. Expectations have increased; women with diseases such as cystic fibrosis and lupus erythematosus now expect to enjoy the birth of a child. Indications and contraindications for epidural blockade in obstetrics are classified in Table 1.

ABSOLUTE CONTRAINDICATIONS

Patient refusal

Epidurals must only be sited with the woman's agreement and cooperation. If a woman appears reluctant despite the advice of the attendant midwife and obstetrician, the anaesthetist is advised to ensure that a clear verbal consent is obtained and recorded in the case sheet.

Written consent is inappropriate in the delivery room, especially when the patient is in pain or has received systemic narcotics. Written informed consent can only be given antenatally when the woman is not in labour or in any way sedated; since it is impossible to predict who will have epidural analgesia, consent would have to be obtained from everyone, which would be a misuse of resources. Patients should be asked how much information they require about

Table 1. Indications and contraindications for epidural blockade in obstetrics.

Contraindications	Indications

Patient refusal
Absence of adequate staff and
    facilities
Local or systemic sepsis
Hypovolaemia
Anticoagulant therapy, bleeding
    diathesis
	Maternal
	1. **Any patient in whom intubation**
	   is expected to be difficult or
	   impossible
	2. Maternal disease:
	    respiratory
	    cardiovascular
	    renal
	    neurological/neuromuscular
	    endocrine
	    orthopaedic
	3. Pain
	
	Labour
	1. Incoordinate uterine action and
	    prolonged labour
	2. Trial of labour
	3. Previous Caesarean section
	4. Operative or instrumental
	    delivery
	5. Operative management of third
	    stage
	
	Fetal
	1. Prematurity and intra-
	    uterine growth retardation
	2. Breech presentation
	3. Multiple fetuses

the procedure, and their questions answered frankly. We have a moral obligation to inform our patients. Readers are referred to an excellent review on informed consent by Gild (1989).

Absence of adequate staff and facilities

Epidural analgesia should only be offered to patients if there are sufficient obstetricians, anaesthetists and midwives to care for them safely.

It is futile to site an epidural catheter if prompt top-ups cannot be provided. In units relying on midwives topping-up, adequate staffing is clearly essential. It is not safe to overcome a midwife shortage by using epidural infusions, however, since these too require careful supervision (see Chapter 4).

Originally it was felt that it was acceptable to use epidural analgesia provided 'a doctor' was available to resuscitate the patient. This led to obstetrician-based services. However the obstetrician's first duty should always be the obstetric care of the patient, and it is doubtful if one specialty can maintain expertise in aspects of patient care which are the province of another specialty.

There is now a consensus of opinion that resident, readily available anaesthetic cover is mandatory when epidural analgesia is in progress (*Anaesthetic Services for Obstetrics: a Plan for the Future*, 1987).

Local and systemic sepsis

It is only common sense not to site an epidural when there is skin sepsis over the lumbar area. However, what of systemic sepsis, bacteraemia or viraemia?

Epidural blockade is frequently performed without problems in patients who are pyrexial due to urinary tract infection, chorioamnionitis or the common cold. Once infection becomes systemic with bacteraemia, multi-system disturbance and leucocytosis, then caution is required in siting an epidural catheter because of the risk of epidural abscess or meningitis.

Diseases such as genital herpes and acquired immune deficiency syndrome (AIDS) assume more importance as their incidence increases. Genital herpes is caused by HSV-1 and HSV-2 viruses. The majority of primary infections and almost all recurrent episodes are caused by HSV-2. Primary systemic symptoms include fever, lymphadenopathy and headaches, and are accompanied by viraemia. Epidural blockade is not recommended in primary genital herpes but is not contraindicated in secondary infection provided there are no active lesions over the lumbar area (Ramanathan et al, 1986). There is also the possible association of HSV-1 reactivation with epidural morphine (Douglas and McMorland, 1987).

The patient who is HIV positive, in other words who has AIDS antibodies, needs careful assessment. In the absence of severe systemic manifestations of AIDS such as coagulopathy, hypovolaemia, neuropathy and dementia, epidural blockade is not contraindicated.

Hypovolaemia

Hypovolaemia remains a unanimously accepted contraindication. Controversy exists about the use of epidural blockade in the patient who may bleed, such as one who has a small antepartum haemorrhage or a minor degree of placenta praevia. Decisions about the potential significance of a small antepartum haemorrhage should be taken jointly with the obstetrician before instituting epidural blockade.

Epidural anaesthesia is frequently provided for Caesarean section in the presence of unexpected placenta praevia; this situation has to be efficiently managed. However, knowingly embarking upon epidural anaesthesia for Caesarean section for placenta praevia (especially anterior, and particularly if associated with a previous Caesarean section) may be living dangerously. Despite the conclusions of Chestnut et al (1989) that epidural analgesia is relatively safe with placenta praevia, most obstetric anaesthetists would recommend general anaesthesia in such cases. Not every patient with a placenta praevia will be anaesthetized by a consultant working in optimal conditions (DHSS, 1989).

Anticoagulant therapy or bleeding diathesis

Abnormal clotting or disseminated intravascular coagulation remain unanimously accepted contraindications to epidural blockade.

The use of subcutaneous heparin to prevent deep vein thrombosis and the administration of aspirin to prevent the development of pre-eclampsia and intrauterine growth retardation (IUGR) have provided obstetric anaesthetists with controversy. This subject has been succinctly reviewed by Letsky (1987). Discussions with haematologists and perusal of the literature have led to formulation of the following policy.

1. Patients in whom there is abnormal clotting clinically or on routine laboratory testing do not have epidural catheters sited. All patients with fulminating pre-eclampsia have a full blood count and clotting screen. If the platelets are less than 100 000, epidural blockade is contraindicated.
2. Patients on subcutaneous heparin may have epidural catheters sited expertly (Odoom and Sih, 1983), since this therapy does not interfere with haemostatic mechanisms or platelet function (Letsky, 1987).
3. Patients who have ingested aspirin. Aspirin affects platelet function, the bleeding time is prolonged and thrombin formation may be inhibited (Letsky, 1987). A bleeding time should therefore be performed, and if it is greater than 10 minutes epidural blockade is contraindicated.

It may be argued that many epidural catheters must have been sited in patients on aspirin in the 1960s and 1970s, but technical difficulties with siting and bleeding into the catheter do occur in up to 18% (McNeill and Thorburn, 1988) and the potential danger of *low dose* aspirin cannot be ignored.

INDICATIONS FOR EPIDURAL BLOCKADE

Any patient in whom intubation is expected to be impossible or difficult

The maternal mortality reports (DHSS, 1989) provide evidence that this is an important indication. Should operative intervention be required, the epidural block can easily be extended. It is out of all proportion to suggest that accidental total spinal anaesthesia, as a remote complication of epidural blockade, might necessitate urgent intubation.

Maternal disease

Respiratory disease

Asthma is probably the most common respiratory disorder encountered in the delivery suite. Epidural analgesia by infusion is probably better than intermittent doses, since avoidance of painful episodes between top-ups may prevent hyperventilation which can precipitate wheezing.

Most other respiratory disorders such as bronchitis, bronchiectasis and the common cold are best managed with epidural blockade for labour or operative delivery. Patients with emphysematous bullae are rare, but avoidance of intermittent positive-pressure ventilation and maternal effort in the second stage is advisable. Chest drains should always be available in consultant maternity units.

Patients with cystic fibrosis illustrate our changing clientele. More sufferers are reaching childbearing years, with about half surviving until their late teens (Hodson, 1989). Many desire children (Walter and Hodson, 1987), and although childbirth does not increase the overall death rate (Cohen et al, 1980), pregnancy should be avoided unless the clinical score is high (Walter and Hodson, 1987; Cohen et al, 1980). Hospitals with successful cystic fibrosis units can expect to see more of these patients in the maternity unit (and hence more carriers of cystic fibrosis). The success of heart transplantation in this group of patients will provide further challenges.

Cardiovascular disease

The pregnant patient with cardiovascular disease presents a challenge to the obstetric anaesthetist. These patients need careful assessment (Sullivan and Ramanathan, 1985). The New York Heart Association's classification of functional impairment is useful; classes I and II with minimal impairment do well, and may be offered epidural blockade for labour and delivery. Continuous infusions of a low concentration of bupivacaine with a suitable opioid such as fentanyl may confer greater haemodynamic stability. Classes III and IV experience symptoms and suffer functional impairment which leads to a high maternal mortality (up to 90% in class IV) and a high perinatal mortality (Ostheimer and Alper, 1975).

Patients with class III and IV cardiac disease or other potentially serious conditions such as Eisenmenger's syndrome, primary pulmonary hypertension or ischaemic heart disease should be referred to maternity units that can offer high-quality obstetric, anaesthetic and cardiological cover. Invasive monitoring, not only of central venous pressure but also of pulmonary capillary wedge pressure, and full intensive care facilities should be available. Injudicious use or management of epidural blockade can lead to maternal death (Alderson, 1987). Anaesthetists faced unexpectedly with a cardiac patient with functional impairment should use the anaesthetic technique with which they feel most competent, and general anaesthesia may at times be appropriate.

Successful management of the cardiac patient requires thorough antenatal discussion between obstetrician and anaesthetist so that a plan of action covering all eventualities can be agreed.

Hypertensive diseases of pregnancy are responsible for 18% of maternal deaths (DHSS, 1989). Pre-existing hypertension may be aggravated by pregnancy. Epidural blockade should be available for these patients for the following reasons (James, 1988).

1. Superior analgesia is achieved.
2. The hypertensive response to pain (which is exaggerated in these patients) is attenuated.
3. Control of the hypertension is facilitated.
4. Intervillous blood flow is improved.
5. Renal blood flow is improved.
6. Side-effects of narcotic analgesia, such as depressed respiration and a rise in Pco_2, are avoided.
7. Excellent analgesia is provided for elective forceps delivery.
8. Maternal expulsive efforts in the second stage can be prevented if required.

Controversy does exist over fulminating pre-eclampsia characterized by diastolic blood pressure > 100 mmHg, proteinuria > 4 g per 24 hours and systemic symptoms, especially epigastric pain or visual disturbances – when haemostatic dysfunction may constitute a contraindication to epidural blockade. Increasingly these patients are delivered by Caesarean section. Regional block is not routinely used for the following reasons.

1. Haemostatic dysfunction may be present (this should always be checked).
2. Patients who are hyperreflexic, or have other signs of central nervous system involvement such as headache, may have a fit.
3. Phenytoin is the anticonvulsant of choice; intravenous diazepam may have to be used in emergencies. The sedated patient may inhale during Caesarean section under epidural blockade.
4. Epidural narcotics are contraindicated with concurrent sedation.

General anaesthesia, despite its inherent risks, may have a place in the control of cerebral blood flow and intracranial pressure, and it allows insertion of central venous lines with minimum disturbance to the patient. The hypertensive response to laryngoscopy and intubation can be obtunded by pretreatment with intravenous fentanyl and a hypotensive agent. The depressant effects on the baby are reversible by resuscitation; care of the mother is of paramount importance.

On the other hand, epidural blockade may be particularly indicated, for example in the presence of gross oedema of the face, tongue or airway. Fluid balance needs careful control and infusion of colloid may be appropriate (Joyce and Loom, 1981; Wright, 1983; James, 1988).

Renal disease

The success of renal dialysis and transplantation means that patients with end stage renal failure may now become pregnant. During labour and delivery, their management must take account both of their renal disease (Weir and Chung, 1984) and their obstetric welfare. Fluid balance must be managed carefully during labour and hypotension avoided, especially in the hypertensive patient with a renal transplant.

Neurological and neuromuscular disease

Epidural blockade is indicated in any condition where a rise in intracranial pressure during labour or delivery would be dangerous (Crawford, 1983). Siting an epidural catheter in a patient with raised intracranial pressure requires skill, since inadvertent dural puncture must be avoided. Management of epidural analgesia must be meticulous and topping-up prompt, to avoid further rises in intracranial pressure (Hilt et al, 1986), or an epidural infusion may be indicated.

The obstetric patient who is paraplegic or quadriplegic may require little analgesia for labour, depending on the sensory loss. Epidural blockade can be performed but siting the catheter may be difficult because of deformity secondary to wheelchair life.

Management of blood pressure may prove difficult due to autonomic dysfunction (Stirt et al, 1979), which suggests scope for the use of epidural narcotics in these patients.

Controversy still surrounds the use of epidural blockade in patients with multiple sclerosis (Jones and Healey, 1980). Provided these patients are counselled antenatally, there is surely no reason to deprive them of this superior analgesia (Crawford et al, 1981; Crawford, 1985).

Epidural blockade is indicated in most neuromuscular disorders unless there is associated severe cardiomyopathy or respiratory embarrassment. One refinement would be the use of small doses of fentanyl both to reduce the amount of bupivacaine and to prevent shivering (Matthews and Corser, 1988), which may be important in the myotonic diseases. The literature contains many case reports of the successful use of epidural blockade in the rarer disorders such as McArdle's disease, a hereditary myopathy (Coleman, 1984).

Epileptic patients benefit from epidural blockade, and narcotic analgesia is best avoided to minimize the likelihood of fits during labour. Anticonvulsants should be continued with careful monitoring (Knott et al, 1986).

Endocrine disorders

Probably no single obstetric anaesthetist gains much experience in the management of the obstetric patient with the rarer endocrinological disorders such as Cushing's disease, phaeochromocytoma, thyrotoxicosis, myxoedema, hyperthyroidism and hypothyroidism. These disorders may develop during pregnancy and require surgical correction (Geelhoed, 1983).

There is little information in the literature on epidural blockade in these conditions, and its use will depend on the policy in the delivering unit. However, the stress hormone response to labour and to Caesarean section is reduced by epidural anaesthesia (Shnider et al, 1983), making management of the endocrine disorders easier (Loughran et al, 1986). Epidural blockade can also confer haemodynamic stability during Caesarean section and excision of phaeochromocytoma (Hopkins et al, 1989).

Diabetes is a common medical problem during pregnancy. The obstetric anaesthetist's aim should be to optimize placental blood flow and blood glucose levels during labour and delivery. Hypotension must be avoided to minimize fetal acidosis (Datta et al, 1982). The changes in oxygen transport and delivery that occur in the diabetic pregnant patient may mean that oxygen saturation should also be monitored (Madsen and Ditzel, 1982). Close cooperation between the diabetic patient, obstetrician, diabetologist, anaesthetist and neonatologist can do much to reduce perinatal mortality in diabetes.

The morbidly obese pregnant patient presents a challenge to the obstetric anaesthetist. There is evidence that such women do better under epidural than under general anaesthesia (Hodgkinson and Husain, 1980). Readers are referred to an excellent review by Dewan (1988).

Orthopaedic disease

Orthopaedic disease of the vertebral column is not in itself a contraindication to epidural blockade. It may render siting a little difficult and hinder the achievement of a perfect block. Adhesions in the epidural space as a result of surgery or the disease process may limit the spread of the anaesthetic agent. Patients should be warned of this possibility prior to siting, although epidural narcotics may achieve a satisfactory block. It has also been suggested that a double catheter technique may be useful (Schachner and Abram, 1982). Epidural blockade is useful in the patient with rheumatoid arthritis or ankylosing spondylitis, in whom intubation may be difficult. Associated pathology, for example in the cardiovascular system, must also be considered and antenatal assessment is mandatory.

The success of neonatal surgical correction of neural tube defects means that these patients may present yet another challenge to the obstetric anaesthetist, especially as scoliosis and impaired respiratory function may have developed during the course of the disease. The epidural space may be absent, making dural puncture likely. It is probably advisable to site the epidural above the lesion (McGrady and Davis, 1988).

Epidural anaesthesia for Caesarean section in achondroplasia is desirable since intubation may be impossible (Kalla et al, 1986).

Maternal request for pain relief

Despite advances in all branches of medicine over the last hundred years, pain relief remains a Cinderella (Rosen, 1989). The National Birthday Trust's Survey (Morgan, 1985) showed that only 139 out of 524 maternity units provided epidural analgesia on request. The current problem is that consumer groups rarely demand an epidural service. A recent enquiry in a unit where two-thirds of primiparous women requested epidural analgesia in labour, showed that only 13% of these women believed beforehand that they would want it (Rickford and Reynolds, 1987).

Labour indications

Epidural analgesia is indicated in labours in which problems might be anticipated that would otherwise necessitate general anaesthesia, with its inherent dangers. Thus prolonged labour, incoordinate uterine action, trial of labour and previous Caesarean section may presage the need for operative intervention and should therefore prompt staff to encourage these women to have an epidural catheter sited. The potential of superior postoperative analgesia with epidural narcotics is a further advantage.

Previous Caesarean section is no longer a contraindication provided mother and fetus are carefully monitored (Uppington, 1983), and a limited dose of local anaesthetic is used.

Epidural blockade offers vastly superior anaesthesia to pudendal block for forceps delivery. In this situation spinal anaesthesia may be the technique of choice, particularly when speed of onset of complete anaesthesia is desirable.

For Caesarean section the possible complications of epidural blockade must be considered. The death rate is lower than with general anaesthesia (DHSS, 1989), especially in units where epidural blockade is routinely practised. There is less morbidity (Morgan et al, 1984) and earlier discharge from hospital, particularly if epidural narcotics are used for postoperative analgesia (Stenkamp et al, 1989).

The place of epidural blockade in Caesarean section for fetal distress is more controversial. The anaesthetist and obstetrician together must weigh the time taken to institute the block with the urgency of delivery. It must be emphasized that in units with resident anaesthetic cover and regular combined obstetric and anaesthetic labour ward rounds, patients who may require operative delivery should already have epidurals *in situ*. In many centres, however, spinal anaesthesia may be used for Caesarean section for fetal distress, particularly in the absence of effective epidural analgesia.

Operative management of the third stage

Provided bleeding is not excessive, epidural analgesia may be used for manual removal of the placenta, suturing a third-degree tear or evacuation of a vulval haematoma. If these procedures are rendered urgent by haemorrhage, neither intrathecal nor epidural block is appropriate.

Fetal indications

Prematurity and intrauterine growth retardation

These are the most important fetal indications for epidural blockade both for labour and Caesarean section. These babies may be spending some time in the neonatal intensive care unit or special care baby unit, and it is pleasurable for the parents to participate in the birth.

Breech presentation

Epidural blockade is indicated for breech delivery (Crawford and Weaver, 1982). Compared to conventional narcotic analgesia, epidural blockade is superior both for mother and baby.

During the last ten years obstetricians have actively debated the mode of delivery when the breech presents, and in many units vaginal breech delivery is rare, particularly in primiparous women (Confino et al, 1985).

Multiple pregnancy

Twin delivery (whether vaginal or by Caesarean section), like breech presentation, was originally a contraindication but is now an indication for epidural blockade (Crawford and Weaver, 1982; James, 1982; Crawford, 1987). It must be remembered that twin pregnancies are often associated with complications such as breech presentation, hypertension, anaemia and oedema; the epidural block should be managed accordingly.

What of triplets, quads and even more babies? Although it is not perhaps ideal for the human to give birth to more than two babies at the same time, the treatment of infertility has produced increased numbers of these patients, usually for premature delivery by Caesarean section. A crowded operating theatre precludes full parental participation, and maternal bonding to three, four or five babies may be difficult. Each patient, her personality, her associated complications and the operative skill of the attendant obstetrician should be logically assessed. Finally the height and girth of the patient must be examined, and it may be sensible on occasion to elect for general anaesthesia.

CONCLUSION

During the last ten years most of the original contraindications to epidural blockade in obstetrics have been swept away. What of the future? Spinal anaesthesia is supplanting epidural blockade in many situations, and should further reduce the number of obstetric patients undergoing general anaesthesia. The most recent controversies – epidural blockade and aspirin, epidural blockade and fulminating pre-eclampsia, the role of regional blockade in the management of fetal distress – are being resolved. Will continuous infusion replace intermittent top-ups? Will epidural opioids be used increasingly, or will they be superseded? What new drugs and techniques will become available? One thing is certain, that serious effort should be made to provide a universal service, so that every woman can at least have the choice of regional blockade for labour and delivery.

REFERENCES

Alderson JD (1987) Cardiovascular collapse following epidural anaesthesia for Caesarean section in a patient with aortic incompetence. *Anaesthesia* **42**: 643–645.

Anaesthetic Services for Obstetrics: a Plan for the Future (1987) Association of Anaesthetists of Great Britain and Ireland.

Chestnut DH, Dewan DM, Lloyd F, Redick LF, Caton MD & Spielman FJ (1989) Anesthetic management for obstetric hysterectomy: a multi-institutional study. *Anesthesiology* **70**: 607–610.

Cohen LF, Di Sant'Agnese PA & Friedlander J (1980) Cystic fibrosis and pregnancy. *Lancet* **ii**: 842–844.

Coleman P (1984) McArdle's disease: problems of anaesthetic management for Caesarean section. *Anaesthesia* **39**: 784–787.

Confino E, Gleicher N, Elrad H et al (1985) The breech dilemma. A review. *Obstetric Gynecological Survey* **40**: 330–337.

Crawford JS (1983) *Principles and Practice of Obstetric Anaesthesia*, 5th edn, p. 365. Oxford: Blackwell Scientific Publications.

Crawford JS (1985) Some maternal complications of epidural anaesthesia for labour. *Anaesthesia* **40**: 1219–1225.

Crawford JS (1987) A prospective study of 200 consecutive twin deliveries. *Anaesthesia* **42**: 33–43.

Crawford JS & Weaver JB (1982) Anaesthetic management of twin and breech deliveries. *Clinics in Obstetrics and Gynaecology* **9**: 291–296.

Crawford JS, James FM, Nolte H, Van Steenberge A & Shah JL (1981) Regional analgesia for patients with chronic neurological disease and similar conditions (letter). *Anaesthesia* **36**: 821.

Datta S, Kitzmiller JL, Naulty JS, Ostheimer GW & Weiss JB (1982). Acid base status of diabetic mothers and their infants following spinal anesthesia for Caesarean section. *Anesthesia and Analgesia* **61**: 662–665.

Dewan D (1988) The obese parturient. In James FM, Wheeler AS & Dewan DM (eds) *Obstetric Anesthesia: The Complicated Patient*, Philadelphia: Davies.

DHSS (1989) *Report on Confidential Enquiries into Maternal Deaths in England and Wales 1982–84*. London: HMSO.

Douglas MJ & McMorland GH (1987) Possible association of herpes simplex type 1 reactivation with epidural morphine administration. *Canadian Journal of Anaesthesia* **34**: 426.

Geelhoed GW (1983) Surgery of the endocrine glands in pregnancy. *Clinical Obstetrics and Gynecology* **26**: 865–889.

Gild MW (1989) Informed consent. A review. *Anesthesia and Analgesia* **68**: 649–653.

Hilt H, Gramm HJ & Link J (1986). Changes in intracranial pressure associated with extradural anaesthesia. *British Journal of Anaesthesia* **58**: 676–680.

Hodgkinson R & Husain FJ (1980) Caesarean section associated with gross obesity. *British Journal of Anaesthesia* **52**: 919–923.

Hodson ME (1989) Managing adults with cystic fibrosis (editorial). *British Medical Journal* **298**: 471–2.

Hopkins P, Macdonald R & Lyons G (1989) Caesarean section at 27 weeks gestation and excision of phaeochromocytoma. *British Journal of Anaesthesia* **63**: 121–124.

James FM (1982) Anesthetic considerations for breech or twin delivery. *Clinical Perinatology* **9**: 77–94.

James FM (1988) Pregnancy induced hypertension. In James FM, Wheeler AS & Dewan DM (eds) *Obstetric Anesthesia: the Complicated Patient*, pp 411–487. Philadelphia: Davies.

Jones RM & Healy TEJ (1980) Anaesthesia and demyelinating disease. *Anaesthesia* **35**: 879–884.

Joyce T & Loow M (1981) Pre-eclampsia: effect of albumin 25% infusion. *Anesthesiology* **55**: 3, A313.

Kalla GN, Gening E & Obiaya MO (1986) Anaesthetic management of achrondo-plasia. *British Journal of Anaesthesia* **58**: 117–119.

Knott C, Williams CP & Reynolds F (1986) Phenytoin kinetics during pregnancy and the puerperium. *British Journal of Obstetrics and Gynaecology* **93**: 1030–1031.

Letsky E (1987) Haemostasis in pregnancy. In Morgan B (ed.) *Foundations of Obstetric Anaesthesia*, pp 189–207. London: Farrand Press.

Loughran PG, Moore J & Dundee JW (1986) Maternal stress response associated with caesarean delivery under general and epidural analgesia. *British Journal of Obstetrics and Gynaecology* **93**: 943–949.

McGrady EM & Davis AG (1988) Spina bifida occulta and epidural anaesthesia. *Anaesthesia* **43**: 867–869.

McNeill MJ & Thorburn J (1988) Cannulation of the epidural space: a comparison of 18- and 16-gauge needles. *Anaesthesia* **43**: 154–155.

Madsen H & Ditzel J (1982) Changes in red blood cell oxygen transport in diabetic pregnancy. *American Journal of Obstetricis and Gynecology* **143**: 421–424.

Matthews NC, Corser G (1988) Epidural fentanyl for shaking in obstetrics. *Anaesthesia* **43**: 783–785.

Morgan BM (1987) Anaesthetic facilities. In Chamberlain GVP (ed.) *Birthplace. Confidential Enquiries into Facilities at the Place of Birth*, pp 167–202. London: John Wiley. (1987).

Morgan BM, Aulakh JM, Barker JR et al (1984) Anaesthetic morbidity following Caesarean section under epidural or general anaesthesia. *Lancet* i: 328–330.

Odoom JA & Sih IL (1983) Epidural analgesia and anticoagulant therapy. Experience with one thousand cases of continuous epidurals. *Anaesthesia* **38**: 254–259.

Ostheimer GW & Alper MH (1975) Intrapartum anesthetic management of the pregnant patient with heart disease. *Clinical Obstetrics and Gynecology* **18**: 81–97.

Ramanathan S, Sheth R & Turndorf H (1986) Anesthesia for Cesarean section in patients with genital herpes infection: a retrospective study. *Anesthesiology* **64**: 807–809.

Rickford WJK & Reynolds F (1986) Expectations and reality of labor pain and analgesia. *Proceedings of the Society of Obstetric Anesthesiology and Perinatology*, Halifax, NS, p 163.

Rosen M (1989) An interview on pain relief. *Frontiers of Pain* **1**: 4–7.

Schachner SM & Abram SE (1982) Use of two epidural catheters to provide analgesia of unblocked segments in a patient with lumbar disc disease. *Anesthesiology* **56**: 150–151.

Shnider SM, Abboud TK, Artal R et al (1983) Maternal catecholamines decrease during labor after epidural anesthesia. *American Journal of Obstetrics and Gynecology* **147**: 13–15.

Stenkamp J, Easterling TR & Chadwick HS (1989) Effect of epidural and intrathecal morphine on the length of hospital stay after Cesarean section. *Anesthesia and Analgesia* **68**: 66–69.

Stirt JA, Marco A & Conklin KA (1979) Obstetric anesthesia for a quadriplegic patient with autonomic hyperreflexia. *Anesthesiology* **51**: 560–562.

Sullivan JM & Ramanathan KB (1985) Management of medical problems in pregnancy: severe cardiac disease. *New England Journal of Medicine* **313**: 304–309.

Uppington J (1983) Epidural analgesia and previous Caesarean section. *Anaesthesia* **38**: 336–341.

Walter S & Hodson ME (1987) *Fertility, Pregnancy and Contraception in Cystic Fibrosis*. London: Cystic Fibrosis Trust/Association of Cystic Fibrosis Adults.

Weir PHC & Chung FF (1984) Anaesthesia for patients with chronic renal disease. *Canadian Anaesthetists Society Journal* **31**: 468–480.

Wildsmith JAW (1986) Extradural blockade and intracranial pressure (editorial). *British Journal of Anaesthesia* **58**: 579.

Wright JP (1983) Anesthetic considerations in pre-eclampsia – eclampsia. *Anesthesia and Analgesia* **63**: 590–601.

Current Research 1

Relationship between spine length and spread of drugs within the epidural space: the advantage of the paramedian approach

J.K. MOORE and N.J. DENNIS

It would be useful to be able to predict the spread of drugs within the epidural space. Previous workers have used height as an indication of spine length and hence volume of the epidural space. At best they were able to demonstrate only a weak correlation between height and extent of neural blockade (Bromage, 1962; Burn et al, 1973). We have assessed the relationship between back length and height, and quantified the influence of back length on the epidural spread of 0.5% bupivacaine in the labouring patient.

METHOD

Sixty patients were studied: 38 patients had epidural catheters sited by a midline approach, 22 by a paramedian approach. All injections of local anaesthetic were given with the patient in the left lateral position. Height was plotted against spine length, and spread of analgesia was plotted against weight, height, spine length and body mass index.

RESULTS

We found that height was poorly related to spine length. We also found that when a paramedian approach to the epidural space was used, spine length was inversely related to the extent of neural blockade ($P < 0.01$) (Figure 1). No such relationship was seen with a midline approach. This may be because catheters inserted via a midline approach travel in unpredictable directions, whereas those inserted via a paramedian approach reliably pass cranially and in the midline (Blomberg, 1988), so that local anaesthetic is delivered to a predictable site in all patients.

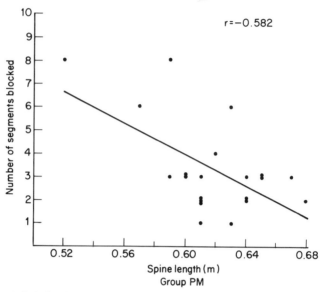

Figure 1. Relationship between spine length and number of segments blocked to pin-prick in paramedian group.

CONCLUSION

The ability to predict the extent of neural blockade is a major advantage. Spine length is easily measured and we therefore recommend that the paramedian approach should receive greater attention in obstetric anaesthesia.

References

Blomberg RG (1988) Technical advantages of the paramedian approach for lumbar epidural puncture and catheter introduction. *Anaesthesia* **43**: 837–843.

Bromage PR (1962) Spread of analgesic solutions in the epidural space and their site of action: a statistical study. *British Journal of Anaesthesia* **34**: 161–178.

Burn JM, Guyer PB & Langdon L (1973) The spread of solutions injected into the epidural space. *British Journal of Anaesthesia* **45**: 338–345.

SECTION I – DISCUSSION

CHAIRMAN: DR M. TUNSTALL, Aberdeen

Dr Reynolds On the subject of both anatomy and approach, and of contraindications: abnormal anatomy is of course not necessarily a contraindication, but more often a challenge (Doughty, 1980). I would like to describe a case that illustrates this.

Figure 1 shows a lateral view of the lumbar spine of a 32-year-old primipara with osteogenesis imperfecta. She would have been 97 cm tall if she had been able to stand, and weighed 35 kg at 37 weeks, when she presented for Caesarean section because of progressive respiratory difficulty. She requested epidural anaesthesia which was indicated because of a risk of hyperpyrexia with general anaesthesia in this condition (Roberts and Solomons, 1975). However X-rays of her lumbar spine, which were actually taken to assess the condition of the baby, revealed not only a scoliosis of 80° but also a lumbar lordosis of 90°, while externally her lumbar region was represented by a horizontal crease between thorax and buttock. The right laminae of the second and third lumbar vertebrae were, however, relatively superficial, and with the patient sitting but suspended from her axillae to minimize the scoliosis, Andrew Doughty successfully inserted an epidural catheter using the paramedian approach. Even then, the problem was not over: even using her pregnant weight, the maximum safe dose of bupivacaine 0.5% was 14 ml, which eventually produced satisfactory anaesthesia, while two episodes of hypotension, one associated with the onset of blockade, and the second with blood loss, were accompanied by extreme cyanosis and dyspnoea. Each was corrected by fluid and blood replacement. This case (Price and Reynolds, 1987) illustrates both the absence of respiratory reserve characteristic of the severe scoliotic, and the tiny blood volume associated with such a crippling disease.

Dr Gutsche Dr Macdonald, do you really think epidural anaesthesia is contraindicated in placenta praevia? In our hospital it is the technique of choice.

Dr Macdonald We teach our trainees that epidural anaesthesia is contraindicated in the presence of placenta praevia, particularly anterior and with previous Caesarean section.

35

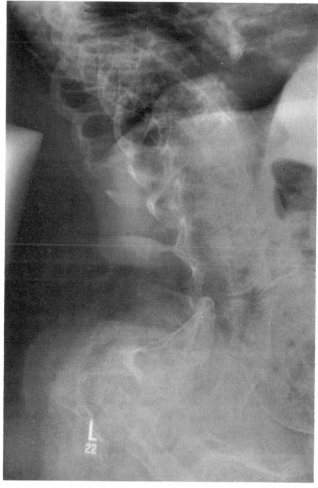

Figure 1. Lateral X-ray of abdomen of a woman with osteogenesis imperfecta at 37 weeks' gestation. Caesarean section was carried out under epidural anaesthesia.

Dr Gutsche   Do you think it would be unsafe for me and my Senior Resident?

Dr Macdonald   Probably not; but in the UK you only have to read the maternal mortality reports to realize that many women with placenta praevia are anaesthetized by trainees working alone, and often with a trainee obstetrician. I think general anaesthesia is safer in these circumstances.

Dr Naulty I am interested in your remarks about consent for epidural analgesia. We take a written consent.

Dr Macdonald Written consent is impracticable during labour; but verbal consent with some discussion of side-effects is possible. We really try to gauge just how much information each patient wishes to receive.

Dr Reynolds Informed consent, whether written or verbal, implies a knowledge of recognized side-effects. We attempt to provide brief written information on all forms of analgesia for every woman in the antenatal period, so that at least we can say that information about side-effects was available to them all. Incidentally, people make remarkably little fuss about consent to an injection of pethidine, yet how many women know that it delays gastric emptying?

References

Doughty A (1980) The 'impossible' epidural. In *Epidural Analgesia in Obstetrics*, p 183. London: Lloyd Luke.

Price J & Reynolds F (1987) Management of pregnancy complicated by osteogenesis imperfecta. *Journal of Obstetrics and Gynaecology* **7**: 178–180.

Roberts JM & Solomons CC (1975) Management of pregnancy in osteogenesis imperfecta: new perspectives. *Obstetrics and Gynaecology* **45**: 168–170.

SECTION II

Management of Labour

3

Test doses

MICHAEL J. JORDAN

The invention of the epidural test dose is usually attributed to Dogliotti (1933). Dogliotti's technique of epidural anaesthesia involved the use of very large volumes (50–80 ml) of procaine or cinchocaine with adrenaline. His 'test dose' was 15–20 ml which, he said, '. . . should be injected under moderate pressure within ten to fifteen seconds. One then waits three to four minutes before injecting the remaining 30 cc. During this interval the condition of the patient is carefully watched in order that any manifestations of intolerance to the anaesthetic may be noted . . . One should also ascertain that no deep anaesthesia such as follows the ordinary subarachnoid spinal anaesthetics has set in . . .'. In the intervening years since Dogliotti's description, the exact components of the test dose, and even the need for one, have been fiercely debated.

The original *raison d'être* for test dosing was to detect the inadvertent intrathecal placement of an epidural needle before injection of a large volume of local anaesthetic resulted in total spinal anaesthesia. The introduction of bupivacaine, and the realization of its cardiotoxicity (Albright, 1979) made it as important to detect accidental intravascular injection, with its risk of convulsions or cardiac arrest.

Ideally, an epidural test dose in the obstetric patient would detect not only intrathecal or intravascular injection but also subdural administration. There would be a reliable and unambiguous result within 5 minutes and the mother and fetus would not be subjected to additional hazard in the process. It is universally agreed that no single test dose can meet these requirements. One conspicuous area of failure is the detection of subdural injection.

Test doses and subdural block

Subdural block, resulting from inadvertent injection into the potential space between the dura and the arachnoid, typically takes 20 minutes to develop. Case reports (Brindle Smith et al, 1984; Pearson, 1984; Abouleish and Goldstein, 1986) have mentioned the absence of sensory or motor impairment 5 minutes after a test dose, while motor sparing may persist despite high sensory blocks. This may be due to the anatomy of the subdural space around nerve roots (Pearson, 1984). It seems that this complication cannot reliably be prevented by test dosing unless at least 20 minutes is allowed to elapse, possibly doubling the time for the procedure in an attempt to detect a very rare occurrence. Moreover, subdural block is usually relatively easy to manage, though there is a small risk of late arachnoid tear (Reynolds and Speedy, 1990).

'Single shot' versus catheter techniques

Opinions differ on the need for a test dose in 'single shot' epidural techniques, not involving the placement of a catheter. At least one paper (Laishley and Morgan, 1988) described test dosing in this context, but its use requires the needle to remain in the epidural space for at least 5 minutes, increasing the chance of dural puncture. Neurological examination at the end of that time must be performed by a third party and is hampered by the need for the patient to remain still. Furthermore, the information obtained only relates to the position of the needle 5 minutes previously.

There is no evidence that injections through the needle are any less safe than catheter techniques, indeed the reverse may be true (Dain et al, 1987). The placement of an epidural catheter is accompanied by a higher incidence of epidural vein puncture, a further risk of dural (or at least arachnoid) puncture and the added hazards of knotting, breakage and migration of the catheter. Although both epidural vein and dural puncture with the needle usually reveal themselves, intrathecal or intravenous placement of the catheter may not be apparent even after aspiration, particularly with a single end-hole catheter. In one series, a third of intravenous catheter placements were not detected by an aspiration test (Kenepp and Gutsche, 1981). Moreover, a test dose may reveal subarachnoid injection following a negative aspiration test. Majority opinion, therefore, favours both an aspiration test and a test dose when a catheter has been sited.

Physical tests of catheter placement

Vigorous aspiration of an epidural catheter lying within a vein will tend to collapse the wall and reduce the chance of aspirating blood. Cartwright (1987) has recommended opening the proximal end of the fluid-filled catheter to air and lowering it below the level of the patient. Shah (1982) describes injection of a small volume of air before aspiration. The distal end of the catheter should then be lying in an air-filled cavity and only air should come out. Whatever test is performed at insertion of the catheter, a *gentle* aspiration test must always precede any injection down it.

If clear fluid is aspirated, various tests have been suggested to aid in its identification, including temperature (cerebrospinal fluid being warmer than recently injected saline or local anaesthetic) and pH (Lee et al, 1982). The measurement of glucose content is not a wholly reliable test for the presence of cerebrospinal fluid (CSF). Not only may Clinistix (Berry, 1958) and BM test strips (Saddler, 1985) show a positive reaction with blood and saline, but local anaesthetic aspirated from the epidural space after as little as 10 minutes may have an appreciable glucose content (Scott, 1979).

As Prince and McGregor (1986) have concluded, the best evidence that an epidural catheter is lying within the CSF is the aspiration of a larger volume of fluid than has been injected.

Detection of intrathecal catheter placement

There is now a large body of evidence that bupivacaine is not suitable as the local anaesthetic component of an epidural test dose. Many British anaesthetists still use 0.5% bupivacaine in doses of 2–3 ml, waiting for 5 minutes before interpreting the result. The manufacturer's current data sheet recommends a 3–5 ml test dose for all concentrations of Marcain. Should the catheter be lying intrathecally, such doses may produce a dangerously high block in obstetric patients; case reports have described blockade to T1 (Stonham and Moss, 1983), C4 (Kumar et al, 1985) and even trigeminal nerve block (Fine and Wong, 1984) after 3 ml 0.5% bupivacaine. Even volumes as low as 1.6 ml have produced blocks to C6 (Kumar et al, 1985). It has often been suggested that the unusually high intrathecal blocks in obstetric patients result from engorgement of epidural veins secondary to aortocaval compression causing compression of the dural sac and cranial movement of the local anaesthetic within. However, Shah (1984) has shown that epidural space pressures measured supine, lateral and prone are not significantly different between groups of pregnant and non-pregnant patients. It is nonetheless true that marked cranial extension of subarachnoid block in the parturient occurs on turning from the lateral to the supine position, and the patient should not be turned following an epidural test dose until the results are known.

If smaller volumes of 0.5% bupivacaine are used in an attempt to avoid excessive cranial spread, the onset of intrathecal block may be slowed to a point where it is missed at 5 minutes (*see Discussion*). Nicholas (1984) has observed the variability of speed of onset of intrathecal bupivacaine in a variety of doses. The use of 0.75% solution has been suggested (Fargas-Babjak et al, 1980) but it has an even greater potential for cardiotoxicity injected intravenously and is not recommended for use in obstetrics.

Van Zundert et al (1987) suggested a standard dose of 10 ml of 0.125% bupivacaine containing 12.5 μg adrenaline, which has been used successfully for epidural analgesia in labour. Injected intrathecally in patients for urological surgery, the mean upper level of sensory block produced was T8. They did not, however, report the effects of intrathecal administration of such a dose in pregnant women.

Reviews of epidural test doses (Prince and McGregor, 1986; Biehl, 1987; Dain et al, 1987) have recommended 1.5–2% lignocaine as the drug of choice. Intrathecally, 2 ml of 1.5% solution in 7.5% dextrose produces unambiguous evidence of a sensory block in 2 minutes, with an average cephalad spread to T9 (Abraham et al, 1986).

Ideally, the test dose should be a hyperbaric solution, allowing control of cranial spread should it be deposited intrathecally. At present, a 1.5% or 2% hyperbaric lignocaine solution is not generally available in the UK. Casey (1985) suggested 3 ml of 5% hyperbaric solution, but this may cause appreciable epidural block in its own right and thus create difficulties in interpretation. Until a hyperbaric 2% solution becomes available it seems reasonable to use the isobaric preparation, which is freely available in almost every obstetric department.

Detection of intravascular catheter placement

Plain solutions of local anaesthetics injected intravenously in test dose quantities seldom give rise to symptoms. Much of the recent controversy concerning test doses has centred on whether adrenaline-containing test doses are useful in the detection of intravascular catheter placement. The original study by Moore and Batra (1981) was an attempt to discover a single solution that would reliably detect intrathecal and intravascular injection within 2 minutes. They examined 3 ml test doses of 0.75% bupivacaine, 1.5% mepivacaine,

1.5% lignocaine and 3.0% chloroprocaine, and 175 patients received one of these solutions with 15 μg adrenaline (equivalent to a 1:200 000 solution) as an intravenous injection while their electrocardiogram (ECG) was recorded and heart rate monitored. Forty control subjects received the plain solutions. None of these controls showed a change in heart rate, but the subjects receiving adrenaline-containing solutions increased their heart rates from 79 ± 14 to 111 ± 15 beats per minute within 23 ± 6 seconds. On Moore and Batra's evidence, intravascular and intrathecal injection *were* reliably detectable with a single test dose. Following their paper many anaesthetists adopted a criterion of an increase in heart rate of 30 beats per minute within 1 minute of injection of 15 μg adrenaline as being indicative of intravascular injection.

Unfortunately for the obstetric anaesthetist, Moore and Batra's patients differed in two important respects from women in labour. Their patients were heavily premedicated, having received 100 μg fentanyl and 10–15 mg diazepam intravenously 15 minutes previously, and none of them was pregnant. Their baseline heart rates were thus lower and less variable than those of parturients. Furthermore, there is a reduced chronotropic response to β-agonists in pregnancy (DeSimone et al, 1987). Leighton et al (1988) examined the effects of 15 μg adrenaline compared with normal saline injected intravenously in labouring patients. On the accepted criteria, only 5 out of 10 subjects receiving adrenaline were correctly identified, and 2 of 10 controls were wrongly identified as having received adrenaline. Two fetuses in the adrenaline group showed transient signs of fetal distress following the injection.

Cartwright et al (1986) observed heart-rate changes following an epidural test dose of 3 ml of *plain* 0.5% bupivacaine in 100 labouring patients. Although none of the epidural catheters was lying intravenously, 24 subjects showed an increased heart rate of more than 20 beats per minute, and 12 of more than 30 beats per minute.

Tom (1988) examined the implications of these studies. In a random group of 100 obstetric patients, perhaps 2 will have intravascular catheter placement. On the basis of the response to an adrenaline test dose only 1 will be correctly identified, while another 12 patients will have their epidural catheters resited unnecessarily. The conclusion must be that however useful such test doses may be in a general surgical context, they are unreliable in the obstetric patient.

Moore (1986) stated that since the introduction of the adrenaline test dose, his institution had not had a single systemic toxic reaction in 8500 surgical and 6000 obstetric epidural blocks, whereas prior to 1980 there were about 3 cases of anaesthetic-induced convulsions per year.

SUGGESTED PROTOCOL

A careful aspiration test is a vital part of the procedure of siting an epidural catheter, and it is essential that every injection via the catheter be preceded by gentle aspiration. A test dose of 2 ml of 2% plain lignocaine should be given once the catheter has been secured in position. After 5 minutes there should be little if any sensory blockade, no objective evidence of motor blockade, and the arterial pressure should not have fallen significantly (this may be the earliest sign of subdural block).

While doubts remain about the test dose as a detector of intravascular placement, every epidural catheter must be treated as potentially lying intravenously. All subsequent injections of plain solutions should be given slowly, so that not more than 20 mg of bupivacaine per minute are injected, while the patient is questioned directly about symptoms related to intravenous injection, such as sensations of a metallic taste, tinnitus or circumoral numbness. If an adrenaline-containing solution is used to establish the block, ECG monitoring should be instituted and the heart rate and rhythm observed during injection. Unreliable though the adrenaline test dose may be, larger quantities injected intravenously will invariably produce a tachycardia before the onset of symptoms related to the local anaesthetic component.

Test doses and top-ups

The use of a test dose before every top-up in intermittent techniques has been advocated, but the interpretation can be difficult in the presence of existing partial epidural block. One of the most common reasons for an obstetric epidural to be branded unsatisfactory, namely persistent L1 pain, is often abolished by the test dose after resiting the catheter (personal observation). Certainly, it is not reasonable to expect midwifery staff to interpret the results of test doses, and it is therefore held by some that all top-ups should be performed by anaesthetists (Rees and Rosen, 1979). However, midwives are likely to find the aspiration test easier to interpret than the outcome of a test dose, and top-ups by midwives have an excellent safety record (Crawford, 1988).

REFERENCES

Abouleish E & Goldstein M (1986) Migration of an extradural catheter into the subdural space. *British Journal of Anaesthesia* **58**: 1194–1197.
Abraham RA, Harris AP, Maxwell LG & Kaplow S (1986) The efficacy of 1.5%

lidocaine with 7.5% dextrose and epinephrine as an epidural test dose for obstetrics. *Anesthesiology* **64**: 116–119.

Albright GA (1979) Cardiac arrest following regional anesthesia with etidocaine or bupivacaine. *Anesthesiology* **51**: 285–287.

Berry A (1958) Test for spinal fluid. *Anaesthesia* **13**: 100–101.

Biehl D (1987) The dilemma of the epidural test dose (editorial). *Canadian Journal of Anaesthesia* **34**: 545–548.

Brindle Smith G, Barton FL & Watt JH (1984) Extensive spread of local anaesthetic solution following subdural insertion of an epidural catheter during labour. *Anaesthesia* **39**: 355–358.

Cartwright PD (1987) Obstetric epidural test doses. *Anaesthesia* **42**: 556.

Cartwright PD, McCarroll SM & Antzaka C (1986) Maternal heart rate changes with a plain epidural test dose. *Anesthesiology* **65**: 226–228.

Casey WF (1985) Epidural test doses in obstetrics. *Anaesthesia* **40**: 597.

Crawford JS (1988) Epidural test dose in obstetrics (letter). *Canadian Journal of Anaesthesia* **35**: 441–442.

Dain SL, Rolbin SH & Hew EM (1987) The epidural test dose in obstetrics: is it necessary? *Canadian Journal of Anaesthesia* **34**: 601–605.

DeSimone CA, Leighton BL, Norris MC, Chayen B & Menduke H (1987) The chronotropic effect of isoproteronol is reduced in pregnant women. *Anesthesiology* **67**: A460.

Dogliotti AM (1933) Segmental peridural spinal anesthesia. *American Journal of Surgery* **20**: 107–118.

Fargas-Babjak A, McChesney J, Morison DH (1980) The efficacy of bupivacaine 0.75% as an epidural test dose. *Canadian Anaesthetists Society Journal* **27**: 500–501.

Fine PG & Wong KC (1984) Cranial nerve block after test dose through an epidural catheter in a pre-eclamptic parturient. *Canadian Anaesthetists Society Journal* **31**: 565–567.

Kenepp NB & Gutsche BB (1981) Inadvertent intravascular injections during lumbar epidural anesthesia. *Anesthesiology* **54**: 172–173.

Kumar CM, Dennison B & Panchal HI (1985) Epidural test dose (letter). *Anaesthesia* **40**: 1023.

Laishley RS & Morgan BM (1988) A single dose epidural technique for Caesarean section. *Anaesthesia* **43**: 100–103.

Lee JA, Atkinson RS & Rushman GB (1982) *A Synopsis of Anaesthesia*. London: Wright PSG.

Leighton BL, Norris, MC, DeSimone CA & Epstein R (1988) The epinephrine test dose revisited, again (letter). *Anesthesiology* **68**: 807.

Moore DC (1986) Epidural test doses in obstetrics – let us face facts. *Anaesthesia* **41**: 1159.

Moore DC & Batra MS (1981) The components of an effective test dose prior to epidural block. *Anesthesiology* **55**: 693–696.

Nicholas ADG (1984) The optimal test dose for epidural anesthesia. *Anesthesiology* **60**: 79.

Pearson RMG (1984) A rare complication of extradural analgesia. *Anaesthesia* **39**: 460–463.

Prince G & McGregor D (1986) Obstetric epidural test doses – a reappraisal. *Anaesthesia* **41**: 1240–1250.

Rees GA & Rosen M (1979) Test dose in extradural analgesia (letter). *British Journal of Anaesthesia* **51**: 70–71.

Reynolds F & Speedy H (1990) The subdural space. The third place to go astray. *Anaesthesia* **45**: 120–123.

Saddler JM (1985) Falsely positive reaction to glucose test strips. *Anaesthesia* **40**: 601.

Scott DB (1979) Test doses in extradural analgesia (letter). *British Journal of Anaesthesia* **51**: 910.

Shah JL (1982) A test to show correct placement of epidural catheter. *Anaesthesia* **37**: 426–427.

Shah JL (1984) Effect of posture on extradural pressure. *British Journal of Anaesthesia* **56**: 1373–1377.

Stonham J & Moss P (1983) The optimal test dose for epidural anesthesia (letter). *Anesthesiology* **58**: 389–390.

Tom WC (1988) The epidural test dose and the identification of rare events (letter). *Canadian Journal of Anaesthesia* **35**: 441–442.

Van Zundert A, Vaes L, Soetens M et al (1987) Every dose given in epidural analgesia for vaginal delivery can be a test dose. *Anesthesiology* **67**: 436–440.

4

Epidural analgesia by continuous infusion

DAVID GAYLARD

The administration of epidural drugs by continuous infusion, as first described by Dawkins (1957), appears to be increasing in popularity.

The aim of epidural analgesia in labour is to provide continuous and safe pain relief; Crawford (1985) stated that epidural analgesia for labour and delivery, including topping-up by well-informed midwives, is characterized by an extremely high level of safety for the mother. In a consecutive series of over 27 000 lumbar epidural blocks, 9 potentially life-threatening complications occurred; only 3 caused real concern for the mother's safety, and 6 occurred with the first dose given by the anaesthetist. In all 9 cases the local anaesthetic was apparently given either intravenously or intrathecally. Despite this excellent safety record, the intermittent top-up technique has some disadvantages which may potentially be overcome by continuous infusion.

Pain relief

Fluctuations in pain control ('roller-coaster' analgesia) are an almost inevitable result of the intermittent top-up technique of epidural analgesia. Delays between the request for a top-up and the onset of analgesia are inevitable. Infusions overcome this to a large degree, and the infusion rate can be altered to introduce an element of fine tuning and provide a level of block that suits the patient (Hicks et al, 1988). Despite this, with all regimens described, occasional top-ups are still required to maintain satisfactory analgesia (Li et al, 1985; Ewen et al, 1986).

Hypotension

Similarly, fluctuations in blood pressure occur, episodes of hypotension usually being associated with a bolus injection, most commonly the initial dose (Abboud et al, 1984). While preloading and selection of an appropriate initial dose can diminish the frequency of these episodes, those occurring as a result of additional top-ups can be reduced by the use of continuous infusions (Clark, 1982; Ewen et al, 1986). Regular checks on the height of the block should prevent inappropriately high sympathetic block and subsequent hypotension from this cause. It has been shown that there is good agreement between medical staff and midwives in assessment of block height. Jones et al (1988) studied the ability of midwives to assess accurately the level of epidural blockade by loss of sensation to a cold stimulus. The anaesthetist and midwife agreed in 71.5% of cases. The midwife overestimated in 9.5% of cases and never underestimated by more than three spinal segments. These important checks therefore may most appropriately and conveniently be performed by midwives, in conjunction with assessment of pain.

Inadvertent intravenous or intrathecal injection

Inadvertent intravenous and intrathecal injections of local anaesthetic are probably the most potentially serious complications, and may be attributed to epidural catheter migration (Philip and Brown, 1976; Robson and Brodsky, 1977). Another possibility is accidental subdural analgesia in which the spread of solution may be slow, and an extensive block delayed (Boys and Norman, 1975). Careful aspiration and the use of a test dose, prior to each top-up, may be helpful in detecting a misplaced catheter, but neither of these manoeuvres is absolutely reliable. Continuous infusions offer possible advantages since either intravenous or intrathecal infusion should produce gradually increasing symptoms and signs and therefore allow more time for recognition and appropriate treatment (see also Chapter 8). Injection of 15–20 mg of bupivacaine intrathecally produces a block which does not usually progress above T4 and then regresses at approximately two segments per hour (Chambers et al, 1981; Kalso et al, 1982; Sheskey et al, 1983). Li et al (1985) stated that theoretically at an infusion rate of 12.5 mg per hour of bupivacaine it is unlikely that total spinal block would occur rapidly following dural puncture. They recommended 2-hourly sensory testing. Certainly midwives and patients should be aware of the symptoms and signs of intravenous and intrathecal local anaesthetic injection and report these immediately. If in doubt the infusion can be stopped until medical advice is obtained.

Ensuring an impeccable technique by proper training, reliable equipment and constant midwife vigilance is obviously of paramount importance. However, should any of these fail, and if occasional disasters are to be avoided, it is essential that a high level of training in the skills of resuscitation of pregnant women is maintained by all members of staff working in the delivery suite. In a survey carried out by Langton (1989) only 41% of midwives knew the correct posture for the resuscitation of a pregnant woman and only 32% said they would be confident of ventilating the lungs with a mask and airway during an emergency. The resuscitation skill of qualified medical staff is also a cause for concern (Skinner et al, 1985). These studies of the provision of basic life support have shown a worrying need for improvement, and the value of regular practice and assessment. The presence of an experienced anaesthetist with duties exclusive to the labour ward must be considered a minimum requirement.

Closed systems

There is always a potential for mistakes with multiple tubes and administration systems. A number of methods of preventing such errors have been described (Taylor, 1983; Gaylard et al, 1987). Infusions, by reducing the number of injections required, will reduce the chance of the incorrect drug or dose being administered. A closed system is also less susceptible to contamination. The fear that the extra tubing further limits mobility has not posed a problem in practice. Women in labour requesting epidural analgesia will inevitably have their activities restricted and the use of an infusion should not be an additional factor. Infusions of weak concentrations of bupivacaine have generally been found to produce neither greater nor more prolonged motor blockade than standard top-ups, and therefore should not further restrict mobility (Li et al, 1985; Gaylard et al, 1987; Hicks et al, 1988).

Delivery

Whether the use of epidural anaesthesia increases the rate of forceps delivery remains a matter of debate and is now unlikely to be settled by prospective controlled studies (Bailey, 1989). In any event infusions can be maintained or stopped if necessary to provide conditions suitable for the preferred management of the second stage (Chestnut et al, 1987) and should not be worse than top-ups in this respect. Infusion regimens consistently produce no adverse effects on the fetus (Clark, 1982; Abboud et al, 1984).

Medical and midwife workload

Infusions have been shown to reduce both medical and midwife workload. Caldwell and Bradwood (1984) found that medical time involved in maintaining epidurals fell from an average of 40 minutes to 13 minutes when infusions were used. Gaylard et al (1987) showed a reduction in midwife workload from 76 minutes to 35 minutes per labour, which should allow greater time for patient observation and care.

Techniques

The administration of local anaesthetics by infusion requires a reliable delivery system. A number of methods have been described, including gravity drips, capillary tube devices and various mechanical infusion pumps (Scott and Walker, 1963; Spoerel et al, 1970; Evans and Carrie, 1979; Davies and Fettes, 1981). The safety aspects of these methods are important: they include maintenance of equipment and staff familiarity with the devices. Gravity drips may result in variable flow rates, and capillary tube devices depend upon infusion bags being maintained at constant pressure. Mechanical infusion pumps overcome these problems and are now of convenient size, have suitable alarm systems and are more widely available.

Over the past ten years a variety of regimens for the continuous infusion of bupivacaine into the epidural space for pain relief during labour have been described (Table 1). It is difficult to compare these studies with a view to producing a recommendation for optimum concentration and rate of infusion. Analgesia, episodes of hypotension, degree and duration of motor block, mode of delivery and the condition of the fetus are either not reported or measured in different ways. Not all results exclude patients with a short interval from epidural blockade to delivery, in which the initial dose may still be effective. It is difficult to compare the top-up requirements using different concentrations and infusion rates, since they are also expressed differently. For example, results may be shown as patient groups requiring one or no top-up, or as groups requiring one or more top-ups. Details of top-up timing are not always given, and may be important since the single top-up may be for the second stage.

However, a dose of 0.125% bupivacaine at 10 ml per hour consistently provides good analgesia with approximately 70% of patients requiring one or no top-ups. Plasma concentration and total dose remain well below the recommended safe maximums and duration of motor block is not excessive. Li et al (1985) concluded that this regimen was the best compromise between significant

Table 1. Reported dosage regimens for continuous epidural analgesia with bupivacaine.

Date	Author(s)	Loading dose	Infusion conc.	Flow rate (ml h^{-1})	Top-ups	Remarks
1977	Glover	0.25% 10 ml	0.125%	10	40% 1 top-up	Variable infusion rate
1979	Evans & Carrie	0.25% 10 ml	0.25%	6	16% 1 top-up	Infusion increased if
		0.25% 7–10 ml	0.25%	7–10		analgesia inadequate
1982	Clark	0.125% 10 ml	0.25%	14 or 19		3 patients additional
						10 ml for delivery
1983	Taylor	0.25% 9–12 ml	0.25%	6	70% 1 or none	
			0.3%	6	90% 1 or none	
			0.375%	6	87% 1 or none	
1985	Li et al	0.5% 10 ml	No infusion	–	32% 1 or none	
		0.5% 10 ml	0.0625%	10	35% 1 or none	
		0.5% 10 ml	0.125%	5	45% 1 or none	
		0.5% 10 ml	0.125%	10	69% 1 or none	
		0.5% 10 ml	0.125%	15	70% 1 or none	
1986	Ewen et al	0.5% 11 ml	0.08%	25	40% 1 or more	
		0.5% 11 ml	0.25%	8	68% 1 or none	
1987	Bogod et al	0.5% 6–10 ml	0.125%	10	76% 1 or none	
		0.5% 6–10 ml	No infusion	–	58% 1 or none	
1987	Gaylard et al	0.5% 8–10 ml	0.25%	7–9	90% 1 or none	Variable rate
1988	Hicks et al	0.5% 6–8 ml	Top-ups	(0.25% 6–8 ml)	33% 1 or none	
			0.075%	15	74% 1 or none	

prolongation of the block and patient safety. Variable dose regimens have been described, with medical staff varying infusion rates according to analgesia (Glover, 1977), or adjustment by midwives according to a flow chart system (Gaylard et al, 1987) (Figure 1). These systems would appear to provide more flexibility in terms of pain relief while maintaining the safety features of constant infusions. A regimen of regular timed top-ups of bupivacaine has also been described (Purdy et al, 1987), and found to produce analgesia superior to conventional on-demand therapy, without increasing complications.

Systemic toxicity

Plasma concentrations of bupivacaine during prolonged infusions (or top-ups) may be a cause for concern. The UK manufacturer's data sheet recommends a maximum safe dose of bupivacaine of 2 mg kg^{-1} in any 4-hour period. Following reasonably steady administration a bupivacaine concentration of 1.6 μg ml^{-1} is associated with mild toxic symptoms (Reynolds, 1971). In studies of epidural infusions in which plasma bupivacaine concentration has been measured, it is well below this level (Glover, 1977; Clark, 1982; Abboud et al, 1984). Although the ultimate steady-state concentration will depend upon the dose rate, Reynolds et al (1973) found that the bupivacaine concentration in maternal plasma at delivery following intermittent extradural analgesia was dependent on total dose and not on dose rate. From their data they predicted that using plain bupivacaine there was a 5% chance of mild intoxication with a total dose of 320 mg. Although a number of studies have shown an increase in total dose with infusions when compared to top-ups, this usually falls well below 320 mg (Bogod et al, 1987; Gaylard et al, 1987; Hicks et al, 1988).

Occasionally doses exceeding 300 mg have been reached. Li et al (1985) had three patients in whom the total dose of bupivacaine exceeded 300 mg, all with infusions lasting longer than 12 hours. Gaylard et al (1987) had two patients who received more than 300 mg of bupivacaine, both with infusions longer than 14 hours. It is apparent that high total doses of bupivacaine occur in patients who have infusion times greater than 12 hours. If these patients then proceed to Caesarean section under epidural anaesthesia, the extra bupivacaine required for operative analgesia may exceed the recommended doses, producing an acute on chronic toxicity. In practice these excessive doses have rarely been reported to produce clinical problems (Thorburn and Moir, 1984). It remains difficult to give strict guidelines regarding maximum doses. Nevertheless, this

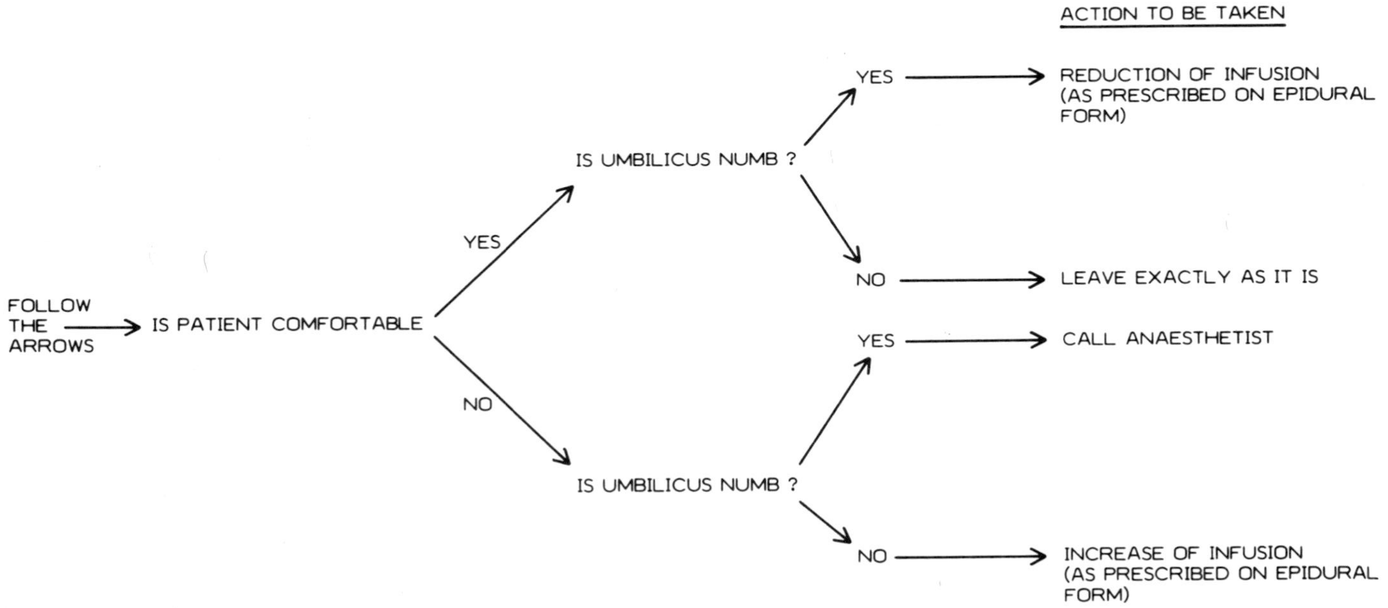

ACTION TO BE TAKEN

FOLLOW THE ARROWS → IS PATIENT COMFORTABLE

YES → IS UMBILICUS NUMB ?

YES → REDUCTION OF INFUSION (AS PRESCRIBED ON EPIDURAL FORM)

NO → LEAVE EXACTLY AS IT IS

NO → IS UMBILICUS NUMB ?

YES → CALL ANAESTHETIST

NO → INCREASE OF INFUSION (AS PRESCRIBED ON EPIDURAL FORM)

ALL NORMAL CARE AND OBSERVATIONS TO BE PERFORMED EXACTLY AS USUAL FOR EPIDURAL ANALGESIA. WHEN IN DOUBT ABOUT THE INFUSION, CALL ANAESTHETIST.

Figure 1. Flow chart for midwife control of continuous epidural infusion.

group of patients requires extra vigilance in checking for symptoms and signs of toxicity.

Opioid infusions

Epidural opioids have several advantages over local anaesthetic agents, such as absence of sympathetic and motor block. A major concern, however, has been the potential for causing neonatal respiratory depression.

Continuous epidural administration of alfentanil has been studied, and shown to provide inadequate analgesia for labour (Heytens et al, 1987). Skerman et al (1985) found that combining low-dose fentanyl with bupivacaine by infusion produced more profound pain relief than bupivacaine alone (assessed by visual analogue scale). No neonatal depression or differences in Apgar score were observed. Chestnut et al (1988) compared 0.0625% bupivacaine combined with fentanyl (0.0002%) versus 0.125% bupivacaine alone. The pain scores in the two groups were similar, but those receiving the combination experienced less intense motor blockade, with the only side-effect being mild pruritus. Top-ups of bupivacaine and fentanyl for perineal pain during labour have been shown to produce consistently reliable analgesia which was quicker in onset and of longer duration than bupivacaine alone (Reynolds and O'Sullivan, 1989). It is possible, therefore, that the addition of an opioid to a local anaesthetic infusion increases its success rate partly because it improves perineal analgesia. Site of pain is rarely reported. The value of opioid infusions in labour is further discussed in Chapter 12.

Continous spinal anaesthesia

When used for general surgery, continuous spinal anaesthesia has been shown to have a low incidence (< 1%) of postdural puncture headache (Denny et al, 1987). It is postulated that this is due to an inflammatory reaction developing at the puncture site so that when the catheter is removed the hole is sealed by oedema. Potential advantages of this technique are rapid onset of action and the small doses of local anaesthetic and or opioid that may be used. Although spinal anaesthesia has some popularity for Caesarean section there are no reports of elective spinal infusions for labour. The expected high incidence of headache in this group of patients would seem to preclude this, although it has been suggested that this might be an appropriate course of action following inadvertent dural puncture (Scott, 1989).

REFERENCES

Abboud TK, Afrasiabi A, Sarkis F et al (1984) Continuous infusion epidural analgesia in parturients receiving bupivacaine chloroprocaine or lidocaine-maternal, fetal and neonatal effects. *Anesthesia and Analgesia* **63**: 241–248.

Bailey PW (1989) Epidural anaesthesia and instrumental delivery. *Anaesthesia* **44**: 171–172.

Bogod DG, Rosen M & Rees GAD (1987) Extradural infusion of 0.125% bupivacaine at 10 ml h^{-1} to women during labour. *British Journal of Anaesthesia* **59**: 325–330.

Boys JE & Norman PF (1975) Accidental subdural analgesia. *British Journal of Anaesthesia* **47**: 1111–1113.

Caldwell JE & Bradwood JM (1984) Epidural analgesia by infusion. *Anaesthesia* **39**: 493–494.

Chambers WA, Edstrom HH & Scott DB (1981) Effect of baricity on spinal anaesthesia with bupivacaine. *British Journal of Anaesthesia* **53**: 279–282.

Chestnut DH, Vandewalker GE, Owen CL, Bates JN & Choi WW (1987) The influence of continuous epidural bupivacaine analgesia on the second stage of labour and method of delivery in nulliparous women. *Anesthesiology* **66**: 774–780.

Chestnut DH, Owen CL, Ostman LG, Bates JN & Choi WW (1988) Continuous infusion epidural analgesia during labor. *Anesthesiology* **68**: 754–759.

Clark MJ (1982) Continuous mini-infusion of 0.125% bupivacaine into the epidural space during labour. *Journal of American Obstetric Association* **81**: 484–491.

Crawford JS (1985) Some maternal complications of epidural analgesia for labour. *Anaesthesia* **40**: 1219–1225.

Davies AO & Fettes IW (1981) A simple safe method for continuous infusion epidural analgesia in obstetrics. *Canadian Anaesthetists Society Journal* **28**: 484–487.

Dawkins M (1957) Relief of post operative pain by continuous epidural drip. *Survey of Anesthesiology* **1**: 616–617.

Denny N, Masters R, Pearson D, Read J, Sihota M & Selander D (1987) Post dural puncture headache after continuous spinal anesthesia. *Anesthesia and Analgesia* **66**: 791–794.

Evans KRL & Carrie LES (1979) Continuous epidural infusion of bupivacaine in labour: a simple method. *Anaesthesia* **34**: 310–315.

Ewen A, McLeod DD, MacLeod DM, Campbell A & Tunstall ME (1986) Continuous infusion epidural analgesia in obstetrics: a comparison of 0.08% and 0.25% bupivacaine. *Anaesthesia* **41**: 143–147.

Gaylard DG, Wilson IH & Balmer HGR (1987) Forum. An epidural infusion technique for labour. *Anaesthesia* **42**: 1098–1101.

Glover DJ (1977) Forum. Continuous epidural analgesia in the obstetric patient: a feasibility study using a mechanical infusion pump. *Anaesthesia* **32**: 499–503.

Heytens L, Cammu H & Camu F (1987) Extradural analgesia during labour using alfentanil. *British Journal of Anaesthesia* **59**: 331–337.

Hicks JA, Jenkins JG, Newton MC & Findley IL (1988) Continuous epidural infusion of 0.075% bupivacaine for pain relief in labour. *Anaesthesia* **43**: 289–292.

Jones MJT, Bogod DG, Rees GAD & Rosen M (1988) Midwives' assessment of the upper sensory level after epidural blockade. *Anaesthesia* **43**: 557–559.

Kalso E, Tuominen M & Rosenberg PH (1982) Effect of posture and some CSF characteristics on spinal anaesthesia with isobaric 0.5% bupivacaine. *British Journal of Anaesthesia* **54**: 1179–1184.

Langton JA (1989) Skills in basic life support. *Anaesthesia* **44**: 258.

Li DF, Rees GAD & Rosen M (1985) Continuous extradural infusion of 0.0625% or 0.125% bupivacaine for pain relief in primigravid labour. *British Journal of Anaesthesia* **57**: 264–270.

McGrady EM, Brownhill DK & Davies AG (1989) Epidural diamorphine and bupivacaine in labour. *Anaesthesia* **44**: 400–403.

Philip JH & Brown WU (1976) Total spinal anesthesia late in the course of obstetric bupivacaine epidural block.*Anesthesiology* **44**: 340–341.

Phillips GH (1987) Epidural sufentanil/bupivacaine combinations for analgesia during labor: effect of varying sufentanil doses. *Anesthesiology* **67**: 835–838.

Purdy G, Currie J & Owen H (1987) Continuous extradural analgesia in labour. *British Journal of Anaesthesia* **59**: 319–324.

Reynolds F (1971) A comparison of the potential toxicity of bupivacaine, lignocaine and mepivacaine during epidural blockade for surgery. **43**: 567–571.

Reynolds F & O'Sullivan G (1989) Forum. Epidural fentanyl and perineal pain in labour. *Anaesthesia* **44**: 341–344.

Reynolds F, Hargrove RL & Wyman JB (1973) Maternal and foetal plasma concentrations of bupivacaine after epidural block. *British Journal of Anaesthesia* **45**: 1049–1053.

Robson JA & Brodsky JB (1977) Latent dural puncture after lumbar epidural block. *Anesthesia and Analgesia* **56**: 725–735.

Scott DB (1989) Subarachnoid spread of epidural local anaesthetic following dural puncture. *Anaesthesia* **44**: 74–75.

Scott DB & Walker LR (1963) Administration of continuous epidural analgesia. *Anaesthesia* **18**: 82–83.

Sheskey MC, Rocco AG, Bizzarri-Schmid M, Francis DM, Edstrom H & Covino BG (1983) A dose response study of bupivacaine for spinal anesthesia. *Anesthesia and Analgesia* **62**: 931–935.

Skerman, JH, Thompson BA, Goldstein MT, Jacobs MA, Gupta A & Blass NH (1985) Combined continuous epidural fentanyl and bupivacaine in labor. *Anesthesiology* **63**: A450.

Skinner DV, Camm AJ & Miles S (1985) Cardiopulmonary resuscitation skills of preregistration house officers. *British Medical Journal* **290**: 1549–1550.

Spoerel WE, Thomas A & Gerula GR (1970) Continuous epidural analgesia: experience with mechanical injection devices. *Canadian Anaesthetists Society Journal* **17**: 37–51.

Taylor HJC (1983) Clinical experience with continuous epidural infusion of bupivacaine at 6 ml per hour in obstetrics. *Canadian Anaesthetists Society Journal* **30**: 277–285.

Thorburn J & Moir DD (1984) Bupivacaine toxicity in association with extradural analgesia for Caesarean section. *British Journal of Anaesthesia* **56**: 551–552.

5

Epidural analgesia and the management of the second stage of labour: a failure to progress

PHILIP W. BAILEY

Despite the acknowledged efficacy of epidural analgesia in relieving pain in labour and delivery, there is widespread apprehension that there will be an 'inevitable, sharp increase' (O'Driscoll and Meagher, 1980) in the need for forceps delivery when the technique is widely used. For some this may be of little concern, since the presence of epidural analgesia allows the elective use of forceps to shorten the second stage (Crawford, 1984). But others feel that any increased use of forceps introduces trauma for both mother and child (O'Driscoll and Meagher, 1980).

Two questions arise for discussion:

1. How real is this increase in the use of forceps?
2. Can obstetric practice be modified in the presence of epidural analgesia to reduce the use of forceps?

Is the increase in forceps delivery well founded?

Bailey and Howard (1983) described the effect of the sudden impact of widespread use of epidural analgesia on a stable obstetric scene at Doncaster Royal Infirmary. There was very little alteration in the overall use of forceps despite the rapid establishment of widespread epidural analgesia (Table 1). The changes were not significant.

Figure 1 shows the continuing annual trends in deliveries, and Figure 2 those for primiparous patients. There has been little change in the forceps delivery rate. The transient increase in the first year may have resulted from nervousness about the new technique and

Table 1. Patterns of delivery before and after the introduction of an epidural service in 1978.

	No epidural service		Epidural service available		
	1976	1977	1978	1979	1980
No. of mothers delivered	1285	1446	1684	1688	1722
Spontaneous delivery (%)	74.2	74.0	68.6	70.6	71.3
Forceps delivery (%)	13.8	14.3	16.8	15.0	15.4
Caesarean section (%)	7.9	7.1	9.6	8.8	8.5
Epidural anaesthesia (%)	–	–	26.9	36.7	43.3

the expectation of an increase in the need for forceps. The recent decline may be the result of more careful attention to obstetric policy, which is discussed later.

The manner of reporting results can distort the apparent use of forceps. Many people describe the results only of their epidural patients. For example, figures for 1988 presented in Table 2 would suggest a 23% forceps delivery rate, as against the overall forceps

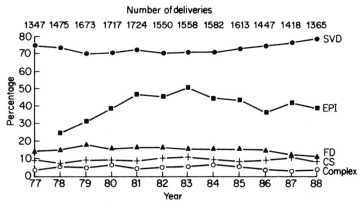

Figure 1. Annual trends in deliveries in one obstetric unit (all deliveries). SVD, spontaneous vaginal delivery; EPI, epidural analgesia; FD, forceps delivery; CS, Caesarean section.

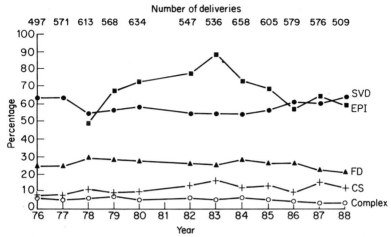

Figure 2. Annual trends in deliveries to primiparae in one obstetric unit. SVD, spontaneous vaginal delivery; EPI, epidural analgesia; FD, forceps delivery; CS, Caesarean section.

rate of 11%. This reflects the fact that patients coming to forceps delivery commonly have good indications for earlier epidural analgesia.

The different use made of epidural analgesia in the various modes of delivery is evident. Only 28% of people coming to spontaneous delivery had needed epidural analgesia, whereas 77% of those having forceps deliveries had had epidural analgesia. This does not

Table 2. Analysis of deliveries in one obstetric unit in 1988 – all deliveries.

	All patients (% deliveries)	Epidural patients (% deliveries)	% use of epidural analgesia
Spontaneous vaginal delivery	1059 (78%)	299 (61%)	28%
Instrumental delivery	145 (11%)	112 (23%)	77%
Caesarean section	112 (8%)	45 (9%)	40%
Complex delivery (breech/twin)	49 (4%)	32 (7%)	65%
TOTALS	1365 (100%)	486 (100%)	36%

Table 3. Analysis of deliveries in one obstetric unit in 1988 – primiparae.

	All primiparae (% deliveries)	Epidural patients (% deliveries)	% use of epidural analgesia
Spontaneous vaginal delivery	326 (64%)	164 (55%)	50%
Instrumental delivery	108 (21%)	84 (28%)	78%
Caesarean section	59 (12%)	40 (13%)	68%
Complex delivery (breech/twin)	16 (3%)	12 (4%)	75%
TOTALS	509 (100%)	300 (100%)	59%

signify that the use of epidural analgesia induced forceps deliveries, but rather shows the clinical acumen of the obstetric and midwifery staff in identifying likely forceps deliveries and requesting a prior epidural.

Since primiparae have a higher forceps delivery rate and a greater use of epidural analgesia than multiparae, the rest of the discussion concerns this group of patients; Table 3 shows the relevant figures for 1988. There was an overall forceps rate of 21%, and epidural analgesia was requested in 59% of primiparae.

It is difficult to compare these data with those of previously published reports (Table 4) using their criteria of presentation, because of the greatly differing techniques and high selectivity of their cases.

Nicholas et al (1970) dealt with caudal epidural blockade in 86% of cases. Crawford (1972) with his second thousand cases described his preferred 'tendency to perform simple forceps delivery as early as possible in the second stage'. Hoult et al (1977) excluded Caesarean sections and complex deliveries from their results, and the percentages given were divided between spontaneous deliveries and various instrumental deliveries. Studd et al (1980) selected only patients who had spontaneous onset of labour, and excluded complex deliveries. Morgan et al (1980) studied 200 patients in uneventful labour out of 1972 women using epidural analgesia in 3400 deliveries, and specifically excluded medical and obstetric abnormalities.

Table 4. Outcome of labour in selected epiduralized primiparous patients.

	No. of primiparae	Spontaneous vaginal delivery (%)	Forceps delivery (%)	Caesarean section (%)	Complex delivery (%)	Comment
Nicholas et al (1970)	100	14	74	11	–	86% caudal
Crawford (1972)	1000	31	61	7	1	Early forceps delivery preferred
Hoult et al (1977)	125	29	71	Excl.	Excl.	Caesarean sections and complex deliveries excluded
Studd et al (1980)	833	34–37	64–57	3–8	Excl.	Only spontaneous onset Study of oxytocin augmentation Complex deliveries excluded
Morgan et al (1980)	114	45	55	Excl.	Excl.	Selected from 1972 epidurals in 3400 deliveries Abnormal deliveries excluded
Romine et al (1970)	376	–	93	1	Excl.	Administered by obstetrician
Taylor et al (1977)	–	59	30	9	–	Administered by obstetrician

Table 5. Outcome of labour in unselected primiparae.

	No. of primiparae	Spontaneous vaginal delivery (%)	Forceps delivery (%)	Caesarean section (%)	Complex delivery (%)	Comment
Potter & MacDonald (1971)	1533	71	24	2	–	65% epidural use
Bailey & Howard (1983)	571	63	24	8	5	Pre-epidural use
	613	54	29	11	6	50% epidural use
Bailey (this report)	509	64	21	12	3	59% epidural use

Romine et al (1970) and Taylor et al (1977) dealt with epidural analgesia administered by obstetricians. It is interesting to note the differing calls for forceps between these two obstetric units.

These papers all referred only to epidural patients. No indication is given of what the forceps rate would have been without the use of epidural analgesia, nor how the introduction of epidural analgesia influenced the forceps rate in the overall obstetric scene. Potter and MacDonald (1971), Bailey and Howard (1983) and this report (Table 5) attempt to do this, describing the proportions using epidurals among the whole primiparous population. There is widespread use of epidural analgesia in these patients, yet the use of forceps is not unreasonably high.

In conclusion, Figure 2 shows the trend of deliveries in primiparae in one unit over the years from the time before epidurals were used until 1988. Clearly the extensive use of epidural analgesia has had minimal impact on the need for forceps delivery. It does seem sad that despite observations like these, the association of increased use of forceps with epidural analgesia persists in most people's minds, is perpetuated in textbooks, and is the first to be quoted in the list of the few remaining objections to the use of epidural analgesia in labour.

Can the obstetric management of the second stage be modified as a result of epidural use?

Many years ago, Doughty (1969, 1978) illustrated how different obstetric practices are a major determinant of the forceps rate. Table 6 shows the extremes from one consultant who only allowed a short second stage and used forceps frequently, to another who allowed a longer time in the second stage and achieved a higher spontaneous delivery rate. It is stating the obvious to point out that forceps deliveries are done by obstetricians, not by epidurals. So what makes an obstetrician decide to terminate the second stage of labour?

Table 6. Length of second stage in primiparae with epidural analgesia (Doughty, 1978).

	No. of patients	Forces delivery rate (%)	Spontaneous delivery (min)	Forceps delivery (min)
Obstetrician A	70	94%	22.8	27.1
Obstetrician H	71	20%	59.4	75.6

Some definitions of fundamental obstetric concepts are given below to help clarify the following discussion.

Labour is the process of expulsion of the fetus from the womb. How it is *initiated* is complex and not fully elucidated, but it is *maintained* almost entirely by oxytocic activity.

Progress is measured by (a) progressive dilatation of the cervix and (b) descent of the presenting part in the birth canal.

The *second* stage starts when the cervix is fully dilated. An awareness has now developed of *two phases* of the second stage, divided by the descent of the presenting part to the perineum (O'Driscoll and Meagher, 1980).

Delay is defined by the application of time limits at various stages.

Failure to progress may be the result of (a) misdiagnosis of the onset of labour and onset of the second stage; (b) inefficient uterine contractions; (c) malposition of the fetus; or (d) obstructed labour.

MANAGEMENT OF LABOUR WITHOUT EPIDURAL ANALGESIA

First stage

Classically, *natural progress* is expected. Delay is only diagnosed after 48 hours in primiparae or 24 hours in multiparae. *Analgesia* is classically with pethidine, which is more often than not ineffective and has many other disadvantages, which are well documented elsewhere. *IV infusions* are rare, although the benefits of maintaining maternal hydration when using epidural analgesia have resulted in more frequent infusions in non-epidural labours also.

Nowadays, a more *active approach* to labour is usually taken, for with a longer labour there is increasing development of maternal acidosis, catecholamine release and maternal dehydration, not to mention maternal despair. A rate of cervical dilatation of 1 cm per hour is expected, and *oxytocic stimulation* used if progress is slow. Nonetheless, if vaginal examinations are only made at 4-hour intervals then there can often be long delays in the appreciation of a slow labour.

Diagnosis of onset of second stage

The exact moment of transition is usually unknown. The urge to push is often the first alert. This implies that the presenting part is low in the birth canal and distending the perineum – that is, phase 2 of the second stage has been reached. The presenting part becomes visible at the vulva, also indicating that phase 2 has been reached.

Vaginal examination often follows to confirm the previous signs.

Sometimes an examination is made for other reasons and full dilatation is discovered with the head high in the birth canal, with no distension of the perineum – that is, phase 1 of the second stage.

All of these may signal full dilatation of the cervix, but none indicates the exact moment that it occurred. This could be some hours earlier if examinations are only 4-hourly.

Active pushing

Traditionally, this begins as soon as full dilatation is discovered, for the fully open birth canal is seen as the opportunity to curtail distress to the mother and to speed delivery. The mother welcomes the chance to become active in her labour. Pushing is encouraged even with the head high in the birth canal.

Oxytocic stimulation of uterine activity may be continued into the second stage, but is less important since Ferguson's reflex causes a boost of endogenous oxytocin from the pituitary gland as the perineum is distended (Goodfellow et al, 1983).

Indications for intervention in the second stage

Maternal distress

Although the discovery of full dilatation is greeted with relief, for active involvement of the mother is possible, mothers are often very tired and distressed by poorly relieved first-stage pain, and disorientated by analgesic drugs. If a mother does not deliver rapidly, it is a kindness to cut short the second stage with a forceps delivery. Any suggestion that pushing should be delayed is not well received.

Fetal distress

Fetal well-being depends on maternal well-being, oxygenated blood circulating to the placenta and continuing fetal circulation. Interference with any of these may give rise to fetal distress. Not much can be done about mechanical interference with the fetal circulation by such factors as cord compression. However, maternal metabolic disturbances will be reflected in fetal metabolic disturbances, and circulating catecholamines and maternal dehydration have been shown to reduce placental perfusion (Barrier and Surreau, 1982).

Delay

Pearson and Davies (1974) showed that the longer the time spent pushing, the greater the metabolic disturbance in both mother and infant. Also hypoxaemia in the mother is common with pushing. It is thus usual to have a time limit imposed on pushing of one hour for primiparae and half an hour for multiparae. Such time limits when applied to a whole second stage, however, ignore the unknown time that a woman may have been fully dilated before she started pushing.

Failure to progress

If there is no early prospect of delivery, then some feel that it is kinder to the mother to curtail the labour with forceps delivery (Crawford, 1984).

MANAGEMENT OF LABOUR WITH EPIDURAL ANALGESIA

The effects of epidural analgesia are:

1. *Maternal benefits* from excellent pain relief, decreased metabolic disturbances and dehydration (Pearson and Davies, 1973; Barrier and Sureau, 1982). Mothers are more relaxed and cooperative; they are more physiologically normal.
2. *Fetal benefits* are reflected from the mother, and improved placental circulation results from good hydration, vasodilatation and the obligatory lateral position. Fears of hypotension and possibly reduced placental circulation have proved unfounded in a well-managed epidural block.

First stage

An active management is very feasible. Labour may be accelerated as required without causing any increased distress to the mother. Proper analgesia must be ensured. A low-dose, selective policy is appropriate, using for example 7–10 ml aliquots of 0.25% bupivacaine in the horizontal position for uterine pain, and a larger dose, sloped head up for perineal pain. IV infusion is obligatory and maintains hydration.

Diagnosis of onset of second stage

Commonly, full dilatation of the cervix is only discovered by chance vaginal examination, because there may be perineal analgesia and no urge to push. Often, the presenting part is visible, waiting to be delivered. Not uncommonly, there is an urge to push, especially with a selective epidural technique when there may be perineal awareness.

Active pushing

It is important to remember that maternal efforts supplement uterine contractions and do not replace them. If the head is high and there is no distension of the perineum, there would be no urge to push even without epidural blockade. These are the conditions describing phase 1 of the second stage. Physiologically this is simply an extension of the first stage of labour and management is the same as for the first stage. Any active pushing at this time will introduce metabolic upset (Pearson and Davies, 1974), and impose a time limit when there may be a long way to go. Prolonged pushing is also very tiring for the mother. Top-ups should not be withheld during phase 1 of the second stage (Phillips and Thomas, 1983).

It is desirable to await phase 2 of the second stage, when there may be an urge to bear down (Maresh et al, 1983), before instituting pushing. It is reasonable to do this since the mother is pain-free (provided epidural blockade is maintained), no major physiological disturbance occurs, and the fetal condition is optimized. The effect on labour is to extend the first stage situation for perhaps an hour, or two at the most. This is acceptable provided the fetus is continuously monitored and there are no signs of fetal distress.

It has been shown that blunting of perineal sensation by epidural blockade may reduce or abolish the Ferguson's reflex boost of oxytocin, and an extra infusion of oxytocin may be required (Goodfellow et al, 1983). The main force to progress in labour is provided by effective uterine contractions (O'Driscoll and Meagher, 1980).

During phase 2, expulsive efforts should be encouraged with contractions – prompted either by palpating the abdomen, or by perineal awareness. It is not necessary to wait for perineal sensation to recur if the head is already well down the birth canal. The use of oxytocin should be increased as necessary to simulate Ferguson's reflex.

Indications for intervention in the second stage

Maternal distress

This is not a problem with good epidural analgesia, and the need for intervention is decreased. Contractions can be stimulated and progress awaited without distressing the mother. She can maintain her energy and morale.

Fetal distress

Fetal heart monitoring is necessary. With epidural blockade, the mother must remain in the lateral position, good hydration is maintained and maternal metabolic disturbances are minimal. All these should improve the condition of the fetus and reduce the need for intervention. If supplementary oxytocin is being used, watch must be kept for over stimulation which might lead to reduced placental perfusion and fetal distress.

Failure to progress

Progress (descent through the birth canal) is expected. Failure to progress should not be diagnosed in the absence of adequate uterine contractions, stimulated by oxytocin if necessary (O'Driscoll and Meagher, 1980). Once full dilatation has been detected, progress to delivery should occur within an hour: if not, then further examination is indicated at that time. If examinations are made 4-hourly or longer at this stage then there may well be delay in diagnosing failure to progress and even obstruction.

Delay

Crawford (1984) stated: 'If there is no evidence of fetal distress, and if the mother displays no sign of undue fatigue, then there is no recognizable limit to the time which can be invested in the delivery process'. And indeed, Cohen (1977) showed in 4403 primiparous patients that a prolonged second stage had no deleterious effect so long as the fetus was monitored. Some very long second stages have been recorded in this hospital by following this policy. Table 7 is taken from a study of 360 primiparae: 55% had a total second stage of less than 60 minutes and 22% were longer than 120 minutes. However, 52% delivered within 30 minutes of pushing and only 2% were not delivered within 120 minutes of the start of pushing. Recent evidence suggests that few patients will deliver normally beyond 3 hours in the second stage (Kadar et al, 1986).

CONCLUSION

There are many instances where obstetric opinion can influence the decision to intervene or not to intervene. Conservative attitudes and entrenched prejudices have meant that there has often been no progress in the management of the second stage with epidural analgesia, and many mothers are denied the joy of a spontaneous delivery because of ill-advised obstetric intervention. The policy

Table 7. Duration of second stage in primiparae.

Total second stage		Pushing phase	
Duration (min)	No. of patients (%)	Duration (min)	No. of patients (%)
<60	198 (55)	<30	189 (52)
61–120	81 (23)	30–60	108 (30)
121–240	69 (19)	60–120	56 (16)
<240	12 (3)	<120	7 (2)
TOTAL	360	TOTAL	360

advocated aims to create a safe environment for mother and baby, and to promote the progress of labour with effective uterine activity. Mothers are not encouraged to begin pushing until the baby is well placed for delivery. Figures 1 and 2 show that this management is effective in preventing significant increases in forceps deliveries.

REFERENCES

Bailey PW & Howard FA (1983) Epidural analgesia and forceps delivery: laying a bogey. *Anaesthesia* **38**: 282–285.

Barrier G & Sureau C (1982) Effects of anaesthetic and analgesic drugs on labour, fetus and neonate. *Clinics in Obstetrics and Gynaecology* **9**: 351–367.

Cohen WR (1977) Influence of the duration of second stage labor on perinatal outcome and puerperal morbidity. *Obstetrics and Gynecology* **48**: 266–269.

Crawford JS (1972) The second thousand epidural blocks in an obstetric hospital practice. *British Journal of Anaesthesia* **44**: 1277–1287.

Crawford JS (1984) *Principles and Practice of Obstetric Anaesthesia.* Oxford: Blackwell Scientific Publications.

Doughty A (1969) Selective epidural analgesia and the forceps rate. *British Journal of Anaesthesia* **41**: 1058–1062.

Doughty A (1978) Epidural analgesia in labour: the past, the present and the future. *Journal of Royal Society of Medicine* **71**: 879–884.

Goodfellow CF, Hull MGR, Swaab DF, Dogterom J & Buijs RM (1983) Oxytocin deficiency at delivery with epidural analgesia. *British Journal of Obstetrics and Gynaecology* **90**: 214–219.

Hoult IJ, MacLennan AH & Carrie LES (1977) Lumbar epidural analgesia in labour: relation to fetal malposition and instrumental delivery. *British Medical Journal* **1**: 14–16.

Kadar N, Cruddas M & Campbell S (1986) Estimating the probability of spontaneous delivery conditional on time spent in the second stage. *British Journal of Obstetrics and Gynaecology* **93**: 568–576.

Maresh M, Choong KH & Beard RW (1983) Delayed pushing with lumbar epidural analgesia in labour. *British Journal of Obstetrics and Gynaecology* **90**: 623–627.

Morgan B, Rehor S & Lewis PJ (1980) Epidural analgesia for uneventful labour. *Anaesthesia* **35**: 57–60.

Nicholas ADG, Tipton RH, Wheatley CJ & Bircumshaw J (1970) Obstetric practice and epidural analgesia. *Journal of Obstetrics and Gynaecology of the British Commonwealth* **77**: 457–461.

O'Driscoll K & Meagher D (1980) *Active Management of Labour.* London: WB Saunders.

Pearson JF & Davies PD (1973) The effect of continuous lumbar epidural analgesia on the acid-base status of maternal arterial blood during the first stage of labour. *Journal of Obstetrics and Gynaecology of the British Commonwealth* **80**: 218–224.

Pearson JF & Davies PD (1974) The effects of continuous lumbar epidural analgesia upon fetal acid-base status during the second stage of labour. *Journal of Obstetrics and Gynaecology of the British Comonwealth* **81**: 975–979.

Phillips KC & Thomas TA (1983) Second stage of labour with or without extradural analgesia. *Anaesthesia* **38**: 972–976.

Potter N & MacDonald RD (1971) Obstetric consequences of epidural analgesia in nulliparous patients. *Lancet* **i**: 1031–1034.

Romine JC, Clark RB & Brown WE (1970) Lumbar epidural anaesthesia in labour and delivery: one year's experience. *Journal of Obstetrics and Gynaecology of the British Comonwealth* **77**: 722–727.

Studd JWW, Crawford JS, Duignan NM, Rowbotham CJF & Hughes AO (1980) The effects of lumbar epidural analgesia on the rate of cervical dilatation and the outcome of labour of spontaneous onset. *British Journal of Obstetrics and Gynaecology* **87**: 1015–1021.

Taylor ABW, Abukhalil SH, El-Guindi MM, Tharian B & Watkins JA (1977) Lumbar epidural analgesia in labour: a 24-hour service provided by obstetricians. *British Medical Journal* **2**: 370–372.

Current Research 2

Delayed maternal effort in the second stage of actively managed labour in primiparae with epidural analgesia

A. P. GRIFFITH and N. C. GLEESON

Epidural analgesia in labour is associated with an increased incidence of instrumental delivery, particularly rotational deliveries. Studies have shown that delaying pushing in the second stage of labour until the presenting part is visible at the perineum may reduce the rotational delivery rate (McQueen and Mylrea, 1977) and increase the spontaneous vertex delivery rate (Maresh and Chung, 1983). We undertook a prospective study of the benefits of instituting a policy of expectant management of the second stage in primiparae having epidural analgesia in labour.

METHOD

In 194 primiparae with lumbar epidural analgesia, pushing was discouraged until the fetal head was visible at the perineum or until 3 hours had elapsed from full dilatation of the cervix. Their outcome was compared with a similar group of 219 parturients in whom pushing was encouraged as soon as the second stage was diagnosed. Bupivacaine 0.375% 10 ml was used to establish epidural analgesia and for all subsequent top-ups. In the study group, if the desire to push occurred before the head had reached the perineum, a 'sitting up' top-up was given. All labours were actively managed using oxytocin infusions if the rate of cervical dilatation was not optimal.

RESULTS

Table 1.

	Group 1 Late pushing $n = 194$	Group 2 Early pushing $n = 219$	Significance level
Induction rate	15.7%	29.9%	NS
Oxytocin infusion	75.8%	78.7%	NS
First stage (h)	4.3 ± 1.7	4.5 ± 1.7	NS
Second stage (h)	1.6 ± 0.8	1.2 ± 0.5	$P < 0.001$
waiting	0.9 ± 0.7		
pushing	0.7 ± 0.6	1.2 ± 0.5	$P < 0.001$
Vaginal exams	5.3 ± 1.5	6.1 ± 1.7	$P < 0.001$
Bupivacaine (mg)	119 ± 54	110 ± 47	NS
Cervical dilatation at insertion of epidural (cm)	4.7 ± 1.8	4.9 ± 1.9	NS
Method of delivery:			
spontaneous	35.6% (69)	31.5% (69)	NS
forceps			
non-rotational	44.8% (87)	54.8% (120)	$P = 0.04$
rotational	19.1% (37)	15.1% (28)	NS
Caesearean section	0.52% (1)	0.91% (2)	

Values are mean ± standard deviations; values in parentheses are actual values. NS = not significant at $P < 0.05$.

CONCLUSION

The observed difference in spontaneous delivery rates did not reach statistical significance. There was a reduction in non-rotational forceps rates in the study group ($P < 0.05$), but no change in the incidence of rotational forceps deliveries.

References

McQueen J & Mylrea L (1977) Lumbar epidural analgesia in labour. *British Medical Journal* 1: 640–641.

Maresh M & Chung A (1983) Delayed pushing with lumbar epidural analgesia in labour. *British Journal of Obstetrics and Gynaecology* **90**: 623–627.

SECTION II – DISCUSSION

CHAIRMAN: DR W. L. DANN, Derby

Dr Shah (Birmingham) I would like to suggest the use of a simple test as an aid in excluding intravascular placement of the epidural catheter. After injection of 2–3 ml of local anaesthetic the syringe and filter are removed and the catheter is then held vertically to act as a manometer. When jugular pressure is applied the increase in cerebrospinal fluid pressure is transmitted to the epidural space resulting in a rise of the fluid level in the catheter (Figure 1). The catheter tip is thus proved to be lying either in the epidural or in the subarachnoid space and not in a blood vessel, since the epidural veins drain either into the azygos veins or directly into the inferior vena cava and jugular venous compression cannot influence pressure in the thorax or abdomen.

Dr Reynolds What happens if the catheter is subdural?

Dr Shah It has not been possible to investigate this.

Question Dr Jordan, do you really believe test doses are useful?

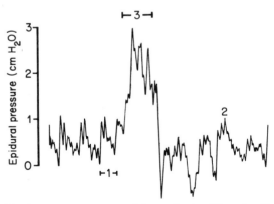

Figure 1. Epidural pressure waves caused by respiration (1), pulse (2) and jugular venous compression (3). From Shah (1981) with permission.

Dr Jordan   The thrust of my presentation was to show that safety measures are not 100% reliable but they are seldom completely useless. I am aware that there is a strong body of opinion that test doses are at best a waste of time and at worst lull one into a false sense of security, but I really cannot accept that they are valueless in a labouring patient, certainly not in the detection of intrathecal catheter placement. But I admit that in 13 years of doing epidurals I have only once discovered anything with a test dose that I hadn't learnt from the aspiration test. In retrospect that was only because I didn't believe the results of the aspiration test and persuaded myself I was aspirating saline, not CSF. But I am not brave enough to say that test doses are a complete waste of time – I still use them.

Dr Naulty   Dr Jordan, you said you couldn't use bupivacaine for the test dose as the onset is too slow. Maybe you are asking the wrong questions. We have done about 150 continuous subarachnoid blocks in labour with bupivacaine. The patients do not report that they cannot move their legs or that they feel any sensations of the onset of sensory block; they just don't feel the pain of the next contraction.

Dr Jordan   Yes, thank you for making that point. I think that the patients' response to the next contraction in labour is an extremely important part of assessing the test dose. But of course not all catheters are put into labouring patients and the length of time between contractions may be variable. So an objective test of a developing subarachnoid block is still necessary.

Dr Russell   I fully agree. If you give a spinal anaesthetic to a woman in labour, she doesn't feel the next contraction. I must confirm that, in my hands, 2–2.5 ml of 0.5% plain bupivacaine has just as fast an onset as 1.5 ml of 5% heavy lignocaine. It is not slow, the patients will often comment during the injection that their legs tingle or have gone numb and warm all over. But if you are using a test dose, and you want to assess the full effects, you must turn the patient over and stir up the CSF.

Dr Jordan   I think that's an extremely dangerous suggestion. I think it is vital that you assess the results of the test dose before you move the patient.

Dr Russell   Well, you won't know where it is, because it won't spread.

Dr Jordan   Well, you'll know where it is after you move the patient: somewhere around C6. We now know that when the patient changes position that is exactly when the major spread in a cranial direction occurs. I agree absolutely with the recommendation of Prince and

McGregor (1986) that you do not move the patient until you know the result of the test dose.

Dr Reynolds   Over a series of 14 000 epidurals I have encountered 2 in which a positive test dose followed negative aspiration. The test dose was 2 ml of 0.5% plain bupivacaine and the women noted the effects of high block at once. The explanation for the negative aspiration test, I believe, is that the catheter may be subdural but the pressure of the injection tears the arachnoid, and so the test dose is positive. This supports the use of a bupivacaine test dose.

Question   Do you think midwives should use test doses, in view of the danger of catheter migration?

Dr Jordan   It is a very difficult question, as you are looking at an extremely rare complication. How far do we go to eliminate the possibility of rare events? Safety is not a black-and-white issue, it is a value judgement. I too believe that catheter migration is not through the dura but through the arachnoid. All I can say is that the outcome of a huge series of midwife top-ups suggests that they are extraordinarily safe (Crawford, 1985). We cannot ignore that. Moreover the interpretation of a test dose in the presence of a previous epidural is much harder than the interpretation of an aspiration test.

Dr Dann (Derby) called for a vote by a show of hands on the following questions:

1. *How many delegates routinely use test doses?* [*great majority*]
2. *How many do not use test doses?* [*tiny minority*]
3. *How many routinely use epidural infusion in preference to intermittent top-ups?* [*over one-third of the delegates*]

Dr Fayek (Jeddah)   I have been using infusions of bupivacaine for four years, and though I haven't seen a case of catheter migration I recognize the potential risk. I would like to know how frequently Dr Gaylard would suggest checking the level of the block. Also how do you avoid inadvertent injection of drugs intended for intravenous injection, into the epidural infusion? Do you have distinctive giving sets?

Dr Gaylard   The first question: we routinely check the level of the block every hour. There are those who suggest 2-hourly is sufficient, but since the midwives check other things hourly, it seems reasonable that they should also do that hourly. In answer to the second question, we use a different type of tubing for the epidural infusion; there is a syringe attached to one end of it and there are no injection ports on the infusion circuit. The chance of an attempted intravenous injection is very remote.

Dr Fayek   One further question concerning the efficacy of epidural infusions in long labours. We have found that in labours lasting 10–12 hours there is a demand for extra top-ups every 1–2 hours. Have you any explanation for this?

Dr Gaylard   I suppose there is the possibility of tachyphylaxis occurring with bupivacaine in very long labours; I have no personal experience of epidurals continuing beyond 12 hours. [Editor's note: absence of perineal analgesia with the infusion is another explanation. Attention should always be paid to the site of pain.]

Dr Macdonald   Dr Bailey, I am worried that you use oxytocin in the second stage of labour. If the patient already has an oxytocin infusion then it is fine to continue, but if not then she needs very careful assessment because failure to progress in the second stage, especially in a multiparous patient, may herald disproportion and the injudicious use of oxytocin could be disastrous. I do hope you involve the obstetricians.

Dr Bailey   My policy essentially applies to primiparas for that very reason. A multipara is less likely to need epidural analgesia and is less likely to have undue delay in the second stage or to need extra oxytocin, while a primiparous uterus is less liable to rupture. The use of oxytocin is a decision that must be taken by the obstetricians; I am merely trying to get them to think in terms of extra oxytocin in the second stage for mothers with epidural analgesia.

References

Crawford JS (1985) Some maternal complications of epidural analgesia for labour. *Anaesthesia* **40**: 1219–1225.
Prince C & McGregor D (1986) Obstetric epidural test doses. A reappraisal. *Anaesthesia* **41**: 1240–1250.
Shah JL (1981) Influence of cerebrospinal fluid on epidural pressure. *Anaesthesia* **36**: 629.

SECTION III

Complications

6

Local anaesthetic toxicity

R. S. LAISHLEY

BUPIVACAINE TOXICITY

The American experience

One of the hazards of epidural block remains the toxicity of local anaesthetic agents. Albright (1979) first alerted the medical establishment to the possible potent cardiovascular toxicity of the then newly introduced agents bupivacaine and etidocaine. He reported 7 cases from America (6 involving bupivacaine and 1 etidocaine) of presumed accidental intravenous administration and cardiovascular collapse. Three cases involved brachial plexus block, one intravenous regional anaesthesia, two caudal blocks and one lumbar epidural for Caesarean section. He then presented at the 1982 European Congress of Anaesthesiology a further collection of 15 cases of maternal death in the USA following the epidural injection of bupivacaine (Albright, 1982).

The United States Food and Drug Administration conducted an enquiry into the toxicity of local anaesthetic agents to which Albright presented information on 36 obstetric cases and 20 others (Writer et al, 1984). Following this, the FDA withdrew their recommendation for the use of 0.75% bupivacaine in obstetric anaesthesia, as this concentration was employed in many of the reported cases. They also stated that bupivacaine was contraindicated in obstetric paracervical block and not recommended for intravenous regional anaesthesia (IVRA) (FDA, 1983). This edict in the USA had a rapid 'knock-on' effect in the pharmaceutical industry, and similar recommendations were announced by drug companies in Canada and the UK without further enquiry or consultation with the medical profession (Writer et al, 1984; Scott, 1984).

The British experience

Deaths from bupivacaine toxicity have been reported in the UK following intravenous regional anaesthesia (IVRA) (Heath, 1982) and may be associated with inadvertent cuff release. Despite full precautions and meticulous technique, bupivacaine may also leak past an inflated tourniquet (Davies et al, 1981, 1984). This has led to the use of IVRA being questioned (Fowler, 1982) and a Committee on Safety of Medicines (CSM) bulletin recommending the discontinuation of bupivacaine for IVRA (CSM, 1983). Although obstetric accidental intravenous administration of bupivacaine has been reported in the UK (Ryan, 1973), the fact remains that no maternal deaths from bupivacaine toxicity have been reported in this country. This is in direct contrast to many cases occurring in the USA. However, there have been nine maternal deaths reported in association with epidural analgesia since the introduction of bupivacaine in the UK (DHSS, 1975, 1979, 1982, 1986, 1989). The first died from neglected supine hypotensive syndrome. In four cases there was inadequate resuscitation following total spinal block. Two women died from aspiration of vomit while under sedation and epidural analgesia. One case resulted from inadequate postoperative care following general anaesthesia in combination with epidural anaesthesia. The ninth case was an unstable diabetic with severe pre-eclampsia who had seizures followed by a cardiac arrest after an epidural block with bupivacaine. This death was judged to have other more significant causes.

Systemic toxicity of local anaesthetics injected epidurally results either from accidental intravenous injection or from administration of an excessive dose into the epidural space. Most of the epidural deaths associated with bupivacaine in the USA appear to be due to accidental intravenous injection. One possible explanation for the relative absence of this serious complication in British practice is a difference in the practical techniques of establishing epidural analgesia. In the UK, a clear epidural catheter (for use with a 16-gauge Tuohy needle) with a sealed end and three side-holes is commonly used. In contrast, in the USA, a smaller catheter for a 17 or 18-gauge needle is used, sometimes with a single end-hole and a stylet. It is suggested (Reynolds, personal communication) that intravascular placement is more likely with a stylet and less clearly detected with the narrower single-hole catheter. Michael et al (1989) noted a lower incidence of bloody taps with a single-hole catheter, but this may imply a lower detection rate as opposed to actual incidence. The single hole could be more easily occluded by the wall of an epidural vein and give a false negative result when the aspiration test is performed. To avoid intravascular injection it is necessary to pay meticulous attention to practical technique and to realize that test doses and catheter aspiration tests can give false negative results. Slow, fractionated injection of the local anaesthetic will reduce the risk of the serious sequelae of accidental intravascular injection.

Although there have been no British case reports of maternal death from accidental intravascular injection of local anaesthetic, non-fatal cases of bupivacaine toxicity have been reported (Crawford, 1985). In labour, toxicity from correctly placed epidural bupivacaine administration is unlikely. Low doses of 25–50 mg are usually given at approximately two-hourly intervals and bupivacaine is very slow to accumulate at this dose frequency. The patients more likely to suffer toxicity are those receiving larger doses for Caesarean section under epidural block, especially emergency Caesarean section following labour with epidural analgesia (Thorburn and Moir, 1984). Thorburn and Moir (1984) reported 2 cases of convulsions in obstetric patients who had received epidural bupivacaine for labour followed by a top-up for emergency Caesarean section. These cases are summarized in Table 1. In both cases the epidural block was difficult to extend for Caesarean section and unfortunately in neither case was blood taken for bupivacaine plasma concentrations. Both women had convulsions 20 minutes after the last dose and this almost certainly represented toxicity by systemic absorption from the epidural space. Crawford et al (1986) described 5 further cases of systemic bupivacaine toxicity occurring in a series of 993 patients undergoing elective Caesarean section under epidural anaesthesia. These cases are also summarized in Table 1. Interestingly, 4 out of 5 of them were associated with the use of 0.75% bupivacaine. In all 7 cases toxicity resulted from systemic absorption from the epidural space and accidental intravenous injection was not implicated.

It has consistently been found that, in accordance with basic pharmacological principles, maximum bupivacaine plasma concentrations are dependent on total dose rather than dose rate (Reynolds et al, 1973; Laishley et al, 1988). In the more recent study (Laishley et al, 1988) bupivacaine dose (mg kg^{-1}) correlated well with maximum plasma bupivacaine concentrations (μg ml^{-1}) (correlation coefficient 0.61; $P < 0.0001$). From the regression line plotted, the threshold for symptomatic toxicity at 1.6 μg ml^{-1} (Reynolds, 1971) could be achieved with a mean epidural dose of approximately 5.5 mg kg^{-1}. This is in close agreement with Reynolds et al (1973) in which an average total dose of approximately 440 mg correlated with 1.6 μg ml^{-1}. Using 95% confidence limits this latter study also predicted that in 5% of patients a total dose of 320 mg would result in plasma levels exceeding 1.6 μg ml^{-1}. These doses are far in excess of the recommended maximum dose of 2 mg kg^{-1} in any 4-hour period given in the manufacturer's data sheet for 1987. The 1989 data sheet provided more detailed information depending on the

Table 1. Data of seven case reports of patients with symptomatic bupivacaine toxicity.

Caesarean section	Bupivacaine concentration (%)	Total dose (mg)	Time period	Emergency Caesarean Dose (mg)	Period (min)	Dose (mg kg^{-1})	Toxic symptoms
Emergency[1]	0.375 0.5	357.5	10 h	98.5	60	4.9	Convulsion
Emergency[1]	0.35 0.5	356.25	9 h	225	70	6.48	Convulsion
Elective[2]	0.5	300	3 h 7 min			4.47	Convulsion
Elective[2]	0.75	382.5	118 min			5.97	Convulsion (plasma conc. 2.5 µg ml^{-1})
Elective[2]	0.75	225	48 min			2.71	Drowsiness
Elective[2]	0.5	90	8 min			1.32	Convulsion (probably eclamptic)
Elective[2]	0.75	525	60 min			7.09	Slurred speech, confusion

[1] From Thorburn and Moir (1984).
[2] From Crawford et al (1986).

site of nerve block, and recommended 150 mg as a maximum safe single dose, with subsequent maximum doses of 50 mg 2-hourly.

Thompson et al (1985) investigated venous plasma bupivacaine concentrations in 47 women undergoing epidural Caesarean section with plain 0.5% bupivacaine and documented mean maximum values of 1.56 μg ml^{-1} for emergency sections and 1.51, 1.27 and 1.00 μg ml^{-1} for elective sections (depending on injection schedule: bolus, 10- and 20-minute increments respectively). The highest elective level occurred with single bolus injection, whereas the lower levels occurred using incremental techniques. The plasma concentrations corresponded with mean total doses of bupivacaine of 187 mg for the emergency sections and 127, 130 and 106 mg for elective sections respectively. In this series, no patients exhibited symptoms of bupivacaine toxicity.

The effect of adrenaline

Laishley et al (1988) investigated plasma bupivacaine concentrations following a single, fractionated dose of 100 mg 0.5% bupivacaine for elective and emergency Caesarean sections, and also investigated the effect of adrenaline. Bupivacaine concentrations were significantly higher in the emergency group compared with the elective group (Table 2). Adrenaline was associated with significant reductions in plasma concentrations in the elective group only. Adrenaline was also noted to promote a better block, but only in the elective series. Burm et al (1986) showed significant reductions of plasma bupivacaine concentrations following epidural adrenaline with 100 mg of bupivacaine, albeit in a group of predominantly male general surgical patients and using central venous blood sampling.

Overall, it appears that adrenaline reduces epidural absorption and plasma concentrations to a greater extent with lignocaine

Table 2. Maximum bupivacaine concentrations (μg ml^{-1}) during epidural blockade for Caesarean section.

	Elective		Emergency	
	Mean ± SD	Range	Mean ± SD	Range
Plain	0.80 ± 0.35	0.26–1.97	1.11 ± 0.34	0.66–1.86
With adrenaline	0.62 ± 0.12	0.44–0.94	1.02 ± 0.26	0.63–1.53

From Laishley et al (1988).

(30–40%) (Scott et al, 1972; Braid and Scott, 1965; Mather et al, 1976) compared to bupivacaine (5–25%) (Wilkinson and Lond, 1970; Appleyard et al, 1974; Reynolds and Taylor, 1971).

PHYSICOCHEMICAL AND PHARMACOKINETIC EFFECTS

The interpretation of blood concentrations is dependent on physico-chemical properties, that is pKa, lipid solubility and protein binding (Table 3). As the pKa of local anaesthetics is close to the physiological pH of 7.4, the degree of ionization of these agents is sensitive to small changes in pH. Increasing the hydrogen ion concentration increases the proportion of cation. Because weak acids and bases tend to cross membranes by non-ionic diffusion, their distribution in cells and organs such as brain is influenced by the ion-trapping effect. Thus weak bases, such as local anaesthetics, tend to become concentrated in more acidotic tissues, and this effect is more prominent with stronger bases (those with higher pKa values) (Reynolds and Knott, 1989). Thus local anaesthetic toxicity is enhanced if brain or heart tissue pH falls more than plasma pH, because of convulsions or ventricular fibrillation and under perfusion.

Lipid solubility affects potency and toxicity by influencing the penetration of the drug to the membrane active site. Hence the greater the lipid solubility, the greater is the potency and toxicity.

One important influence on toxicity is the variation in protein binding between agents. It is generally held that the toxic effects of local anaesthetics are more closely related to the non-protein bound (free) plasma concentrations than total (free plus bound) concentrations (Denson et al, 1984). Amide agents are bound mainly to α_1-acid glycoprotein (AAG) and variation in the plasma

Table 3. Physicochemical and pharmacokinetic properties of local anaesthetics.

	Molecular wt	pKa	Partition coefficient (N–heptane/ buffer)	Protein binding (%)
Ester				
Chloroprocaine	271	8.7	0.14	–
Amides				
Prilocaine	220	7.9	0.9	55
Lignocaine	234	7.9	2.9	64.3
Bupivacaine	288	8.1	27.5	95.6
Ropivacaine	274	8.1	6.1	94
Etidocaine	276	7.7	141	94

From Tucker & Mather (1980), Rosenberg et al (1986).

concentrations of this protein is a major source of variability in free drug fraction. Thus there may be an eightfold difference in lignocaine binding between newborns and cancer patients (Figure 1). As bupivacaine is even more protein-bound than lignocaine, one might expect this tendency to be even greater with bupivacaine.

In comparing toxicity studies, it must be remembered that plasma and whole blood concentrations are not the same, and the ratio of the two varies with each drug (Tucker and Mather, 1979). Thus, based on plasma concentrations, bupivacaine is approximately 2.5 times as toxic as lignocaine; while based on whole blood concentrations, it is approximately 3.5 times as toxic. This is because the cellular content of blood also binds local anaesthetics to a varying extent.

Another source of difficulty in comparing studies is the variation beween arterial and venous blood concentrations of local anaes-thetics. These are only likely to be equal in steady-state conditions which do not prevail with intermittent bolus injections. One cause of disparity between arterial and venous concentrations is the uptake of drug by lung tissue, which tends to buffer blood concentration after accidental intravenous injection. In rat lung the affinity for bupivacaine was found to be greater than for lignocaine (Post et al, 1979).

From this discussion one can deduce that there is no theoretically straightforward answer to the question of relative toxicity between

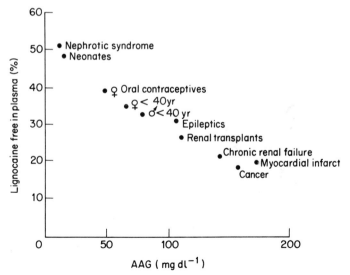

Figure 1. Relationship between the mean percentage of lignocaine unbound in plasma and the mean plasma α_1-acid glycoprotein (AAG) concentration in different types of patients. From Tucker (1986) with permission.

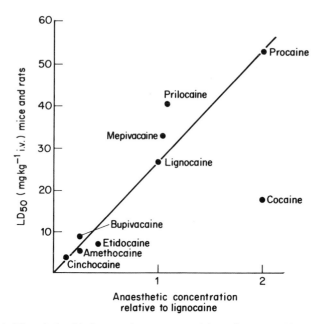

Figure 2. The relationship between intravenous toxicity and potency. The correlation is good except in the case of cocaine, which has a separate mechanism for producing toxicity. From Reynolds (1987) with permission.

agents. Site of injection, pH and AAG binding, for example, all profoundly affect the potential toxicity of a single injection. However, it has been stated that provided equipotent doses are used, the danger from intravenous injection is generally similar for all agents (Reynolds, 1987). The relationship between intravenous toxicity and potency is almost a straight-line correlation (Figure 2).

In contrast, agents exhibit differences in toxicity when administered extravenously for regional block, when blood levels depend on absorption and elimination which are partly independent of potency. These differences are shown by the variation in toxicity following subcutaneous or intravenous injection in animals (Table 4). For example, prilocaine and mepivacaine have similar intravenous LD_{50} values in mice of 35 and 40 mg kg^{-1} respectively, but very different subcutaneous LD_{50} values (900 and 270 mg kg^{-1} respectively), indicating the basis for the renowned relative safety of prilocaine (Reynolds, 1970).

The actual safety margin of a drug is the difference between the maximum effective dose (ED) and minimum toxic dose (TD) (Reynolds, 1987). This is entirely different from the therapeutic index (ratio of TD_{50} to ED_{50}). The maximum ED and minimum

Table 4. Animal toxicity data.

	LD$_{50}$ (mice)	
	intravenous (mg kg^{-1})	subcutaneous (mg kg^{-1})
Amethocaine	8	30
Bupivacaine	8	82
Lignocaine	30	400
Prilocaine	35	900
Mepivacaine	40	270

From Reynolds (1987).

TD may overlap despite a wide difference between TD$_{50}$ and ED$_{50}$ (Figure 3).

CARDIOTOXICITY – IS THERE A DIFFERENCE?

Since Albright's editorial (1979) on deaths due to toxicity of bupivacaine, some workers have suspected that bupivacaine is relatively more cardiotoxic than other local anaesthetic agents (Marx, 1984). Reynolds (1987) summarized the cardiovascular complications

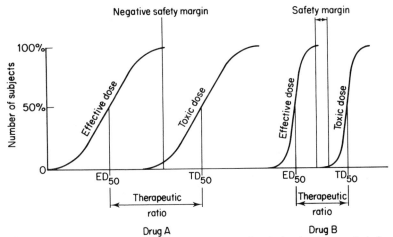

Figure 3. Theoretical quantal dose-effect curves, used to derive the therapeutic index or ratio (TD$_{50}$:ED$_{50}$). In practice the actual safety margin (interval between maximum effective dose and minimum toxic dose) does not necessarily bear a direct relationship to the theoretical therapeutic ratio. From Reynolds (1987) with permission.

occurring with the older agents, and indicated that cardiovascular toxicity is not a new phenomenon associated with bupivacaine. The cardiovascular system (CVS) is more resistant than the central nervous system (CNS) to the toxic effects of local anaesthetics (Reynolds, 1984), and mild CNS toxicity symptoms may occur following systemic absorption from correctly sited regional blocks. In contrast, CVS toxicity usually occurs with the much higher plasma concentrations of local anaesthetics that may follow accidental intravenous injection.

Animal investigations and *in vitro* techniques have been used to investigate the relative toxicity between agents and their CVS and CNS toxic thresholds (Tables 5 and 6). These data suggest that there is a greater margin between cardiovascular and CNS toxicity with bupivacaine than with lignocaine. One of the difficulties in interpreting various studies has been the use of different end-points and variables, such as contractility (Buffington, 1989), duration of action potentials (Moller and Covino, 1988), arrhythmias (Kotelko et al, 1984) and cardiovascular collapse (Morishima et al, 1985). One example of a misleading study is the work by Kotelko et al (1984), in which non-equipotent doses of lignocaine and bupivacaine were given to convulsing sheep. However, at least two *in vivo* animal studies using intracoronary injection of lignocaine and bupivacaine support the hypothesis that myocardial depression is proportional to anaesthetic potency (Nath et al, 1986; Buffington, 1989). In contrast, Nath et al (1986) confirmed that bupivacaine is much more arrhythmogenic than lignocaine. While the local anaesthetic and cardiodepressant potency ratios for bupivacaine to lignocaine are 4:1, the cardiac electrophysiological toxicity ratio is more in the region of 16:1. There is evidence that the presence of

Table 5. Toxicity data for bupivacaine and lignocaine in humans (except LD_{50} mice).

	Bupivacaine	Lignocaine
LD_{50} IV mice (mg kg^{-1})	7.8	30
Maximum safe dose (mg kg^{-1})		
Intravenous	0.6–2	2
Other: alone	2–3.5	3–4.5
+ adrenaline	4–6	7
Toxic plasma concentrations (μg ml^{-1})		
Mild	1.6–2	3–7
Convulsions	2.3–5	5–10

From Reynolds (1987).

Table 6. CVS to CNS toxic ratios for local anesthetics in animals.

	CVS/CNS ratio	Animal
Bupivacaine	4.5	Awake dogs
	4.8	Ventilated cats
Amethocaine	6.7	Awake dogs
Etidocaine	5.1	Awake dogs
Lignocaine	3.5	Awake dogs
	2.6	Ventilated cats
	3.7	Non-asphyxiated baboon fetuses
	2.3	Asphyxiated baboon fetuses

From Reynolds (1984).

local anaesthetic in the CNS may be involved in the generation of cardiovascular toxicity (Heavner, 1986).

It has been reported that bupivacaine cardiovascular toxicity may be resistant to or require prolonged periods of resuscitation (Albright, 1979). In contrast to many of the cardiovascular toxic threshold studies, there is good evidence that this may be true. The higher pKa and protein binding of bupivacaine would theoretically explain its prolonged retention by cardiac tissue. This is supported by *in vitro* work which showed that recovery from sodium block by bupivacaine was prolonged (mean time constant, 1557 ms) compared with lignocaine (mean time constant 154 ms) (Clarkson and Hondeghem, 1985). A further of influence on cardiac toxicity is the role of hypoxia and acidosis which readily occur during convulsions. In animals, hypoxia and acidosis have been shown to enhance both the CNS and CVS toxicity of lignocaine (Englesson and Matousek, 1975; Morishima and Covino, 1981) and the cardiotoxicity of bupivacaine (Rosen et al, 1985).

ROPIVACAINE

As toxicity remains a hazard from any local anaesthetic procedure, the pharmaceutical industry is continually looking for new local anaesthetics with greater margins of safety. Currently, the newest agent is ropivacaine, which is undergoing initial human evaluation. This is the L-isomer of the propyl derivative of the same homologous series as mepivacaine and bupivacaine. It has a similar pKa and protein binding to bupivacaine, but its lipid solubility is closer to lignocaine than bupivacaine (Table 3). Studies of epidural anaesthesia in dogs suggest that ropivacaine is less potent and has a shorter duration of action than bupivacaine (Feldman et al, 1986). Toxicity studies in dogs (Arthur et al, 1986) indicate that similar doses of ropivacaine and bupivacaine are required to produce convulsive activity. However, ropivacaine may be less cardiotoxic, as the ratio of cardiovascular to convulsive dose was higher for ropivacaine than bupivacaine. In addition, ventricular arrhythmias were observed in 45% of dogs receiving bupivacaine compared to 15% receiving ropivacaine. *In vitro* studies in isolated Purkinje fibre and ventricular muscle preparations indicate that ropivacaine is less cardiodepressant than bupivacaine, but more so than lignocaine (Moller and Covino, 1986). Initial animal studies with ropivacaine have been encouraging and it appears to be a useful agent. Whether ropivacaine will replace bupivacaine as the most useful and popular long-acting agent remains to be seen.

REFERENCES

Albright GA (1979) Cardiac arrest following regional anesthesia with etidocaine or bupivacaine (editorial). *Anesthesiology* **51**: 285–287.

Albright GA (1982) Maternal mortality with bupivacaine regional anaesthesia (abstract). *Proceedings of Sixth European Congress of Anaesthesiology*, 10.

Appleyard TN, Witt A, Atkinson RE & Nicholas ADG (1974). Bupivacaine carbonate and bupivacaine hydrochloride: a comparison of blood concentrations during epidural blockade for vaginal surgery. *British Journal of Anaesthesia* **46**: 530–533.

Arthur GR, Feldman HS, Norway SB, Doncette AM & Covino BG (1986) Acute IV toxicity of LE-103, a new local anesthetic, compared to lidocaine and bupivacaine in the awake dog. *Anesthesiology* **65**: A182.

Braid DP & Scott DB (1965) The systemic absorption of local analgesic drugs. *British Journal of Anaesthesia* **37**: 394–404.

Buffington CW (1989) The magnitude and duration of direct myocardial depression following intracoronary local anesthetics: a comparison of lidocaine and bupivacaine. *Anesthesiology* **70**: 280–287.

Burm AGL, Van Kleef JW, Gladines MPRR, Olthof G & Spierdijk J (1986) Epidural anesthesia with lidocaine and bupivacaine: effects of epinephrine on the plasma concentration profiles. *Anesthesia and Analgesia* **65**: 1281–1284.

Clarkson CW & Hondeghem LM (1985) Mechanism for bupivacaine depression of cardiac conduction: fast block of sodium channels during the action potential with slow recovery from block during diastole. *Anesthesiology* **62**: 396–405.

Crawford JS (1985) Some maternal complications of epidural analgesia for labour. *Anaesthesia* **40**: 1219–1225.

Crawford JS, Davies P & Lewis M (1986) Some aspects of epidural block provided for elective Caesarean section. *Anaesthesia* **41**: 1039–1046.

CSM (1983) Bupivacaine (Marcain plain) in intravenous regional anaesthesia (Bier's block). Committee on Safety of Medicines. *Current Problems 12.*

Davies JAH, Gill SS & Weber JCP (1981) Intravenous regional analgesia using bupivacaine. *Anaesthesia* **36**: 331.

Davies JAH, Wilkey AD & Hall ID (1984) Bupivacaine leak past inflated tourniquets during intravenous regional analgesia. *Anaesthesia* **39**: 996–999.

Denson DD, Myers JA, Hartrick CT, Pither CP, Coyle DE & Raj PP (1984) The relationship between free bupivacaine concentration and central nervous system toxicity. *Anesthesiology* **61**: A211.

DHSS (1975) *Report on Confidential Enquiries into Maternal Deaths in England and Wales 1970–72*. London: HMSO.

DHSS (1979) *Report on Confidential Enquiries into Maternal Deaths in England and Wales 1973–75*. London: HMSO.

DHSS (1982) *Report on Confidential Enquiries into Maternal Deaths in England and Wales 1976–78*. London: HMSO.

DHSS (1986) *Report on Confidential Enquiries into Maternal Deaths in England and Wales 1979–81*. London: HMSO.

DHSS (1989) *Report on Confidential Enquiries into Maternal Deaths in England and Wales 1982–84*. London: HMSO.

Engelsson S & Matousek M (1975) Central nervous system effects of local anaesthetic agents. *British Journal of Anaesthesia* **47**: 241–246.

FDA (1983) The withdrawal of 0.75% bupivacaine. *FDA Drug Bulletin* **13**: 23.

Feldman HS, Hurley RJ & Covino BG (1986) LEA-103 (ropivacaine) a new local anesthetic: experimental evaluation of spinal and epidural anesthesia in the dog and sciatic nerve block in the rat. *Anesthesiology* **65**: A181.

Fowler AW (1982) Standard intravenous regional analgesia. *British Medical Journal* **285**: 732.

Heath ML (1982) Deaths after intravenous regional anaesthesia. *British Medical Journal* **285**: 913–914.

Heavner JE (1986) Cardiac dysrhythmias induced by infusion of local anesthetics into the lateral cerebral ventricle of rats. *Anesthesia and Analgesia* **65**: 133–138.

Kotelko DM, Shnider SM, Dailey PA et al (1984) Bupivacaine-induced cardiac arrhythmias in sheep. *Anesthesiology* **60**: 10–18.

Laishley RS, Morgan BM & Reynolds F (1988) Effect of adrenaline on extradural anaesthesia and plasma bupivacaine concentrations during Caesarean section. *British Journal of Anaesthesia* **60**: 180–186.

Marx GF (1984) Cardiotoxicity of local anesthetics – the plot thickens. *Anesthesiology* **60**: 3–5.

Mather LE, Tucker GT, Murphy TM, Stanton-Hicks MA & Bonica JJ (1976) The effects of adding adrenaline to etidocaine and lignocaine in extradural anaesthesia. II: Pharmacokinetics. *British Journal of Anaesthesia* **48**: 989–994.

Michael S, Richmond MN & Birks RJS (1989) A comparison between open-end (single hole) and closed-end (three lateral holes) epidural catheters. *Anaesthesia* **44**: 578–580.

Moller RA & Covino BG (1986) Cardiac electrophysiologic effects of a new long-acting anesthetic agent (LEA-103). *Anesthesiology* **66**: A183.

Moller RA & Covino BG (1988) Cardiac electrophysiologic effects of lidocaine and bupivacaine. *Anesthesia and Analgesia* **67**: 107–114.

Morishima HO & Covino BG (1981) Toxicity and distribution of lidocaine in non-asphyxiated baboon fetuses. *Anesthesiology* **54**: 182–186.

Morishima HO, Pederson H, Finster M et al (1985) Bupivacaine toxicity in pregnant and non-pregnant ewes. *Anesthesiology* **63**: 134–139.

Nath S, Haggmark S, Johansson G & Reiz S (1986) Differential depressant and electrophysiologic cardiotoxicity of local anesthetics: an experimental study with special reference to lidocaine and bupivacaine. *Anesthesia and Analgesia* **65**: 1263–1270.

Post C, Anderson RGG, Ryrfeldt A & Nilsson E (1979) Physio-chemical modification of lidocaine uptake in rat lung tissue. *Acta Pharmacology and Toxicology* **44**: 103–109.

Reynolds F (1970) Systemic toxicity of local analgesic drugs with special reference to bupivacaine. MD thesis, University of London.

Reynolds F (1971) A comparison of the potential toxicity of bupivacaine, lignocaine and mepivocaine during epidural blockade for surgery. *British Journal of Anaesthesia* **43**: 567–572.

Reynolds F (1984) Local anaesthetic drugs. *Clinics in Anaesthesiology* **2**: 577–603.

Reynolds F (1987) Adverse effects of local anaesthetics. *British Journal of Anaesthesia* **59**: 78–95.

Reynolds F & Knott C (1989) Pharmacokinetics in pregnancy and placental drug transfer. *Oxford Reviews of Reproductive Biology* **11**: 389–449.

Reynolds F & Taylor G (1971) Plasma concentrations of bupivacaine during continuous epidural analgesia in labour: the effect of adrenaline. *British Journal of Anaesthesia* **43**: 436–439.

Reynolds F, Hargrove RL & Wyman JB (1973) Maternal and foetal plasma concentrations of bupivacaine after epidural block. *British Journal of Anaesthesia* **45**: 1049–1053.

Rosen MA, Thigpen JW, Shnider SM, Foutz SE, Levinson G & Koike M (1985) Bupivacaine-induced cardiotoxicity in hypoxic and acidotic sheep. *Anesthesia and Analgesia* **64**: 1089–1096.

Rosenberg PH, Kytta J & Alila A (1986) Absorption of bupivacaine, etidocaine, lignocaine and ropivacaine into *N*-heptan, rat sciatic nerve, and human extradural and subcutaneous fat. *British Journal of Anaesthesia* **58**: 310–314.

Ryan DW (1973) Accidental intravenous injection of bupivacaine: a complication of obstetrical epidural anaesthesia. *British Journal of Anaesthesia* **45**: 907–908.

Scott DB (1984) Toxicity caused by local anaesthetic agents (editorial). *British Journal of Anaesthesia* **56**: 435–436.

Scott DB, Jebson PJR, Braid DP, Ortengren B & Frisch P (1972) Factors affecting plasma levels of lignocaine and prilocaine. *British Journal of Anaesthesia* **44**: 1040–1049.

Thompson EM, Wilson CM, Moore J & McClean E (1985) Plasma bupivacaine levels associated with extradural anaesthesia for Caesarean section. *Anaesthesia* **40**: 427–432.

Thorburn J & Moir DD (1984) Bupivacaine toxicity in association with extradural analgesia for Caesarean section. *British Journal of Anaesthesia* **56**: 551–552.

Tucker GT (1986) Pharmacokinetics of local anaesthetics. *British Journal of Anaesthesia* **58**: 717–731.

Tucker GT & Mather LE (1979) Clinical pharmacokinetics of local anaesthetics. *Clinical Pharmacokinetics* **4**: 241–278.

Tucker GT & Mather LE (1980) Absorption and disposition of local anesthetics: pharmacokinetics. In Cousins MJ & Bridenbaugh PO (eds) *Neural Blockade in Clinical Anesthetics and Management of Pain*. Philadelphia: JB Lippincott.

Wilkinson GR & Lond PC (1970) Bupivacaine levels in plasma and cerebrospinal fluid following peridural administration. *Anesthesiology* **33**: 482–86.

Writer WDR, Davies JM & Strunin L (1984) Trial by media: the bupivacaine story. *Canadian Anaesthetists Society Journal* **31**: 1–4.

7

Lumbar epidural analgesia in obstetrics: taps and patches

BRETT B. GUTSCHE

A common and often troublesome complication of lumbar epidural block is accidental dural puncture. Its occurrence ranges from less than 0.5% to over 2%, the higher figure sometimes being found in teaching institutions (Palahniuk and Cumming, 1989). Holdcroft and Morgan (1976) reported 17 dural punctures in the first thousand epidurals for obstetric patients at their hospital, of whom 13 developed spinal headaches. As the needle used for epidural analgesia is usually 18-gauge or larger, the frequency of headache is high after dural puncture, particularly in parturients, who are more prone to spinal headache than non-pregnant females, males or older patients. In the parturient, a dural puncture with an 18-gauge or larger needle without prophylaxis results in a 70% incidence of headache, which is often severe, even incapacitating (Crawford, 1972; Craft et al, 1973; Bromage, 1987). This high frequency of headache has been attributed to:

1. bearing down in the second stage of labour, which promotes loss of cerebrospinal fluid (CSF) through the dural rent
2. decreased intra-abdominal pressure following delivery which fosters collapse of the epidural veins
3. rapid loss of fluid following delivery from blood loss, diuresis and lactation.

Spinal headache is attributed to the loss of CSF through the dural and arachnoid rent, which allows the brain to sag and to pull on the dura mater, the tentorium and the blood vessels, all of which are pain-sensitive (Brownridge, 1983). The evidence to support the continued loss of CSF as the cause of headache is that larger needles are associated with a higher incidence of headache, particularly in the parturient (Greene, 1950; Eckstein et al, 1982). Kunkle et al

(1943) demonstrated that drainage of 20 ml of CSF from a subject in the upright position resulted in an immediate headache.

Spinal headaches are typically related to position; assuming an upright position exacerbates the headache, recumbency alleviates it. While the severity of spinal headache is rapidly modified within seconds of positional change, headaches from other causes may in some patients respond similarly to position. A useful test to distinguish between these and spinal headache is simply to sit the patient upright and allow the headache to become manifest. Firm, continuous abdominal pressure is applied with a hand on the abdomen and back, while watching the patient's reaction. If the headache improves, usually within a matter of 15–30 seconds, and then on release of pressure rapidly returns, it is characteristic of a spinal headache; headaches from other causes are little affected by this manoeuvre. Stiff neck and photophobia may accompany spinal headache, giving the appearance of meningitis, but the headache and neck stiffness of meningitis are not improved by recumbency or abdominal pressure. Furthermore, the patient with meningitis appears extremely ill. These distinctions are of value, particularly in the presence of fever, in staying the hand of the neurologist who proposes a diagnostic lumbar puncture (usually with a 20-gauge needle) to rule out meningitis.

The site of the headache is not diagnostic and can be occipital, frontal or involving the top of the head. Diplopia, the result of stretching and compression of cranial nerve VI (abducens) may occur. Other symptoms include nausea, vomiting, dizziness and photophobia. The headache may be manifest in as little as several hours or as late as two to three days, although with sudden loss of CSF following a dural puncture in the upright position it may occur at once. Without therapy, it may persist from a few days to several weeks, during which time the mother is often bedridden and unable to take care of her baby or perform other household chores. Rarely the headache persists for weeks or even months, and is associated with residual spasm and pain in the muscles of the neck.

There are three aspects to management: prevention, accurate diagnosis and prompt effective treatment. Many parturients develop postpartum headaches completely unrelated to dural puncture. It is important to distinguish spinal headache from other headaches as treatment is relatively specific, will not benefit other conditions and may subject the patient to needless procedures with potential risks. Once the diagnosis of spinal headache is made, vigorous and effective treatment is essential. Untreated spinal headache has been associated with the rare development of subdural haematoma (Edelman and Wingard, 1980; Jack, 1979).

IMMEDIATE MANAGEMENT FOLLOWING ACCIDENTAL DURAL PUNCTURE

When accidental dural puncture occurs, the loss of CSF should be minimized by replacing the stylet or syringe, or withdrawing the needle. If it is elected to proceed with continuous subarachnoid block (which requires 20% or less of the dose needed for epidural block) before removing the needle, a catheter is passed into the subarachnoid space. As the diameter of the catheter is smaller than the rent caused by the needle the incidence of headache is not increased by this action. However, the notion that continuous spinal block decreases the incidence of spinal headache is controversial (Denny et al, 1987; Harris and Whitehead, 1989). The site of the catheter must be clearly identified as subarachnoid to prevent inadvertent injection of local anaesthetic in epidural doses. Following delivery, an epidural catheter may be sited at another interspace for prophylactic injection of saline or blood. Alternatively at the time of dural puncture the needle is withdrawn to the epidural space and a catheter passed therein. Because this carries a risk of subdural catheter placement, it may be preferable to enter the epidural space at an adjacent interspace. The catheter must then be thoroughly tested to confirm its correct siting. Small incremental doses of local anaesthetic are administered, as some of the drug may be forced through the dural rent if large-volume boluses are injected rapidly. The total dose of local anaesthetic may be decreased by as much as 25% even though the catheter is not subarachnoid. This procedure has three advantages: continuous epidural analgesia with all its benefits is obtained, the incidence of headache is reduced from 70–80% to 55% (Shnider and Levinson, 1987) and after delivery a catheter is available for prophylactic saline or blood injection.

It is extremely important that the interspace where dural puncture occurred be noted to allow an epidural blood patch to be appropriately placed, if necessary, after catheter removal. In addition to documentation on the anaesthetic record, before removing the needle a small needle scratch may be made at the site of the dural puncture, which will identify the puncture site for at least a week.

NON-INVASIVE METHODS OF PROPHYLAXIS AND TREATMENT OF POST-LUMBAR PUNCTURE HEADACHE

The best method of prophylaxis against the development of spinal headache is to avoid dural puncture. As the parturient has a high incidence of spinal headache, is often in severe discomfort and hence a moving target during epidural insertion, and cannot afford to be bedridden because of her baby, she serves as a poor teaching model for the novice mastering the technique. As the rate of headache increases with the size of the needle, it is prudent to use the smallest needle possible. Generally an 18-gauge thin-walled needle is required to allow passage of the epidural catheter. However, there is now available a catheter that can be inserted through a 20-gauge thin-walled Tuohy needle which may replace the 18-gauge needles used today. Great emphasis should always be placed on avoiding dural puncture. Rates considerably lower than 1% are reported in maternity units when the loss of resistance to saline technique is carefully taught by a consultant to successive trainees (Doughty, 1979; Macdonald, 1983; Reynolds, 1988).

Direction of needle bevel

It has been suggested that piercing the dura with the bevel facing the side creates a smaller hole than with the bevel facing caudal or cephalad, as in the former method fibres are split rather than cut (Franksson and Gordth, 1946; Mihic, 1985). Norris et al (1989) found that when the dura was accidentally punctured with a 17- or 18-gauge Hustead needle with the bevel to the side, the incidence and severity of headache and the need for blood patch was significantly lower than when the bevel was perpendicular to the dural fibres. This technique necessitates rotating the needle 90° to allow passage of the epidural catheter, a manoeuvre which might itself predispose to dural puncture, although Norris did not find this to be the case.

Enforced recumbency

As recumbency alleviates spinal headache and the upright position exacerbates it, it is not surprising that following lumbar puncture, patients were exhorted to remain flat in bed with no pillow for periods ranging from 12 to 48 hours. Many parturients have related to me how shortly after a subarachnoid block they sat up for a few minutes to eat or to nurse their baby, then shortly thereafter experienced the onset of a severe headache which they attributed to their failure to follow the admonition of remaining flat in bed. Numerous studies in patients following diagnostic lumbar puncture (Carbaat and Crevel, 1981; Handler et al, 1982) or subarachnoid block (Jones, 1974; Levin, 1944) failed to show any benefit from recumbency either in the supine or prone position. Indeed Baumgarten (1987) suggested that enforced recumbency may increase the frequency of headache by allowing continued leak of CSF, while the upright position will swell the dural sac, thus occluding the hole by compression against the rigid spinal canal. This theory does not however square with the fact that the upright posture induces headache.

Abdominal binder

Compression of the inferior vena cava by the gravid uterus, which caused swelling of the epidural veins, abruptly ceases with delivery. This reduces epidural pressure, so promoting leakage of CSF. Increasing abdominal pressure causes inferior vena caval compression which results in swelling of the epidural veins and may reverse the process. CSF will be forced cephalad and loss of CSF through the dural puncture will be opposed.

An abdominal binder worn for several days after subarachnoid block with a 22-gauge needle significantly decreases the incidence and severity of spinal headache (Beck, 1973; Mosavy and Shafei, 1975). The latter investigators found an abdominal binder as effective as injection of 20–25 ml of epidural saline. An abdominal binder may be worn when upright after planned subarachnoid block with a 26-gauge needle for vaginal or abdominal delivery. Patients often find it comfortable. If a headache develops in the upright position, further compression may be provided by an inflatable bladder or rolled-up towel placed between abdomen and binder. Alternatively the patient may lie prone with a pillow under her abdomen. This places the dural hole uppermost, encourages CSF to leave the area of dural puncture and go towards the brain, and compresses the inferior vena cava causing swelling of the epidural veins.

Hydration, antidiuretic and other drug therapy

There is evidence that prevention of dehydration, and vigorous hydration by the oral or intravenous route, may stimulate CSF production. Both vasopressin (Wolfson et al, 1970) and synthetic arginine vasopressin (Cowan et al, 1980) have been used for prophylaxis and treatment of spinal headache. This treatment, however, does nothing to prevent CSF leakage or to allow the hole to close.

Baumgarten (1987), Jarvis et al (1986) and Sechzer (1979 proposed giving intravenous caffeine and sodium benzoate (0.5–1.0 g) before resorting to epidural blood patch. It is suggested that caffeine prevents the painful dilatation of the intracranial blood vessels. The inhalation of 5–6% CO_2 in oxygen for 10 minutes has been recommended by Sikh and Agawal (1974). Its beneficial effect is attributed to an elevation of CSF pressure because of cerebral vasodilation and an increased secretion of antidiuretic hormone. These two treatments appear somewhat contradictory. Aspirin, paracetamol and ibuprofen may also provide symptomatic relief, particularly if combined with oral codeine or pethidine. Since analgesics do not treat the cause, if the headache does not resolve within a few days, more definitive treatment is needed.

PROPHYLAXIS AND TREATMENT OF SPINAL HEADACHE WITH EPIDURAL SALINE OR AUTOLOGOUS BLOOD PATCH

Epidural saline patch

Rice and Dabbs (1950) first described epidural injection of saline to treat severe spinal headache. In a series of 22 patients they injected a mean volume of 82 ml of saline with immediate relief of headache in 21 patients, permanent relief in 10 and only mild return of symptoms in 12. This treatment gained some popularity, but was largely replaced in the 1970s by epidural injection of autologous blood, while saline came to be used prophylactically. In most instances, it was given through an epidural catheter which had been used to maintain epidural analgesia in labour. Crawford (1972) infused 1.0–1.5 litres of lactated Ringer's solution epidurally over 24 hours following delivery in 16 patients with accidental dural punctures, only 5 of whom developed headache. Continuous infusion may, however, be accompanied by significant back or neck pain, necessitating its discontinuation; moreover, it confines the patient to bed. There is also the danger that the epidural infusion might be mistaken for an intravenous infusion and potentially neurotoxic substances be given into the epidural space.

Intermittent bolus injections of saline to a large extent overcome these problems. Craft et al (1973) found an incidence of headache of 76.5% in 17 patients treated conservatively, compared to 12.5% in 16 patients who received two 60 ml injections of epidural saline in the 24 hours following delivery. Smith (1979) gave 30–60 ml boluses of epidural saline through an epidural catheter every 6 hours for 24 hours. The saline was injected until the patient experienced discomfort, stopped until the discomfort disappeared and resumed until the discomfort returned. Using this protocol only 1 in 13 patients developed a headache, compared to 63.6% in patients treated conservatively. Brownridge (1983) reported similar results with this technique. Though not randomized, these studies do suggest that epidural saline is effective prophylactically. Proper aseptic technique, with separate sterile syringes for each injection, is essential. Finally, only preservative-free 0.9% saline should be used. The preservative benzyl alcohol, which may be added to saline in the USA, has been associated with flaccid paralysis following epidural injection (Craig and Habib, 1977).

Epidural blood patch

Epidural injection of autologous non-anticoagulated blood to treat spinal headache by sealing the dural rent was first described by Gormley (1960). He injected 2–3 ml of preclotted autologous blood in seven patients, producing complete relief of headache in 20–30 minutes. Later, success rates of 89% or more were reported using 10 ml of non-anticoagulated blood (DiGiovanni and Dunbar, 1970; DiGiovanni et al, 1972; Ostheimer et al, 1974; Abouleish et al, 1975a). Abouleish found that a second injection in the failures raised the success rate from 89% to 97.5%. Crawford (1980) recommended injection of 20 ml of blood or an amount that caused discomfort, whichever came first. Smaller volumes than 20 ml in Crawford's experience – and 10 ml in the experience of Ostheimer and Abouleish – were associated with a higher failure rate or recurrence after apparent immediate success. Abouleish (1978), using 10 ml of blood, successfully treated three patients with chronic spinal headache of 32, 71 and 180 days' duration. In two cases where blood patches had failed to alleviate headache, Baysinger et al (1986) found epidural saline infusion to be effective.

In these reports no serious sequelae resulted from epidural blood patch. Some patients experienced back pain, neck ache, leg cramp and transient paraesthesiae, all resolving within minutes to hours of injection. Mild fever in 5% of patients (Crawford, 1980) and a case of facial pain (Abouleish et al, 1975a), but no serious or permanent sequelae, have been reported. There is still concern about the consequences of accidental subarachnoid injection of blood and about future identification of the epidural space and the effectiveness of subsequent epidural block. Ravindran et al (1981) injected 2 ml of autologous blood aseptically into the subarachnoid space of ten anaesthetized dogs. All dogs had spasms of their hind legs which resolved, with no detectable residual deficit. Abouleish et al (1975b) and Crawford (1980) reported successful epidural and subarachnoid blocks after epidural blood patch. DiGiovanni et al (1972) injected 10 ml of autologous blood into the epidural space of goats following lumbar puncture at the same site with an 18-gauge needle. Little tissue reaction and no obliteration of the epidural space was found at the time of laminectomy 3 weeks to 6 months later; indeed the findings were indistinguishable from control goats subjected to dural puncture alone. Only one case has been reported of limited cephelad epidural spread, 3 years after blood patch in an obstetric patient (Rainbird and Pfitzner, 1983).

While the safety and efficacy of blood patch for the treatment of spinal headache is well established, its *prophylactic* value after dural puncture has been questioned. Ozdil and Powell (1965) found that 2.5 ml of preclotted autologous blood injected epidurally as the needle was withdrawn from the subarachnoid space was not associated with neurological problems or headache in 100 patients having subarachnoid block. In their original description of epidural blood patch, DiGiovanni and Dunbar (1970) reported five patients in whom 10 ml was used with success prophylactically. Doctor et al (1976) injected 10 ml of blood into the epidural space through the Tuohy needle as it was being withdrawn after dural puncture in eight obstetric patients, only one of whom experienced a mild headache. On the other hand Loeser et al (1978) and Palahniuk and Cumming (1979) reported failure rates of 71% and 54% respectively when injecting 5–10 ml of blood through the epidural catheter less than 24 hours after dural puncture. These findings may explain in part why prophylactic blood patch fell into disfavour.

Quaynor and Corbey (1985, 1986) used prophylactic blood patch in ten non-obstetric patients following dural puncture with a 16- or 17-gauge Tuohy needle; 15–20 ml were injected before or after administration of local anaesthetic. No patient developed a headache and all had effective epidural blocks. Later Cheek et al (1988) reported the prophylactic use of epidural blood patch in ten parturients. Each had had a dural puncture with an 18-gauge Hustead epidural needle, following which an epidural catheter was sited in an adjacent space to maintain analgesia for Caesarean section or labour. At least 30 minutes after the last top-up, 17–20 ml of autologous blood was given via the catheter. Three patients had transient backache and one a mild headache. One of a further six patients treated in the same way developed a headache. Ackerman and Colclough (1987) using a similar protocol treated six obstetric patients with 15–20 ml of blood, with no complications and no headaches.

More recently Colonna–Romano and Shapiro (1988), in a randomized trial, reported an incidence of headache after dural puncture with a 17-gauge needle of 76% in controls, compared with 17% when a 15 ml prophylactic blood patch was used. Trivedi et al (1989) reported headache in 87% of controls compared with 5% with a 15 ml blood patch and 67% with a 40–60 ml saline patch.

From these findings it would appear that although 10 ml of blood may be adequate following deliberate dural puncture with a needle of 22 gauge or less, this volume may often be inadequate to seal the rent caused by a 16–18-gauge needle, for which 15–20 ml may be more successful.

RECOMMENDED MANAGEMENT OF DURAL PUNCTURE

1. Following accidental dural puncture, a catheter is sited both for epidural analgesia and for the administration of a blood patch following delivery.
2. The correct placement of the epidural catheter should be confirmed not only by aspiration and a test dose but also by establishing an epidural block with an appropriate dose of local anaesthetic.
3. No blood should be injected if the patient has a fever or any signs of septicaemia. In these circumstances, large boluses (40–80 ml) of preservative-free saline may be injected every 6 hours as suggested by Smith (1979).
4. Blood is not injected for at least 30 minutes following the last dose of local anaesthetic or narcotic. After giving autologous blood, no further injections are made through the epidural catheter.
5. Autologous blood, to which no anticoagulant is added, is obtained using strict aseptic technique.
6. Fifteen to 20 ml of blood is injected over 2–3 minutes. More rapid injection is usually impossible through the epidural catheter. If discomfort occurs during injection, stopping and waiting for 15–30 seconds usually relieves it, following which injection can continue. Blood should not be injected while the patient experiences discomfort or paraesthesiae.
7. The patient should be supine during the injection and should remain so for at least 30 minutes. Following this no restrictions are placed on her, except to avoid straining or picking up heavy objects over the next week.
8. Should a headache recur, it can be treated conservatively with an abdominal binder, fluids, intravenous caffeine and sodium benzoate and analgesics.
9. Should headache persist or become severe, it should be treated without delay with either a second blood patch or epidural saline injections.

CONCLUSION

The incidence of headache after dural puncture with a 16- to 18-gauge needle may be betewen 70% and 80% in the parturient when no prophylaxis is used. It may persist for days or weeks and is often extremely disabling, confining the mother to bed and preventing her attending to and bonding with her new baby. Enforced bed-rest in the supine position for 2 days or less has been found to be of no value in preventing spinal headache. Simple forms of treatment include providing epidural analgesia through a catheter which is not in the subarachnoid space; hydration with 3 litres or more per day; antidiuretic therapy with natural or synthetic vasopressin; the use of an abdominal binder, particularly in the upright position, to increase intra-abdominal pressure; intravenous caffeine and oral analgesics. *Neither hydration nor drug treatment does anything to stop the leak and so allow the hole to heal.* Epidural preservative-free saline in several large boluses or as a continuous infusion of 1.0–1.5 litres per day has been shown to reduce the incidence of headache following dural puncture to 12–30% in the obstetric patient. Epidural administration of 10–20 ml of non-anticoagulated autologous blood effectively treats approximately 90% of headaches on the first occasion and more than 95% on the second. Reports suggest that following dural puncture with a large needle at least 15–20 ml of blood is needed to *prevent* headache in parturients, and may be more effective than epidural saline.

REFERENCES

Abouleish E (1978) Epidural blood patch for the treatment of chronic post-lumbar-puncture cephalgia. *Anesthesiology* **49**: 291–292.

Abouleish E, de la Vega S, Blendinger I & Tio TO (1975a) Long term follow-up of epidural blood patch. *Anesthesia and Analgesia* **54**: 459–463.

Abouleish E, Wadhwa RK, de la Vega S et al (1975b) Regional analgesia following epidural blood patch. *Anesthesia and Analgesia* **54**: 634–636.

Ackerman WE, Colclough GW (1987) Prophylactic epidural blood patch: the controversy continues (letter). *Anesthesia and Analgesia* **66**: 913.

Baumgarten RK (1987) Should caffeine become the firstline treatment for postdural puncture headache? (letter). *Anesthesia and Analgesia* **66**: 913–914.

Baysinger CL, Menk EJ, Harte E & Middaugh R (1986) The successful treatment of dural puncture headache after failed epidural blood patch. *Anesthesia and Analgesia* **65**: 1242–1244.

Beck WW (1973) Prevention of the postpartum spinal headache. *American Journal of Obstetrics and Gynecology* **115**: 354–356.

Bromage PR (1987) Neurologic complications of regional anesthesia for obstetrics. In Shnider SM & Levinson G (eds) *Anesthesia for Obstetrics*, 2nd edn, pp 316–324. Baltimore: Williams & Wilkins.

Brownridge P (1983) The management of headache following accidental dural puncture in obstetric patients. *Anaesthesia and Intensive Care* **11**: 4–15.

Carbaat PAT & Crevel H (1981) Lumbar puncture headache: controlled study on the preventive effect of 24 hrs bed rest. *Lancet* **ii**: 1133–1135.

Cheek TG, Banner R, Sauter J & Gutsche BB (1988) Prophylactic extradural blood patch is effective. *British Journal of Anaesthesia* **61**: 340–342.

Colonna-Romano P & Shapiro BE (1988) Prophylactic epidural blood patch in obstetrics (abstract). *Anesthesiology* **69**: A665.

Cowan JMA, Durward WF, Harrington H et al (1980) DDAVP in the prevention of headache after lumbar puncture. *British Medical Journal* **2**: 224.

Craft JB, Epstein BS & Coakley CS (1973) Prophylaxis of dural puncture headache with epidural saline. *Anesthesia and Analgesia* **52**: 228–231.

Craig DB & Habib CC (1977) Flaccid paraparesis following obstetrical epidural anesthesia: possible role of benzyl alcohol. *Anesthesia and Analgesia* **56**: 219–222.

Crawford JS (1972) The prevention of headache consequent upon dural puncture. *British Journal of Anaesthesia* **44**: 598–600.

Crawford JS (1980) Experiences with epidural blood patch. *Anaesthesia* **35**: 513–515.

Denny N, Masters R, Pearson D et al (1987) Postdural puncture headache after continuous spinal anesthesia. *Anesthesia and Analgesia* **66**: 791–794.

DiGiovanni AJ & Dunbar BS (1970) Epidural injections of autologous blood for post-lumbar-puncture headache. *Anesthesia and Analgesia* **49**: 268–271.

DiGiovanni AJ, Galbert MW & Wahle WM (1972) Epidural injection of autologous blood for post-lumbar-puncture headache. II. Additional clinical experiences and laboratory investigation. *Anesthesia and Analgesia* **51**: 226–232.

Doctor N, DeZoysa S, Shah R et al (1976) The use of the blood patch for post-spinal headaches (letter). *Anaesthesia* **31**: 794–795.

Doughty A (1979) Inadvertent dural puncture – an avoidable accident. *Anaesthesia* **34**: 116.

Eckstein KL, Rogacev Z, Vincente-Eckstein A & Grahovac A (1982) Prospective comparative study of postspinal headache in young patients (less than 51 years). *Regional-Anaesthesie* **5**: 57–61.

Edelman JD & Wingard DW (1980) Subdural hematomas after lumbar dural puncture. *Anesthesiology* **52**: 166–167.

Franksson C & Gordth T (1946) Headache after spinal anaesthesia and a technique for lessening its frequency. *Acta Chirurgica Scandinavica* **94**: 443–454.

Gormley JB (1960) Treatment of postspinal headache. *Anesthesiology* **21**: 565–566.

Greene BA (1950) A 26 g lumbar puncture needle: its value in the prophylaxis of headache following spinal analgesia for vaginal delivery. *Anesthesiology* **11**: 464–469.

Handler CE, Parkin GD, Smith FR & Rose FC (1982) Posture and lumbar puncture headache: a controlled trial in 50 patients. *Journal of Royal Society of Medicine* **75**: 404–407.

Harris A & Whitehead D (1989) Continuous spinal anesthesia does not prevent headaches following unintentional dural puncture in pregnant patients. *Abstracts of the Society for Obstetric Anesthesiology and Perinatology*, Seattle, C3.

Holdcroft A & Morgan M (1976) Maternal complications of obstetric epidural analgesia. *Anaesthesia and Intensive Care* **4**: 108–112.

Jack TM (1979) Post-partum intracranial subdural haematoma. A possible complication of epidural analgesia. *Anaesthesia* **34**: 176–180.

Jarvis AP, Greenwalt JW & Fagraeus L (1986) Intravenous caffeine for postdural puncture headache. *Anesthesia and Analgesia* **65**: 316–317.

Jones RJ (1974) The role of recumbency in the prevention and treatment of postspinal headache. *Anesthesia and Analgesia* **53**: 788–796.

Kunkle EC, Ray BS & Wolff HC (1943) Experimental studies on headaches, analysis of the headache associated with changes in intracranial pressure. *Archives of Neurology and Psychiatry* **49**: 323–358.

Levin MJ (1944) Lumbar puncture headaches. *Bulletin of the US Army Medical Dept* **82**: 107–110.

Loeser EA, Hill GE, Bennett GM & Sederberg JH (1978) Time v success rate for epidural blood patch. *Anesthesiology* **49**: 147–148.

Macdonald R (1953) Dr Doughty's technique for the location of the epidural space. *Anaesthesia* **38**: 71–72.

Mihic DH (1985) Postspinal headache and relationship of needle bevel to longitudinal dural fibers. *Regional Anesthesia* **10**: 76–81.

Mosavy SH & Shafei M (1975) Prevention of headache consequent upon dural puncture in obstetric patient. *Anaesthesia* **30**: 807–809.

Norris MC, Leighton BL & DiSimone CA (1989) Needle bevel direction and headache after inadvertent dural puncture. *Anesthesiology* **70**: 729–731.

Ostheimer GW, Palahniuk RJ & Shnider SM (1974) Epidural blood patch for post-lumbar-puncture headache (letter). *Anesthesiology* **41**: 307–308.

Ozdil T & Powell WF (1965) Post lumbar puncture headache: an effective method of prevention. *Anesthesia and Analgesia* **44**: 542–545.

Palahniuk RJ & Cumming M (1979) Prophylactic blood patch does not prevent post lumbar puncture headache. *Canadian Anaesthetists Society Journal* **26**: 132–133.

Quaynor H & Corbey M (1986) Extradural blood patch. *British Journal of Anaesthesia* **58**: 468–469 (letter).

Quaynor H & Corbey M (1986) *British Journal of Anaesthesia* **58**: 468–469 (letter).

Rainbird A & Pfitzner J (1983) Restricted spread of analgesia following epidural blood patch. Case report with a review of possible complications. *Anaesthesia* **38**: 481–484.

Ravindran RS, Tasch MD, Baldwin SJ & Hendrie M (1981) Subarachnoid injection of autologous blood in dogs is unassociated with neurologic defeats. *Anesthesia and Analgesia* **60**: 603–604.

Reynolds F (1988) Avoiding accidental dural puncture. *British Journal of Anaesthesia* **61**: 515–516.

Rice GG & Dabbs CH (1950) The use of peridural and subarachnoid injections of saline solution in the treatment of severe postspinal headache. *Anesthesiology* **11**: 17–23.

Sechzer PH (1979) Post-spinal anesthesia headache treated with caffeine. II. Intracranial vascular distension a key factor. *Current Therapeutic Research* **26**: 440–448.

Shnider SM & Levinson G (1987) Anesthesia for Cesarean Section. In Shnider SM & Levinson C (eds) *Anesthesia for Obstetrics*, 2nd edn, pp 159–178. Baltimore: Williams & Wilkins.

Sikh SS & Agawal G (1974) Post-spinal headache. *Anaesthesia* **29**: 297–300.

Smith BE (1979) Prophylaxis of epidural 'wet tap' headache (abstract). *Anesthesiology* (supplement) **51**: S304.

Trivedi N, Eddi D & Shevde K (1989) Prevention of headache following inadvertent dural puncture. *Abstracts of the Society for Obstetric Anesthesia and Perinatology*, Seattle, C3.

Wolfson B, Siker ES & Gray GH (1970) Post-pneumoencephalography headache. A study of incidence and an attempt at therapy. *Anaesthesia* **25**: 328–333.

8

Total spinal anaesthesia: the effect of spinal infusions

IAN F. RUSSELL

There is disagreement about the definition of total spinal anaesthesia. It is usually described as the rapid onset of hypotension and analgesia with widespread paralysis and apnoea due to the effects of local anaesthetics within the subarachnoid space. If the local anaesthetic solution reaches the brain then dilated pupils and unconsciousness may ensue. A more conservative view described total spinal anaesthesia as 'any anaesthetic level above T2', on the grounds that there is not much further it can go (Crawford, 1990). The principal symptom differentiating high spinal from total spinal blockade is respiratory failure. If anaesthetic levels reach C1/C2 without respiratory failure then this should be described as 'high spinal anaesthesia' rather than 'total spinal anaesthesia'.

This review concentrates on publications from 1980 onwards, and includes only reports that are felt to be of some relevance to obstetric anaesthetists. This excludes a multitude of cases of total spinal blockade in non-pregnant patients from complications of epidural, brachial plexus, interscalene, stellate ganglion, intercostal and paravertebral blocks, as well as from some more esoteric causes such as 'total spinal blockade during local anesthesia of the nasal passages' (Hill et al, 1983). It should also be noted that cases described as unexpected 'high blocks' after epidural analgesia have been excluded if block height never rose above T4.

Table 1 lists the total spinal or high spinal blocks of uncertain origin in obstetric anaesthetic practice reported since 1980. It is apparent that complications of epidural anaesthesia still form the vast majority of cases, with a remarkable lack of total spinal blockade occurring after intentional spinal anaesthesia. However, though spinal blockade is the most common form of anaesthesia for Caesarean section in North America (Gibbs et al, 1986) and is

Table 1. Publications on unexpected high blocks or total spinal anaesthesia found as a result of a manual search of the English language literature from 1980 to present. 'Total spinal' only includes patients who were intubated or required respiratory support. '?' indicates insufficient information provided on which to base any opinion.

Author(s)	High spinal block		Total spinal anaesthesia
Epidural			
Conklin & Van der Wal (1980)	1		–
Covino (1980)	–		2
Hodgkinson (1981)	3		3
Skowronski & Rigg (1981)	–		1
Soni & Holland (1981)	1		–
Collier (1982a)	?	3 cases	?
Collier (1982b)	?	10 cases	?
Findley & Shandro (1982)	–		1
Brownridge (1983)	1		–
Manchanda et al (1983)	1		–
Russell (1983b)	1		–
Abouleish & Bryant (1984)	–		1
Brindle-Smith et al (1984)	1		–
Carter (1984)	–		1
Pearson (1984)	1		–
Crawford (1985)	2		1
Abouleish & Goldstein (1986)	–		1
Lee & Dodd (1986)	1		–
Okell & Sprigge (1987)	?	3 cases	?
Leach & Smith (1988)	1		–
Crosby & Halpern (1989)	1		–
Spinal			
Stonham & Moss (1983)	–		1
Russell (1985)	–		1
Bembridge et al (1986)	4		–
Spinal + epidural			
Stone et al (1989)	–		1

becoming more popular in the UK, the overall number of spinal or epidural blocks used in pregnant patients – and hence the relative risk of high spinal or total spinal anaesthesia with either technique – is unknown.

High blocks following intended spinal anaesthesia

In view of the frequently expressed concern regarding the risk of total spinal anaesthesia after an intentional spinal anaesthetic, it is probably worth examining these few cases in some detail. Two cases known to the author that antedate 1980 are also included.

Crawford (1979) described a case requiring 'intubation as a precautionary measure' after 2.0 ml of 5% heavy lignocaine. At no time did this patient require assisted ventilation, and the sensory loss did not exceed T2. This is not a total spinal block. Similarly, Crawford (personal communication) also described another total spinal block following 1.5 ml heavy lignocaine; the patient complained of inability to breathe, but at the time of intubation she had a good hand grip. Once again the diagnosis is in doubt.

Stonham and Moss (1983) described total spinal anaesthesia caused by 3 ml of 0.5% plain bupivacaine given for Caesarean section, but no relevant clinical information is given.

Russell (1985) described a total spinal block caused by 2.0 ml of 0.75% plain bupivacaine. All was well until the obstetrician requested transfer of the wedge from the right to the left hip. Within seconds a previously stable anaesthetic level rose rapidly to cause respiratory paralysis. The high block wore off equally rapidly so that extubation was possible a few minutes after delivery of the infant.

Stone et al (1989) failed to obtain adequate analgesic levels with 33 ml of 0.5% bupivacaine given epidurally, and gave 1.6 ml heavy 0.5% bupivacaine intrathecally. They described dyspnoea and 'patient distress' when the analgesic level rose to T2, but without gross motor blockade of the upper limbs. Circumstances did not allow a detailed neurological examination before general anaesthesia was induced. At the end of surgery the patient was extubated with a sensory level still at T2. It is difficult to be sure whether total spinal anaesthesia had occurred, or whether the spinal plus epidural blockade resulted in a greater than usual block of the thoracic motor and sensory nerves, such that the patient was either relying entirely on diaphragmatic respiration or the lack of sensory information from the thoracic nerves caused dyspnoea. This symptom is seen occasionally with conventional spinal anaesthesia. A rapid assessment of the muscle power of the patient's hands and arms should be made, and provided there is reasonable power, reassurance and a confident explanation of the problem to the patient is usually all that is required. Delivery of the infant, indeed release of amniotic fluid, unsplints the diaphragm as well as distracting the mother and dyspnoea is usually no longer a complaint. It is always worth giving the obstetrician a quiet signal to expedite delivery.

The important issue, as always, is to determine the adequacy of respiration. Bembridge et al (1986), using 5% heavy lignocaine, described several high spinal blocks with glottic involvement, but, unlike any of the preceding reports, respiration was assessed with a Wright's respirometer and all the patients were found to have adequate rsepiratory reserve.

High blocks following intended epidural analgesia

With diagnoses ranging from 'massive epidural' (Dawkins, 1969) to total spinal anaesthesia, the situation with high blocks after epidural analgesia is even more confusing. The potential causes of high or total spinal blockade after intended epidural administration include injections directly into the cerebrospinal fluid (CSF), into the subdural space, or into the epidural space after a dural puncture. These causes may occur in isolation, or together in any combination. It seems likely that the older diagnosis of 'massive epidural' may be the same as the more recently described accidental subdural block. Although high epidural blockade may follow rapid injection or a relative overdose of local anaesthetic into a normal epidural space, such cases do not usually cause problems (Collier, 1982b).

In many cases it is impossible to categorize the cause of the abnormal blockade. Even though the authors of reports may reach well-argued conclusions, as do Skowronski and Rigg (1981) for accidental subarachnoid injection, subsequent critical correspondence often suggests an alternative explanation such as subdural injection (Collier, 1982b). In another case where respiratory support by bag and mask was required for 10 minutes, Abouleish and Bryant (1984) concluded that total spinal blockade had occurred. However, it was later suggested that this patient had probably fainted while being topped-up in the sitting position (Christensen and Lund, 1984).

Attempts have been made to specify particular diagnostic pointers to distinguish a subdural extra-arachnoid block from a subarachnoid block. After a moderate volume of drug (10–15 ml) given subdurally, characteristic effects are said to include relative sparing of sympathetic tone and motor power, such that there is usually only moderate hypotension and limited motor block; slow onset of symptoms over 15–20 minutes with gradual progression over the next 20 minutes; slowly progressive respiratory depression with incoordination rather than sudden apnoea; and recovery after two hours (Collier, 1982b).

However, the reliability of these clinical signs in differentiating between subdural and subarachnoid injection is open to question. Evans (1974) has shown in 100 non-pregnant patients that even with intentional total spinal blockade using 40 ml of local anaesthetic solution, 11 patients had no significant hypotension, the onset could be slow (up to 45 minutes), and 5 of his patients, although unconscious, did not have apnoea. There are also obstetric cases where 2–3 ml injections into the 'epidural' space have produced rapid high blocks with hypotension. Subsequent radiological investigation showed the catheter lying within the subdural space (Brindle-Smith et al, 1984).

After such problems an X-ray of the spinal column with contrast medium injected through the catheter is often used to demonstrate the position of the catheter. Even this cannot guarantee that the site of the catheter at X-ray was the same as that at the time the 'epidural' injection was made. Catheters can migrate readily (Phillips and Macdonald, 1987; Mourisse et al, 1989), but it is doubtful whether they can penetrate intact dura mater (Hardy, 1986).

An aspect of the management of many of these abnormal 'epidurals' that is hard to understand is the frequent recourse to intramuscular analgesia for labour or general anaesthesia for operative deliveries. In the presence of these very effective 'epidurals' why are careful, small-volume top-ups not used more frequently, as described by Crawford (1974, 1985) or Brownridge (1983)? At worst the catheter will be in the CSF. Spinal anaesthesia with a catheter is easily controlled, but there still appears to be a fear of this procedure (Leach and Smith, 1988) which is not borne out by current experience.

MANAGEMENT

Irrespective of the cause of potential total spinal anaesthesia, its recognition and treatment are important. Early treatment may prevent progression to total spinal block. If a large dose of local anaesthetic has been injected inadvertently into the CSF through an epidural needle or catheter, it may prove possible to aspirate a considerable volume of this (Covino, 1980). Indeed, spinal irrigation has been used in the past, with saline injected at the cisterna magna and CSF together with local anaesthetic aspirated in the lumbar region (Covino, 1980). The risks associated with aspiration or irrigation may not be acceptable, unless the drug involved is likely to be toxic in large volumes (Covino, 1980) or trouble with intubation or maintaining an airway is anticipated.

If an accidental subarachnoid injection is suspected it is important to ensure that the pregnant patient is nursed on her side. This will prevent caval occlusion and make cardiovascular resuscitation easier. Equally important, avoiding caval occlusion will reduce the volume of blood in the azygos system, thus ensuring that the volume of blood in the spinal and vertebral venous plexus is kept to a minimum.

This will maximize the volume available within the lower spinal canal for other fluids. Since many of the solutions intended for the epidural space are hypobaric or isobaric with CSF they will not spread rapidly from the site of their injection into the CSF unless they are physically moved by turning the patient on to her back (Kitahara et al, 1956; Russell, 1983a). The slow diffusion of these solutions away from the injection site will allow time to obtain the equipment required for resuscitation and may even make its use unnecessary. A slight head-down tilt may be of value in maintaining venous return and blood pressure as well as encouraging a hypobaric anaesthetic solution within the CSF to move caudally. Too much head-down tilt, however, will embarrass diaphragmatic respiration.

By following these simple guidelines significant problems were avoided after a trainee injected 10 ml of 0.375% bupivacaine into the CSF during a routine epidural for labour (Russell, 1983b). With the patient lying quietly on her side breathing oxygen, it took some 20 minutes for the analgesia to reach C1/C2. Blood pressure and pulse were stable throughout, but the patient did experience some dyspnoea and anxiety. A reasonable hand grip remained at all times. The patient was monitored closely, her hand was held and together with reassurance the situation was explained. The dyspnoea wore off within an hour, but it took over 7 hours for anaesthesia to regress to the sacral segments. Had this patient been turned over, the postural effects of pregnancy on CSF dynamics would have ensured rapid total spinal anaesthesia within seconds.

The postural effects of pregnancy on the spread of conventional doses of bupivacaine for spinal anaesthesia have been described before (Russell, 1983a). The influence of other factors governing the spread of spinal anaesthetic solutions in pregnancy is unclear, since most studies use non-pregnant patients and frequently reach contradictory conclusions (Green, 1985). This has a bearing on the controversy surrounding test doses in association with intermittent epidural top-ups.

One way of avoiding this controversy is to use continuous infusion epidural analgesia (see Chapter 4). However should the catheter inadvertently enter the CSF during such an infusion, little is known of the effects of continuous subarachnoid infusion of local anaesthetic drugs.

SUBARACHNOID INFUSION

It is claimed, hypothetically, that a slow subarachnoid infusion of bupivacaine will result in a slow onset of spinal anaesthesia, allowing easy recognition and discontinuance of the infusion before the anaesthetic level becomes unduly high (Rosenblatt et al, 1983; Li et al, 1985; Gaylard et al, 1987).

The validity of this claim has been studied in patients presenting for elective Caesarean section when 15 mg of bupivacaine was infused, in various dilutions, into the CSF over 30 minutes. The women lay on their *right side* for the duration of the infusion, and were then turned supine with the operating table tilted to the left. A double needle technique was used with placement of an epidural catheter in case anaesthesia was insufficient for the Caesarean section. Five patients had their infusion through 23-gauge catheter placed in the subarachnoid space.

The effects of three solutions only are discussed here: 3 ml of 0.5% bupivacaine (6 patients); 4 ml of 0.375% bupivacaine (10 patients); and 6 ml of 0.25% bupivacaine (10 patients). All three solutions showed the same pattern of onset of analgesia and anaesthesia: a slow onset and spread, predominantly unilateral (left side only), until the patients were turned to a supine wedged position (Figures 1 and 2). The range of analgesic and anaesthetic levels corresponding to Figures 1 and 2 can be seen in Tables 2 and 3. When the patients were turned over, not only was there a rapid rise in the levels of block, but analgesic levels became equal on both sides within 5 minutes, eventually reaching their maximum height at around 10–15 minutes. No patient had any respiratory difficulty.

The five patients with subarachnoid catheters lay supine with the operating table tilted to the left while 6 ml 0.25% bupivacaine was infused, again over 30 minutes. These patients gradually developed analgesia to pin-prick, and by 30 minutes the analgesic levels ranged from T11 to T3. At this time two of the patients had still not developed any anaesthesia and were fully aware of touch, even though analgesia extended to T4 in one case. In another patient anaesthesia was only experienced between the L4 and T10 dermatomes bilaterally, but the patient was aware of touch outside these dermatomes. The final two women developed anaesthesia as expected, a few dermatomes below their analgesic levels. At 30 minutes none of these patients had a level of anaesthesia sufficient for surgery. Rolling the women from side to side only caused one block to extend marginally (from T8 to T6), so the remaining four patients received 0.5% heavy bupivacaine in 0.5–1.0 ml increments through the catheter until adequate anaesthetic levels were obtained.

An unusual feature in these five patients was the onset of motor block to the lower limbs. Considerable motor block was often present despite an inability to determine any level for anaesthesia to touch. Whether this is due to the hypobaric nature of 0.25% bupivacaine enabling it to reach the anterior (motor) nerve roots earlier than the more posterior (sensory) roots is unknown.

It is clear from these results that the onset of spinal anaesthesia is not as slow as the 'two hours to reach T10' suggested by Li et al (1985). The limited results also imply that posture during the infusion has a marked effect on the subsequent spread of the subarachnoid

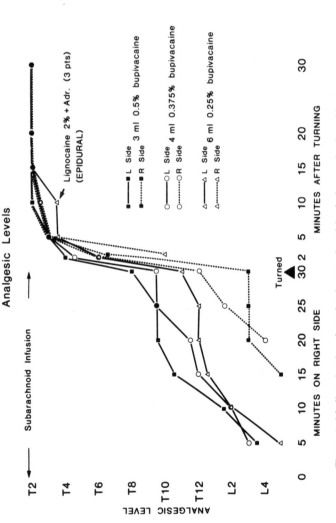

Figure 1. Median levels of analgesia to pin-prick during and after 30-minute subarachnoid infusions of bupivacaine (15 mg). The patients lay on their right sides during the infusion and were then turned supine with a right hip-up tilt. The essentially unilateral nature of the block before turning can be clearly seen, as can the dramatic effect of repositioning on this unilateral block and the rapid extension

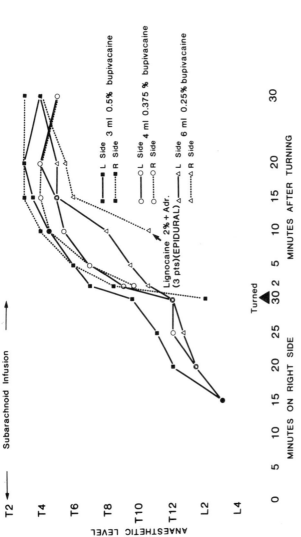

Figure 2. Median levels of anaesthesia to touch during and after 30-minute subarachnoid infusions of bupivacaine (15 mg). The patients lay on their right sides during the infusion and were then turned supine with a right hip-up tilt. The figure illustrates the absence of any anaesthesia on the lowermost (right) side during the infusions, and the rapid rise of anaesthetic levels on both sides following repositioning.

Table 2. Total range of analgesic levels observed (on left and right sides) in the various groups during the spinal infusion at 5, 15 and 30 minutes, and after turning at 2 and 5 minutes, together with the maximum height of block (see Figure 1).

Time interval	Concentration of bupivacaine					
	0.5%		0.375%		0.25%	
	L	R	L	R	L	R
Infusion						
5 min	0/L3	0/0	0/L2	0/0	0/L2	0/0
15 min	L1/T10	0/L3	L2/T11	0/T12	L3/T12	0/0
30 min	T12/T7	0/T6	L1/T6	0/T2	T12/T5	0/T5
After turning						
2 min	T10/T4	L1/T6	T8/T2	T9/T2	T11/T3	0/T3
5 min	T9/T1	T10/T1	T6/T1	T6/T2	T10/T2	T10/T2
Maximum height	T4/C6	T4/C6	T4/C2	T3/C1	T4/C8	T5/C8

Table 3. Total range of anaesthetic levels observed (on left and right sides) in the various groups during the spinal infusion at 5, 15 and 30 minutes, and after turning at 2 and 5 minutes, together with the maximum height of block (see Figure 2).

Time interval	Concentration of bupivacaine					
	0.5%		0.375%		0.25%	
	L	R	L	R	L	R
Infusion						
5 min	0/0	0/0	0/0	0/0	0/0	0/0
15 min	0/T12	0/L3	0/L2	0/L2	0/T12	0/0
30 min	T10/T6	0/T10	L3/T5	0/T5	L3/T11	0/0
After turning						
2 min	T12/T2	0/T2	L1/T4	0/T2	L1/T5	0/T5
5 min	T11/T2	T12/T2	L1/T2	0/T2	L1/T5	0/T5
Maximum height	T8/T1	T8/T2	T7/T1	T5/T1	T9/T3	T7/T3

anaesthetic solution when the position is changed. If the patient is wedged supine during the infusion then the results so far suggest that positional changes may have little effect on the anaesthetic level. This is probably because the vertebral venous plexus is already distended in the supine wedged position, and movement of the patient has little further effect on this. There is thus no further displacement of CSF in a cranial direction with postural changes (unless the patients were to lie prone). If the patient is on her side during the infusion then turning will encourage a significant rise in anaesthetic level, mimicking the onset of a conventional spinal anaesthetic.

Although none of the patients in this study had any cardiorespiratory problems, this may not be so in labour when the unexpected rapid changes in analgesic level and sympathetic block associated with changing position may have potentially serious consequences. Without an adequate fluid preload and prophylactic intravenous ephedrine there may be a sudden fall in blood pressure. Moreover, depending on how long the patient has remained on her side and how much drug has been infused, there is the possibility of total spinal anaesthesia.

From this study there is insufficient evidence to predict the effects of a spinal infusion in the presence of sensory or motor block consequent upon a previous epidural top-up or infusion. Perhaps, if it is specifically sought, the onset of significant motor block in one or both legs may be observed. Motor block of this density would be unusual with epidural infusions of dilute bupivacaine.

On the basis of these results some guidelines are suggested for staff looking after epidural infusions (Table 4). Assessments every 1–2 hours may be all that is required to detect the excessive spread of analgesia from an over-generous *epidural* infusion, but this time interval is too long if the catheter is in the CSF.

The infusions in this series were only for 30 minutes, and were limited to 15 mg of bupivacaine. The effects of longer infusions, larger volumes of more dilute solutions, or larger doses of bupivacaine are largely unknown. However, two further groups are under investigation, using the same protocol but larger volumes: 12 ml of 0.125% bupivacaine (15 mg), and 18 ml of 0.083% bupivacaine (15 mg). Despite these large volumes, initial results indicate an onset and spread of blockade similar to that for the solutions already discussed (0.5%, 0.375%, 0.25%). The use of 10 ml of 0.125% bupivacaine for spinal anaesthesia for Caesarean section with no untoward effects has been described by Van Zundert et al (1988). These workers reported an onset and spread of analgesia and final analgesic levels similar to those observed using more conventional volumes of more concentrated solutions (Russell and Holmqvist, 1987), and furthermore there were fewer high blocks using this large volume of dilute solution.

Table 4. Suggestions for management of an epidural infusion based on observations of the behaviour of intrathecal infusions of bupivacaine.

In addition to the usual monitoring required for management of an epidural infusion, staff should pay particular attention to the following:

A. The patient should be on her side during an epidural infusion
B. The side should be changed every 30 minutes
C. Before changing sides, or repositioning for any obstetric examination or procedure, check analgesic levels to cold or pin-prick, and check blood pressure
D. Three to five minutes after repositioning, check blood pressure and analgesic levels again
E. If there is a discrepancy of two or more segments between C and D above, then suspect a spinal infusion and call the anaesthetist

This evidence suggests that the factors governing spread of spinal anaesthetic solutions are complex, and considerable doubt is cast on the importance of injection volume as a determinant of anaesthetic spread. Furthermore, within the range studied, the spread of effect of drugs given by spinal infusion is faster than previously hypothesized.

CONCLUSION

Total spinal anaesthesia or high blocks of uncertain aetiology are described regularly in the medical literature. The most common cause is inadvertent subdural or subarachnoid injection of local anaesthetic drugs intended for the epidural space. Total spinal anaesthesia after an intentional spinal anaesthetic is a relatively rare occurrence. Whatever the cause of a total spinal or high block, treatment consists of cardiorespiratory support until the effects of the local anaesthetic wear off sufficiently for the patient to maintain airway, respiration and blood pressure. The guidelines presented here for the monitoring of epidural infusions, based on observations of the effects of slow infusions of bupivacaine into the subarachnoid space, should assist in the management of these patients.

REFERENCES

Abouleish EI & Bryant D (1984) Accidental dural puncture. *British Journal of Anaesthesia* **56**: 668.
Abouleish E & Goldstein M (1986) Migration of an extradural catheter into the subdural space. *British Journal of Anaesthesia* **58**: 1194–1197.

Bembridge M, Macdonald R & Lyons G (1986) Spinal anaesthesia with hyperbaric lignocaine for elective Caesarean section. *Anaesthesia* **41**: 906–909.

Brindle-Smith G, Barton FL & Watt JH (1984) Extensive spread of local anaesthetic solution following subdural insertion of an epidural catheter during labour. *Anaesthesia* **39**: 355–358.

Brownridge P (1983) The management of headache following accidental dural puncture in obstetric patients. *Anaesthesia and Intensive Care* **11**: 4–15.

Carter JA (1984) A rare complication of extradural analgesia. *Anaesthesia* **39**: 1033–1034.

Christensen FR & Lund J (1984) Accidental dural puncture. *British Journal of Anaesthesia* **56**: 668–669.

Collier C (1982a) Collapse after epidural injection following inadvertent dural perforation. *Anesthesiology* **57**: 427–428.

Collier C (1982b) Total spinal or massive subdural block? *Anaesthesia and Intensive Care* **10**: 92–93.

Conklin KA & Van der Wal C (1980) Epidural anaesthesia with chloroprocaine. Delayed onset, extensive spread, and prolonged duration. *Anaesthesia* **35**: 202–204.

Covino BG (1980) Prolonged sensory/motor deficits following inadvertent spinal anesthesia. *Anesthesia and Analgesia* **59**: 399–400.

Crawford JS (1974) The strange case of the (inadvertent) continuous spinal. *British Journal of Anaesthesia* **46**: 82.

Crawford JS (1979) Experience with spinal analgesia in a British obstetric unit. *British Journal of Anaesthesia* **51**: 531–535.

Crawford JS (1985) Some maternal complications of epidural analgesia for labour. *Anaesthesia* **40**: 1219–1225.

Crawford JS (1988) Opposer in debate 'Spinals are better than epidurals for elective Caesarean section'. *Controversies in Obstetric Anaesthesia*, Royal Postgraduate Medical School Institute of Obstetrics and Gynaecology, London (in press).

Crosby ET & Halpern S (1989) Failure of lidocaine test dose to identify subdural placement of an epidural catheter. *Canadian Journal of Anaesthesia* **36**: 445–447.

Dawkins CJM (1969) An analysis of the complications of extradural and caudal block. *Anaesthesia* **4**: 554–563.

Evans TI (1974) Total spinal anaesthesia. *Anaesthesia and Intensive care* **2**: 158–163.

Findley I & Shandro J (1982) Delayed onset spinal after epidural analgesia. *Anaesthesia* **37**: 602–603.

Gaylard DG, Wilson IH & Balmer HGR (1987) An epidural infusion technique for labour. *Anaesthesia* **42**: 1098–1101.

Gibbs CP, Krischer J, Peckham BM, Sharp H & Kirschbaum TH (1986) Obstetric anesthesia: a national survey. *Anesthesiology* **65**: 298–306.

Green NM (1985) Distribution of local anesthetic solutions within the subarachnoid space. *Anesthesia and Analgesia* **64**: 715–730.

Hardy PA (1986) Can epidural catheters penetrate the dura mater? An anatomical study. *Anaesthesia* **41**: 1146–1147.

Hill JN, Gershon NI & Gargiulo PO (1983) Total spinal anesthesia during local anesthesia of the nasal passages. *Anesthesiology* **59**: 144–146.

Hogkinson R (1981) Total spinal block after epidural injection into an interspace adjacent to an inadvertent dural perforation. *Anesthesiology* **55**: 593–595.

Kitahara T, Shinnosuke K & Yoshida J (1956) The spread of drugs used for spinal anesthesia. *Anesthesiology* **17**: 205–208.

Leach A & Smith GB (1988) Subarachnoid spread of epidural local anaesthetic following dural puncture. *Anaesthesia* **43**: 671–674.

Lee A & Dodd KW (1986) Accidental subdural catheterisation. *Anaesthesia* **41**: 847–849.

Li DF, Rees GAD & Rosen M (1985) Continuous extradural infusion of 0.0625% or 0.0125% bupivacaine for pain relief in primigravid labour. *British Journal of Anaesthesia* **57**: 264–270.

Manchanda VN, Suha HN, Murad SHN, Shilyanski G & Mehringer M (1983) Unusual clinical course of accidental subdural local anaesthetic injection. *Anesthesia and Analgesia* **62**: 1124–1126.

Mourisse J, Gielen MJM, Hasenbos AWM & Heystraten FMJ (1989) Migration of thoracic epidural catheters: three methods for evaluation of catheter position in the thoracic space. *Anaesthesia* **44**: 574–577.

Okell RW & Sprigge JS (1987) Unintentional dural puncture. A survey of recognition and management. *Anaesthesia* **42**: 1110–1113.

Pearson RMG (1984) A rare complication of extradural analgesia. *Anaesthesia* **39**: 460–463.

Phillips DC & Macdonald R (1987) Epidural catheter migration during labour. *Anaesthesia* **42**: 661–663.

Rosenblatt R, Wright R, Denson D & Raj P (1983) Continuous epidural infusions for obstetric analgesia. *Regional Anesthesia* **8**: 10–15.

Russell IF (1983a) Spinal anaesthesia for Caesarean section: the use of 0.5% bupivacaine. *British Journal of Anaesthesia* **55**: 309–314.

Russell IF (1983b) Total spinal or massive subdural? *Anaesthesia and Intensive Care* **11**: 386–388.

Russell IF (1985) Inadvertent total spinal for Caesarean section. *Anaesthesia* **40**: 199–200.

Russell IF & Holmqvist ELO (1987) Subarachnoid analgesia for Caesarean section. A double blind comparison of plain and hyperbaric 0.5% bupivacaine. *British Journal of Anaesthesia* **59**: 347–353.

Skowronski GA & Rigg JRA (1981) Total spinal block complicating epidural analgesia in labour. *Anaesthesia and Intensive Care* **9**: 274–276.

Soni N & Holland R (1981) An extensive lumbar epidural block. *Anaesthesia and Intensive Care* **9**: 150–153.

Stone PA, Thorburn J & Lamb KSR (1989) Complications of spinal anaesthesia following extradural block for Caesarean section. *British Journal of Anaesthesia* **62**: 335–337.

Stonham J & Moss P (1983) The optimal test dose for epidural anesthesia. *Anesthesiology* **58**: 389–390.

Van Zundert AA, De Wolf AM, Vaes L & Soetens M (1988) High-volume spinal anesthesia with bupivacaine 0.125% for Cesarean section. *Anesthesiology* **69**: 998–1003.

SECTION III – DISCUSSION

CHAIRMAN: DR R. W. JOHNSON, Bristol

Dr Johnson (Bristol)   Dr Gutsche, did I understand you to say that you have been using subarachnoid analgesia deliberately through a catheter in labour?

Dr Gutsche   Yes but we have not yet used the very fine subarachnoid catheters that are now available.

Dr Naulty   By what mechanism does a blood patch alleviate dural puncture headache?

Dr Gutsche   I assume that the blood coagulates around the area of the puncture like a tyre patch and prevents further leakage of fluid from the subarachnoid space.

Dr Shah   Immediate relief of dural puncture headache produced by a blood patch may be due to the rise in intracranial pressure. I have found that during labour and in the immediate postpartum period the mean epidural pressure was 15 cmH$_2$O, while in women with dural puncture headache the mean epidural pressure was 5 cmH$_2$O. I think the reduced epidural pressure reflects the reduced intracranial pressure. It is possible that the blood patch by pushing the remaining spinal CSF towards the head increases the intracranial pressure, and thus relieves the headache in the first instance.

It was shown 40 to 50 years ago that jugular compression increased the severity of spinal headaches, probably by dilatation and stretching the intracranial dural veins. I have used this test several times to confirm the existence of unrecognized dural taps in patients thought not to have had a dural puncture. Free CSF was later demonstrated in the epidural space of these patients and all were cured with a blood patch.

Dr Erwin (London)   Dr Gutsche, have you ever had experience with ACTH in the management of dural puncture headache? It can be remarkably effective, given as Synacthen Depot 1 mg intramuscularly.

Dr Gutsche I have read about it but have never tried it. Many other drugs have been used, for example tolazoline, which is a powerful vasodilator.

Dr Macdonald Why do some people have so many dural punctures? Dr Doughty had to train 135 people before there were 13 taps. At St James's we've trained 60 novices and have had 40 taps in about 17 000 epidurals. We should be discussing prevention of inadvertent dural puncture, instead of treatment of the headache. Just because we can do epidural blood patches is not an excuse for a high tap rate, which I believe to be a reflection on the poor quality of technique taught and on the laxity of supervision by the teachers.

Question May I ask Dr Russell how he manages hypotension with spinals?

Dr Russell The patients in my study of spinal infusion were all preloaded during the infusion period with 1.5 litres of Hartmann's solution and then just as they were being repositioned they received 10–12 mg of ephedrine IV.

Dr Rubin (London) Dr Russell, we all respect your various studies on the role of posture in spinal anaesthesia for Caesarean section, but surely it is preposterous to say that everybody in labour who has an epidural infusion must be in the lateral position. Many of our consumers criticize epidurals because they have to stay in bed. It surely isn't necessary to be in any one posture throughout the whole of labour. Could you not allow at least the maximum mobility within the bed?

Dr Russell I thought it was fairly standard practice that women in labour should lie on their sides.

Dr Rubin We all accept the problems of caval compression, but most of my patients having epidurals spend most of their labour in the sitting position.

Dr Gutsche Our patients having continuous epidural infusions during labour are generally at least 45° upright. In the sitting position the uterus is brought forward to decompress the vena cava and the aorta.

Dr Russell The problem with sitting up is that if the catheter *does* enter the subarachnoid space the local anaesthetic will go up to the head and make the patient unconscious.

Participant But the solution is isobaric!

Dr Russell Although often regarded as isobaric, there is good evidence that the bupivacaine solutions we give epidurally are hypobaric compared with CSF. Moreover, the subarachnoid infusions

I described [Chapter 8] were slow so there would be no turbulent mixing, and in every single case the blockade was confined to the *upper* side until the patient was turned over.

Question   Was the bupivacaine mixed with saline?

Dr Russell   Yes.

SECTION IV

Caesarean Section

9

Regional or general anaesthesia for Caesarean section

GERALDINE O'SULLIVAN

The Caesarean section rate in the UK has increased from approximately 7% in the early 1970s to 15% in 1988. Obstetric, perinatal and medicolegal considerations are the main reasons for this increase. In the USA the Caesarean rate is approaching 25%, and one in three of these are repeat Caesarean sections. The situation in the USA is such that the President of the American College of Obstetrics and Gynecology in 1987 felt constrained to encourage a reduction in what he believed was an unnecessarily high Caesarean section rate (Editorial, 1988).

The *Report on Confidential Enquiries into Maternal Deaths in England and Wales* forms a unique medical audit which focuses attention on the quality of anaesthetic management. Since anaesthesia is the third most common cause of maternal death the search for the optimum anaesthetic technique for Caesarean section continues. Over 75% of anaesthetic deaths occur in association with emergency Caesarean section, making the choice of anaesthesia in that particular group of paramount importance. Recently regional anaesthesia has, in many centres, become the preferred technique for Caesarean section. Increasing maternal demand and a growing belief that regional anaesthesia, even in the hands of trainee anaesthetists, is intrinsically safer than general anaesthesia are the main factors contributing to this increase (Morgan et al, 1983).

POTENTIAL ADVANTAGES OF REGIONAL ANAESTHESIA FOR CAESAREAN SECTION

The mother

Anaesthesia for Caesarean section should be performed or supervised by a properly trained obstetric anaesthetist. Analysis of the maternal

Table 1. Maternal mortality associated with anaesthesia. Adapted from the
*Report on Confidential Enquiries into Maternal Deaths in England and
Wales* (London: HMSO).

	1970–72	1973–75	1976–78	1979–81	1982–84
Number of deaths associated with anaesthesia	37	27	27	22	18
Rate per 1 000 000 maternities	12.8	10.5	12.1	8.7	7.2
Percentage of direct maternal deaths due to anaesthesia	10.8	11.9	12.4	12.4	13.0
Deaths due to aspiration	14	13	14	8	7
Deaths due to difficult intubation	5	7	16	8	10
Deaths associated with epidural analgesia	1	2	4	1	1

mortality reports reveals that the problems associated with general
anaesthesia frequently occur at the time of its induction, in particular
the pulmonary inhalation of gastric contents and difficulties with
endotracheal intubation (Table 1).

Pulmonary inhalation of gastric contents

The toxic effects of acid on the lung were originally reported in an
experimental study of irritant war gases. The pulmonary response
to the aspiration of solid or liquid gastric contents in obstetric
patients was first described by Hall (1940). He reported a series of
5 deaths in 14 pregnant women who aspirated at induction of
anaesthesia. He noted that solid gastric contents resulted in
mechanical obstruction of the air passages, while gastric fluid caused
a chemical pneumonitis. Similar observations by Mendelson (1946)
received greater attention as he corroborated the clinical observations
with animal experiments, and the syndrome of acid pulmonary
aspiration now bears his name. Mendelson reviewed 44 016 pregnan-

cies in one New York maternity hospital over the period 1932–45 and found that there were 66 (0.15%) cases of pulmonary aspiration. Five subjects (two of whom died) aspirated solid material resulting in massive acute respiratory obstruction, and 40 (all of whom survived) of the remaining subjects exhibited a clinical picture consisting of cyanosis, dyspnoea, wheezing and hypoxia, while the X-rays showed 'irregular, soft, mottled densities'. Mendelson postulated that it was the acidity of the gastric aspirate that was responsible for the damaging effect on the lungs and in support of this hypothesis he introduced various fluids including normal saline, distilled water, 0.1 M hydrochloric acid and solid, liquid and neutralized gastric contents into the lungs of rabbits. When 0.1 M hydrochloric acid or liquid gastric contents were instilled, the animals developed a clinical syndrome similar to that seen in humans. Histologically these lungs, unlike those aspirating neutral liquid, showed marked congestion and oedema. Subsequent research indicated that the severity of the syndrome increases as the pH of the gastric aspirate falls (Lewis et al, 1971) and the volume rises (James et al, 1983). The appropriate preventative and prophylactic measures against this syndrome should aim at producing a high intragastric pH with a low intragastric volume, while during induction of anaesthesia the correct application of cricoid pressure prevents the aspiration of gastric contents. Until recently antacids were the main prophylaxis against acid aspiration, but despite their use maternal mortality did not decrease. Antacids have a short duration of action (O'Sullivan and Bullingham, 1984) and their frequent administration can cause an increase in intragastric volume, particularly if gastric emptying is delayed, as it is following opioid analgesics or when labour is prolonged. In addition, the potentially toxic effects of the particulate antacids on the lungs limits their therapeutic value. Anaesthesia for emergency surgery during labour can be particularly hazardous as most patients will have a significant gastric residual volume predisposing to death from acid aspiration. Emptying the stomach, using either a wide-bore stomach tube or intravenous apomorphine, will not guarantee that it is completely empty and is now rarely indicated prior to induction of anaesthesia. The H_2 antagonists both increase gastric pH and decrease gastric volume but the timing of their administration is critical and thus they are of somewhat limited value when emergency Caesarean section is required. At present varying combinations of oral or parenteral H_2 antagonists and oral antacids are the main prophylactic measures against acid aspiration. However in current obstetric practice the pulmonary inhalation of gastric contents is best avoided by performing elective (and whenever possible emergency) Caesarean section under regional blockade.

Failed or difficult intubation

Intravenous induction with endotracheal intubation is the standard practice for general anaesthesia in the obstetric patient. However, failure to intubate the trachea with consequent anoxia, and the regurgitation and inhalation of gastric contents as a result of inadvertent intubation of the oesophagus, contribute significantly to maternal mortality (Table 1). In Table 1 patients in whom the primary event was difficult intubation but who subsequently died of Mendelson's syndrome are included in both columns. Intubation of the trachea can be more difficult in pregnant women. As anaesthesia is induced with the patient lying in a left or right lateral tilt, this position can result in a relatively incorrect application of cricoid pressure with consequent displacement of the larynx. Too early intubation before the muscle relaxant is exerting its maximum effect can also contribute to difficulties with intubation, as can laryngeal oedema in the patient with pre-eclampsia. Since difficulties with intubation occur more frequently in the obstetric patient (Samsoon and Young, 1987), the anaesthetist should always be prepared for a difficult or failed intubation and should never induce anaesthesia in the pregnant patient without checking that equipment for such a situation is readily available. A failed intubation drill should be understood by all who practise obstetric anaesthesia and be rapidly instituted before the apnoeic patient becomes anoxic. However, the optimum management of the obstetric patient would be a technique that avoids the hazards of unconsciousness, paralysis and the need for tracheal intubation. Careful, controlled regional anaesthesia can fulfil this role.

Unplanned awareness

The problem of awareness during general anaesthesia, particularly during Caesarean section, is now well known to most patients following publicity in both the national newspapers and on television. Awareness during general anaesthesia is very distressing for the patient (Editorial, 1979) and costly for the defence unions. The incidence of awareness and unpleasant dreams can reach approximately 18% during unsupplemented nitrous oxide anaesthesia (Wilson and Turner, 1969). Light general anaesthesia has also been shown to reduce placental blood flow and result in fetal acidosis (Palahniuk and Cumming, 1977). This effect is thought to be mediated by increased levels of catecholamines. The addition of 0.5% halothane to a 50:50 mixture of oxygen and nitrous oxide can reduce the incidence of recall to less than 1% (Moir and Thorburn, 1986). Enflurane 0.6% and isoflurane 0.75% have similarly been shown to decrease the level of awareness during Caesarean section. All volatile agents may, however, cause uterine relaxation.

Most mothers want to participate in the delivery of their babies and obviously view a Caesarean section with anxiety and some disappointment. Performing a Caesarean section under regional anaesthesia avoids the problems of unplanned awareness associated with general anaesthesia and provides greater satisfaction for the mother and for the staff involved. Regional anaesthesia also encourages the active participation of the father in the delivery. Urgent or emergency Caesarean section need not always preclude the father's presence at the delivery.

Pulmonary embolism

A survey of maternal death in Massachusetts from 1954 to 1985 showed that for the years 1982–85 the most common causes were trauma and pulmonary embolism (Sachs et al, 1987). The *Report on Confidential Enquiries into Maternal Deaths in England and Wales* for successive years show that pulmonary embolism and hypertensive disorders of pregnancy are the most common causes of maternal mortality in England and Wales. The risk of death from pulmonary embolism is greatest in women aged over 35 years, in those with severe pre-eclampsia, in the obese and in those who undergo a Caesarean section. Overall, however, there has been a decline in the total number of maternal deaths from pulmonary embolism (Table 2). The reasons for this are probably multifactorial, and include early ambulation and the avoidance of venocaval occlusion with consequent venous stasis. Evidence from hip surgery (Mackenzie et al, 1985) suggests that improved peripheral blood flow resulting from the vasomotor block associated with regional anaesthesia may also result in a reduction in deep vein thrombosis and subsequent pulmonary embolism. Although there has been no study to confirm

Table 2. Maternal deaths from pulmonary embolism. Rates per million vaginal deliveries or Caesarean section are given in parentheses. Adapted from the *Report on Confidential Enquiries into Maternal Deaths in England and Wales* (London: HMSO).

Years	Deaths after vaginal delivery	Deaths after Caesarean section	Total
1970–72	22 (11.6)	15 (145.2)	37
1973–75	13 (7.7)	6 (59.2)	19
1976–78	20 (12.7)	9 (74.6)	29
1979–81	4 (2.3)	7 (41.9)	11
1982–84	4 (2.4)	12 (64.6)	16

this, it is possible that epidural analgesia and anaesthesia have contributed to the decline in maternal mortality from pulmonary embolism.

Blood loss

Blood loss during uncomplicated Caesarean section, though variable, does not normally require replacement. However, in any operation the aim should be to minimize blood loss, and since epidural anaesthesia has been shown to reduce blood loss significantly during Caesarean section (Moir, 1970) this is a further advantage to the mother.

Postoperative morbidity

The incidence of postoperative morbidity such as pyrexia, coughing and gastrointestinal stasis is significantly reduced in patients whose Caesarean section is performed under regional rather than general anaesthesia. Breast-feeding and mobilization have been shown to be more rapidly established in mothers delivered under regional anaesthesia (Morgan et al, 1984).

Postoperative analgesia

Recovery from a major surgical procedure such as Caesarean section is obviously slower than following a vaginal delivery, and every attempt must be made to minimize postoperative pain and encourage ambulation. One of the attractions of regional – in particular epidural – anaesthesia to the mother is that she can be alert and pain-free immediately postpartum. The discovery of opioid receptors in the brain and spinal cord led to the clinical use of intrathecal and epidural opioids for the relief of pain, and the post-Caesarean section patient has been the subject of many studies to prove their efficacy (Carmichael et al, 1982; Macrae et al, 1987).

Most of the narcotic analgesics have been used successfully to relieve pain following Caesarean section, and although the quality of analgesia may not always be superior to parenteral opiate, the dosage required is smaller and the duration of action is longer (see Chapters 12 & 13). Thus the mother should be less drowsy, and transfer of opiate into breast milk should be minimal. Side-effects, though usually minor, are common and include itching, nausea and vomiting. The incidence of urinary retention is difficult to define, as most patients have indwelling catheters following Caesarean section. A more serious side-effect is respiratory depression which has been reported following Caesarean section when larger doses of morphine were used (Carmichael et al, 1982). Respiratory depression following epidural opiates is unpredictable, and though unlikely in young, fit, healthy women, all patients receiving epidural opiates should be monitored carefully. On balance, however, epidural opiates significantly improve the quality of analgesia following Caesarean section.

The fetus

One of the aims of modern obstetrics is to produce a healthy infant and thus achieve a reduction in perinatal morbidity and mortality. The fetus is likely to be compromised if there is a decrease in uteroplacental blood flow or if there is significant placental transfer of depressant drugs. Most studies comparing the effects of general and regional anaesthesia have been confined to elective Caesarean sections in which neither the mother nor the fetus were compromised, and the results cannot necessarily be applied to high-risk situations. These studies also assume that the anaesthetic technique, whether general or regional, is meticulous. The tests usually employed to assess the newborn include measures of biochemical status, neurobehavioural tests and Apgar scoring. The disadvantages of these tests are that they do not necessarily predict the long-term outcome for the baby, and any variation in score cannot always be correlated with anaesthetic technique. Some tests have, however, detected differences between infants delivered by regional and general anaesthesia. Both techniques, when carefully conducted, result in normal blood gases and acid-base status in babies weighing more than 2500 g (Abboud et al, 1985; Evans et al, 1989). In a study of emergency Caesarean sections performed because of fetal distress, the neonatal blood gas and acid-base values were similar in the regional and general anaesthetic groups, although Apgar scores were higher in the former (Marx et al, 1984). The results of studies comparing the effects of anaesthetic technique for elective surgery on neonatal Apgar score are conflicting, with some studies showing no change (Hodgkinson et al, 1978; Downing et al, 1979), and others showing a higher percentage of depressed Apgar scores in babies delivered under general anaesthesia (Evans et al, 1989; Ong et al, 1989). Studies also indicate that the time to the onset of sustained respiration is shorter in the regional anaesthetic group (James et al, 1977). A retrospective study of 3940 babies delivered by elective and non-elective Caesarean section showed that following non-elective surgery Apgar scores were lower and more babies required intubation when the Caesarean section was performed under general anaesthesia (Ong et al, 1989). For further details of neonatal effects, see Chapter 14.

Current evidence suggests that general anaesthesia reduces neuro-behavioural scores in the first 24–48 hours after delivery (Hodgkinson et al, 1978; Abboud et al, 1985). No differences have been detected between the neurobehavioural scores of infants delivered by subarachnoid anaesthesia and those delivered by epidural anaesthesia (McGuiness et al, 1978). However hypotension during regional anaesthesia depresses neonatal reflexes (Hollmen et al, 1978), probably as a result of a reduction in placental blood flow (Jouppila et al, 1978).

Studies to date indicate that the newborn delivered by Caesarean section under regional anaesthesia is more alert and is quicker to establish spontaneous respiration. However, the long-term benefits for the baby of regional over general anaesthesia remain unknown. Both are safe for the baby when optimally administered. The advantages of regional anaesthesia for the mother are of greater significance when a decision to perform a Caesarean section is made.

POTENTIAL DISADVANTAGES OF REGIONAL ANAESTHESIA

The *Report on Confidential Enquiries into Maternal Deaths in England and Wales 1982–84* (DHSS, 1989) showed that one death occurred in association with epidural anaesthesia, and this was caused by a total spinal block following a top-up by a midwife. While regional anaesthesia is probably intrinsically safer than general anaesthesia in the obstetric patient, there is a great potential for morbidity and mortality if careful attention is not paid to technique. During the period 1970–84 there were 9 maternal deaths associated with epidural anaesthesia compared with 123 deaths in association with general anaesthesia.

Hypotension

Hypotension and its inadequate treatment can have serious conse-quences for both mother and baby. Regional anaesthesia adequate for Caesarean section is associated with an extensive sympathetic blockade, and if this is aggravated by venocaval occlusion hypotension can be severe. Regular monitoring of blood pressure and heart rate is essential. The incidence of hypotension can be reduced to less than 10% (Lewis et al, 1983) by the intravenous preload of 1000–2000 ml of balanced salt solution given prior to and during the establishment of the block. Ideally the patient should remain in the lateral position until the block is established and surgery should be performed with the patient in a left lateral tilt. However if hypotension occurs, it should be immediately reversed by increments of intravenous ephedrine, the aim being to maintain placental perfusion and prevent nausea and vomiting which can be a frequent accompaniment of hypotension.

Toxic effects

As the dosage of local anaesthetic required for Caesarean section under epidural anaesthesia is large, the possibility of intravascular injection and toxic reactions should never be forgotten. The epidural should be carefully performed and the local anaesthetic should be injected either very slowly or in fractionated doses following aspiration of the epidural catheter.

Vomiting

Vomiting during regional anaesthesia is theoretically hazardous, as the combination of the left lateral or supine position, the high motor and sensory block and the open abdominal cavity will diminish the ability and power to cough. Vomiting can occur in association with hypotension and during eventration of the uterus, which should be avoided during regional anaesthesia. Intravenous ergometrine is an important cause of vomiting during Caesarean section (Moodie and Moir, 1976) and has already been implicated in a maternal death during regional anaesthesia for Caesarean section (DHSS, 1982). Ergometrine should be avoided during regional anaesthesia and should be replaced by an intravenous injection of 10 units of oxytocin supplemented if necessary by 20–30 units of oxytocin in 500 ml of fluid. For details of adverse reactions, see Section III.

Inadequate anaesthesia

Adequate anaesthesia for Caesarean section requires a sensory block extending from T4 to S5. Although many textbooks claim that a block extending to T6 is sufficient, such a block will not always ensure peritoneal anaesthesia. Careful surgical technique which avoids traction on peritoneal structures is also essential if discomfort is to be avoided during surgery under regional anaesthesia. Pain during surgery under regional anaesthesia is distressing for the patient, the surgeon and the anaesthetist. Confidence will be quickly lost if the anaesthetist does not rapidly treat the pain and in some cases a full general anaesthetic may be required. Alternatively if the baby has been delivered a small dose of epidural opiate will often relieve mild intra-abdominal discomfort. Central chest pain during regional anaesthesia for Caesarean section is not uncommon and this has been attributed to the upward tracking of blood within the abdominal cavity and to peritoneal manipulation. However, a recent study has shown that complaints of chest pain and dyspnoea during Caesarean section are frequently associated with ultrasonic evidence of venous air embolism (Malinow et al, 1987). The emboli that occurred most frequently at the time of hysterotomy were not associated with cardiorespiratory changes. Another study, in which a seven-lead electrocardiogram was recorded in 61 women undergoing Caesarean section, showed that over 50% of the women had ECG changes compatible with myocardial ischaemia and a significant number of these women complained of chest pain and dyspnoea (Palmer et al, 1988). It is possible that venous air emboli are responsible for these ECG changes, but it is clear that complaints of chest pain during regional anaesthesia for Caesarean section are incompletely understood and require further investigation.

Time factor

An argument frequently used against regional anaesthesia, especially in the context of emergency surgery, is the time taken to establish an effective block. However it has been shown that when patients were given general anaesthesia because of urgency, only a few were delivered in a shorter time than would have been possible under epidural block (Davis, 1982). In most urgent situations subarachnoid and even epidural block can be rapidly established. The need for general anaesthesia can be further reduced if the anaesthetist is fully acquainted with the obstetric and medical history of the women in labour. Many women who will ultimately require a Caesarean section can be identified (Table 3); in these women it is prudent to site an epidural catheter early in labour, and should Caesarean section subsequently be required a 20 ml top-up of either lignocaine 2% with adrenaline or bupivacaine 0.5% with adrenaline will usually allow surgery to begin in less than 30 minutes (Laishley and Morgan, 1988). Extending a pre-existing block can be even quicker, while in

Table 3. Factors associated with increased likelihood of Caesarean section.

Obstetric background	Short stature/large baby
	Unfavourable cervix
	Malpresentation
	Multiple pregnancy
	Primigravida over 30
Developments during labour	More than 10 hours in labour
	Slow dilatation of the cervix
	Failure of presenting part to descend
	Impaired fetal well-being

From Davis (1982) with permission.

the absence of epidural analgesia there remains the option of subarachnoid block. On the other hand the time taken in preoxygenation and preparation for surgery under general anaesthesia is not negligible. Therefore, regional anaesthesia need not necessarily delay the onset of urgent surgery. In addition, women requiring urgent Caesarean section may have eaten recently, which adds greater weight to the benefits of regional anaesthesia.

General anaesthesia will always be necessary, however, for immediate Caesarean section in the absence of pre-existing block when there is severe fetal distress or a prolapsed cord, or in the presence of coagulopathy, hypovolaemia and anterior placenta praevia, or when the mother has refused regional anaesthesia. Given careful attention to detail and a skilled anaesthetist, morbidity and mortality should be negligible. However, most obstetric units should aim to maintain the Caesarean section rate under general anaesthesia to a minimum.

At present there are insufficient data to judge whether regional anaesthesia has resulted in a decline in maternal mortality, but current evidence indicates that regional anaesthesia is the technique of choice for both elective and (where possible) emergency Caesarean section.

References

Abboud TK, Nagappala S, Murakawa K et al (1985) Comparison of the effects of general and regional anesthesia for Cesarean section on neonatal neurologic and adaptive capacity scores. *Anesthesia and Analgesia* **64**: 996–1000.

Carmichael FJ, Rolbin SH & Hew EM (1982) Epidural morphine for analgesia after Caesarean section. *Canadian Journal of Anaesthesia* **29**: 359–363.

Davis AG (1982) Anaesthesia for Caesarean section. The potential for regional block. *Anaesthesia* **37**: 748–753.

DHSS (1982) *Report on Confidential Enquiries into Maternal Deaths in England and Wales 1976–78*. London: HMSO.

DHSS (1989) *Report on Confidential Enquiries into Maternal Deaths in England and Wales 1982–84*. London: HMSO.

Downing JW, Houlton PC & Barclay A (1979) Extradural analgesia for Caesarean section: a comparison with general anaesthesia. *British Journal of Anaesthesia* **51**: 367–374.

Editorial (1979) On being aware. *British Journal of Anaesthesia* **51**: 711–712.

Editorial (1988) Holding back the tide of Caesareans. *British Medical Journal* **297**: 569–570.

Evans CM, Murphy F, Gray OP et al (1989) Epidural versus general anaesthesia for elective Caesarean section. *Anaesthesia* **44**: 778–782.

Hall CC (1940) Aspiration pneumonitis. *Journal of the American Medical Association* **114**: 728–733.

Hodgkinson R, Bhatt M, Kim SS et al (1978) Neonatal neurobehavioural tests following Cesarean section under general and spinal anesthesia. *American Journal of Obstetrics and Gynecology* **132**: 670–674.

Hollmen AI, Jouppila R, Koivistu M et al (1978) Neurologic activity of infants following anesthesia for Cesarean section. *Anesthesiology* **48**: 350–356.

James FM, Crawford JS, Hopkinson R et al (1977) A comparison of general anesthesia and lumbar epidural analgesia for elective Cesarean section. *Anesthesia and Analgesia* **56**: 228–235.

James CJ, Modell JH, Gibbs CP et al (1983) Combined effect of pH and volume of the aspirate in the rate. *Anesthesia and Analgesia* **62**: 266–267.

Jouppila R, Jouppila P, Kuikka J et al (1978) Placental blood flow during Caesarean section under lumbar extradural analgesia. *British Journal of Anaesthesia* **50**: 275–279.

Laishley RS & Morgan BM (1988) A single dose epidural technique for Caesarean section. *Anaesthesia* **43**: 100–103.

Lewis RT, Burgess JH & Hampson LG (1971) Cardio-respiratory studies in critical illness: changes in aspiration pneumonitis. *Archives of Surgery* **103**: 335–340.

Lewis M, Thomas P & Wilkes RG (1983) Hypotension during epidural analgesia for Caesarean section. *Anaesthesia* **38**: 250–253.

McGuiness, GA, Merkow AJ, Kennedy RL et al (1978) Epidural anesthesia with bupivacaine for Cesarean section. *Anesthesiology* **49**: 270–273.

Mackenzie PJ, Wishart HY, Gray J et al (1985) Effects of anaesthetic technique on deep vein thrombosis: a comparison of subarachnoid and general anaesthesia. *British Journal of Anaesthesia* **57**: 853–857.

Macrae DJ, Rappa Munishank S & Burrow LM (1987) Double blind comparison of the efficacy of extradural diamorphine, extradural phenoperidine and i.m. diamorphine following Caesarean section. *British Journal of Anaesthesia* **59**: 354–359.

Malinow AM, Naulty JS, Hunt CO et al (1987) Precordial ultrasonic monitoring during Cesarean delivery. *Anesthesiology* **66**: 816–819.

Marx GF, Luykx WM & Cohen S (1984) Fetal-neonatal status following Caesarean section for fetal distress. *British Journal of Anaesthesia* **56**: 1009–1012.

Mendelson CL (1946) The aspiration of stomach contents into the lungs during obstetric anesthesia. *American Journal of Obstetrics and Gynecology* **52**: 191–205.

Moir DD (1970) Anaesthesia for Caesarean section. *British Journal of Anaesthesia* **42**:136–142.

Moir DD & Thorburn J (1986) *Obstetric Anaesthesia and Analgesia* 3rd edn, pp 191–194. London: Baillière Tindall.

Moodie JE & Moir DD (1976) Ergometrine, oxytocin and extradural analgesia. *British Journal of Anaesthesia* **48**: 571–574.

Morgan BM, Aulakh JM, Barker JP et al (1983) Anaesthesia for Caesarean section. *British Journal of Anaesthesia* **55**: 885–889.

Morgan BM, Barker JP, Goroszeniuk T et al (1984) Anaesthetic morbidity following Caesarean section under epidural or general anaesthesia. *Lancet* **i**: 328–330.

Ong BY, Cohen MM & Palahniuk RJ (1989) Anesthesia for Cesarean section – effects on neonates. *Anesthesia and Analgesia* **68**: 270–275.

O'Sullivan GM & Bullingham RES (1984) Does twice the volume of antacid have twice the effect in pregnant women at term? *Anesthesia and Analgesia* **63**: 752–757.

Palahniuk RJ & Cumming M (1977) Foetal deterioration following thiopentone-nitrous oxide anaesthesia in the pregnant ewe. *Canadian Journal of Anaesthesia* **24**: 361–370.

Palmer CM, Morris MC, Guidici MC et al (1988) Incidence of ischemic ECG changes during Cesarean delivery under regional anesthesia. *Abstracts of the Society for Obstetric Anesthesiology and Perinatology*, San Francisco, p. 21.

Sachs BP, Brown DAJ, Driscoll SG et al (1987) Maternal mortality in Massachusetts. Trends and prevention. *New England Journal of Medicine* **316**: 667–672.

Samsoon GL & Young JR (1987) Difficult intubation: a retrospective study. *Anaesthesia* **42**: 487–490.

Thorburn J & Moir DD (1980) Epidural analgesia for elective Caesarean section. *Anaesthesia* **35**: 3–6.

Wilson J & Turner DJ (1969) Awareness during Caesarean section under general anaesthesia. *British Medical Journal* **1**: 280–283.

10

Spinal and/or epidural blockade for Caesarean section

LEN E. S. CARRIE

Historically, a variety of factors have influenced the popularity of spinal and epidural anaesthesia for Caesarean section. In the UK, a dark medicolegal shadow was cast over spinal anaesthesia in the 1950s and it is only in recent years that it has begun to regain its popularity. In the meantime, not only has much expertise in the technique been lost, but anaesthetists have gained extensive experience with epidural analgesia in labour, and it is not surprising that the latter has become the most popular form of regional block for Caesarean section.

In the USA, spinals never fell from favour in the same way and it seems that roughly equal numbers of Caesarean sections are carried out under spinal and epidural blockade, the proportions varying from centre to centre.

The other main factor influencing the choice of technique is the variety of local anaesthetic drugs available. In the UK, the strict requirements of the Committee on Safety of Medicines (CSM) for approval of drugs, allied to the near-monopoly of the local anaesthetic market by one drug company, has resulted in a very restricted choice of agents. For example, there is only one hyperbaric spinal solution (heavy bupivacaine) which is both available *and* approved by the CSM. For epidural anaesthesia for Caesarean section, 0.5% bupivacaine, plain or with adrenaline, is the only agent packaged with the outside of the glass ampoule sterile. In other European countries and the USA, a much wider range of agents is available; while at times this may be confusing, it does give a greater choice of drug to suit each particular situation.

PAIN PATHWAYS FROM THE ABDOMINAL CAVITY

Whichever technique of regional anaesthesia is used, it is essential to have a good understanding of the pain pathways likely to be stimulated by Caesarean section. The somatic nerves involved in the incision through skin, muscle and parietal peritoneum are not extensive, being mainly lower thoracic and upper lumbar. However, unless analgesia extends down into the remaining lumbar and sacral segments, pain is likely to be elicited by direct pressure on these nerves, specially if the fetal head is impacted in the pelvis.

The visceral afferent fibres which run in the sympathetic nerves reach the spinal cord at much higher levels. The highest of these passes in the greater splanchnic nerves through the 5th thoracic ganglia of the sympathetic chain, and the central connections of these fibres may be even higher. The desired upper level of anaesthesia, once thought to be only T7 or T6, is now generally believed to be at least T5 or T4.

The parasympathetic afferent nerves are divided into two components. The lesser of these – the pelvic parasympathetic nerves or nervi erigentes – run to the 2nd to 4th sacral segments of the spinal cord and are blocked by spinal or epidural anaesthesia reaching down to that level. The much larger component of the parasympathetic supply is carried in the vagus nerves. These run no part of their extracranial course in either the subarachnoid or epidural spaces, so will be totally unaffected by either spinal or epidural block to any spinal level. Exactly what surgical manoeuvres stimulate the sensory component of these unblocked nerves are unclear, but with gentle surgery no pain seems to be elicited. Rough surgical handling, either by pulling on peritoneal-clad viscera or the omentum, or at times eventration of the uterus, does cause nausea or retching, sometimes but not always associated with pain, although a lesser incidence of these symptoms occurring with higher blocks suggests that at least in part they are mediated through sympathetic afferents.

One other area of the abdominal cavity is totally unaffected by spinal or epidural block to the upper thoracic levels: this is the lower surface of the diaphragm, with its phrenic innervation to C3–5 segments of the spinal cord. A head-down tilt – traditional for Caesarean section under general anaesthesia – will result in blood and liquor running up under the diaphragm where its subsequent removal by swabs will almost always cause pain. As packs forced into the upper abdomen to prevent the spread of blood and liquor will also cause discomfort, the surgeon must accept a degree of head-up tilt to reduce the cephalad spread of fluids.

Thus effective anaesthesia from T4 down to the lowest sacral segments maintained throughout the Caesarean section can provide excellent pain relief, but its success in a high percentage of cases requires in addition gentle surgical technique.

COMPARISON OF LUMBAR EPIDURAL AND SPINAL ANAESTHESIA

As methods of providing anaesthesia for Caesarean section, lumbar epidural and spinal block can be compared from several aspects.

Rate of onset

There is a variation in the rate of onset of the drugs used for either spinal or epidural block, but in general spinal anaesthesia is quicker. In addition, epidural block usually takes longer to perform. Various modifications to the anaesthetic agent can be made to hasten the onset of epidural anaesthesia.

Alkalinization (pH adjustment)

Alkalinization increases the concentration of the free base, the form in which the local anaesthetic penetrates the nerve sheath. Hydrochloride salts of local anaesthetics are acidic in solution and adrenaline-containing solutions are even more so, because of the antioxidant they contain. The pH of local anaesthetic solutions can be raised by adding small amounts of sodium bicarbonate; this shortens the onset time, particularly in the case of adrenaline-containing solutions (Galindo, 1983; DiFazio et al, 1986).

Carbonation

The effect of carbonation on shortening the latency of lignocaine (by about 33%) and of prilocaine (by about 25%) was first demonstrated by Bromage et al (1967). This effect is thought to be more complicated than a simple increase in pH, although this does happen on opening the ampoule. Penetration of the CO_2 to the nerve axon may cause a reduction in pH at that site, enhancing the entry and effect of the local anaesthetic drug. A third possibility is a direct local anaesthetic effect of CO_2 on the nerve cell membrane. The effect of CO_2 on rate of onset is greater with lignocaine than bupivacaine (Brown et al, 1980).

Warming

Mehta et al (1987) claimed that warming 0.5% bupivacaine to 38°C decreases the onset time by 4–5 minutes without reducing the duration of action. However, it is debatable whether this relatively modest improvement in onset time of about 20% justifies the elaboration of technique (warming the solution to 100°F (38°C) and warming the epidural tray) which they recommend (see also Current Research 4).

Efficacy

Apart from safety, efficacy is perhaps the most important aspect of a local anaesthetic block. To produce anaesthesia from T5 to the sacral segments, the local anaesthetic in the epidural space has to reach sufficient concentration in some 38 spinal nerve roots. This it does by percolating though the fat and veins of the epidural space, and it is perhaps surprising that epidurals work as well as they do. Even in labour epidural blocks may be asymmetrical or patchy, despite increments of local anaesthetic.

Anatomical evidence has accumulated to explain some of these difficulties. Luyendijk, with evidence gained from radiography of the epidural space and from surgical and postmortem dissections, described a median dorsal fold of the dura mater with variable attachment to the ligamentum flavum and vertebral arches (Luyendijk, 1963, 1976; Luyendijk and Van Voorthuisen, 1966). This structure might direct local anaesthetic partly or wholly to one side of the epidural space (but see Chapter 1). It is illuminating, but hardly reassuring, to see how complicated the epidural space can be and the difficulty which at times local anaesthetic solution must have in gaining access to all the nerve roots.

In the subarachnoid space, however, there is no such barrier to the spread of local anaesthetic solution. There may at times be problems in extending or restricting the spread, but patchiness is not a problem, and efficacy is probably the main advantage of spinal over epidural block.

The reported efficacy of epidural anaesthesia for Caesarean section varies with the local anaesthetic drug, the technique and the method of assessing the adequacy of the block. Visual analogue scales are not appropriate to test for peroperative pain, so a simple scoring system or the percentage of patients requiring peroperative analgesic supplementation or sedation may be used. Norton et al (1988), comparing 2% lignocaine plus adrenaline with 0.5% bupivacaine, found only about 50% of patients in both groups completely pain-free and not requiring supplementation, although they stated that pain was not necessarily the reason for giving the supplement. Reid and Thorburn (1988), investigating the same agents, gave supplemental drugs to a similar percentage of those given bupivacaine and to 29% of those given lignocaine. Scott et al (1980) found analgesia for lower abdominal surgery adequate in only 60% of cases using 0.5% bupivacaine, although this could be raised to 90% by the use of a 0.75% solution, which is no longer recommended for obstetric use. Laishley et al (1988), however, showed a significant improvement in the efficacy of 0.5% bupivacaine when adrenaline 1:200 000 was added.

Improving the efficacy of epidural blockade

As well as attempts to speed the onset of epidural block, efforts have been made to improve its efficacy. The choice of agents for Caesarean section under epidural blockade is discussed further in Chapter 11 and Current Research 3.

Epidural opioids. As epidural opioids have been used in the treatment of a wide variety of painful conditions, it is not surprising that they should have been used in an attempt to improve the efficacy of epidural block for Caesarean section. A survey of American obstetric anaesthetists in 1987 (Knapp and Writer, 1988) found that 62% were using epidural narcotics during Caesarean section – an indication of their dissatisfaction with epidural local anaesthetic block. The most popular drug was fentanyl and the usual routine was to inject it immediately after delivery. This figure is probably an underestimate of the percentage of American anaesthetists now adding an opioid to their epidural block. In general, the use of peroperative opioids reduces the percentage of patients requiring parenteral or inhalation supplementation (Gaffud et al, 1986); however, because of potential side-effects, these drugs are perhaps a poor substitute for a really effective local anaesthetic block.

Addition of vasoconstrictor. Adrenaline, usually added to epidural local anaesthetics (especially lignocaine) to prolong their action, may in addition increase the intensity of the block (Laishley et al, 1988). This may be a result of its direct action on α-adrenergic receptors in the spinal cord, stimulation of which has been shown to have an analgesic effect.

Other agents. Various other agents have been tried, mostly only experimentally, to improve the efficacy of epidural block. These include clonidine, somatostatin and ketamine; but their value in improving conduction blockade for Caesarean section has not been investigated.

Toxicity

Spinal block provides extensive anaesthesia with a very small amount of local anaesthetic drug, so is almost entirely lacking in general systemic toxicity. Epidural anaesthesia for Caesarean section, especially if epidural blockade has been used for labour, not infrequently approaches toxic dose limits, and convulsions have been reported in these circumstances (Thorburn and Moir, 1984). This is particularly worrying in the case of bupivacaine, which has been shown more than other local anaesthetic drugs to have a propensity for causing ventricular dysrhythmias (Albright, 1979), although only after intravenous injection (see Chapter 6).

Headache

A severe postural headache in a woman with a new baby is an unpleasant complication, and while it does not follow normal epidural analgesia, it occurs in about 70% of women in whom accidental puncture occurs with the large-bore epidural needle (Crawford, 1972) (see Chapter 7). Women of childbearing age have the greatest susceptibility to post-dural puncture headache, and in the past this was a deterrent against the use of spinal anaesthesia. The situation has changed with refinements in needle manufacture, and there is now a variety of disposable 26-gauge needles available. The incidence of significant spinal headache is about 3–6% with these needles inserted through the dura with the bevel parallel to the long axis of the vertebral canal. This is our experience in over 1500 cases, and although not all the headaches are severe, blood patching is occasionally needed (unpublished observations). This small incidence of postural headache, while not sufficient to discourage the use of spinal anaesthesia with a 26-gauge needle, remains a nuisance, and suggests that it is worth while to explore the practicability (as well as the associated incidence of headache) of using even finer needles. We have just completed 100 cases of combined spinal–epidural anaesthesia for Caesarean section with 29-gauge needles and none of these patients developed any degree of postural headache. Similarly Flaatten et al (1989) had a zero incidence of spinal headache in 46 patients under 30 years old in whom spinal anaesthesia was carried out with this gauge of needle.

Hypotension

The incidence and severity of hypotension depend not only on the height of sympathetic blockade but also on its speed of onset, as this may outstrip the body's ability to compensate. For this reason, hypotension is more common with spinal than with epidural block. Parnass (1987), when investigating the properties of pH-adjusted lignocaine, found a greater incidence of hypotension with that drug than with the normal preparation – a result, it was concluded, of the greater speed of onset of the alkalinized drug.

However, other factors than sympathetic blockade affect the blood pressure during regional block for Caesarean section, and the most important of these is aortocaval occlusion, which may be quite severe even in the wedged position. The importance of this fact is demonstrated by how unusual hypotension is (in the absence of severe blood loss) after delivery.

Another possible cause of hypotension is block of the cardiac accelerator nerves which may occur if the block reaches the highest thoracic segments. While this is theoretically possible, bradycardia is unusual even with very high blocks. The reason for this is not apparent, except that pregnant women tend to have faster pulse rates than non-pregnant women.

For prophylaxis against hypotension with spinal or epidural anaesthesia, the most common measures are fluid preloading and wedging the patient to the left (or providing left uterine displacement). The full lateral position is more effective in minimizing the effects of aortocaval occlusion, and it is not clear why obstetric anaesthetists do not use this position rather than the wedged position more frequently during the establishment of regional blockade. It is even possible, with certain modifications, to maintain the lateral position during the establishment of spinal block. Ephedrine is not normally used prophylactically with epidural analgesia but is reserved for treatment. It is more commonly used with spinal anaesthesia, and the prophylactic method described by Kang et al (1982) using an intravenous infusion has much to recommend it for control and flexibility.

Well-fitting, elasticated antiembolism stockings theoretically help to prevent venous pooling in the lower limbs (Gibbs et al, 1983), although some writers deny their effectiveness (Lee et al, 1987).

The duration of hypotension is important. Several groups of workers have now shown, using a variety of indicators of fetal well-being – Apgar scores (Brizgys et al, 1987), fetal blood gases (Datta et al, 1982), intervillous blood flow (Jouppila et al, 1984), ultrasound measurement of the fetal circulation (Lindblad et al, 1987) and neurobehavioural adaptation scores (Corke et al, 1982) — that transient hypotension does not adversely affect the fetus.

Continuous catheter technique

Until recently, spinal anaesthesia has been regarded as a strictly single-shot technique. Interest in continuous catheter techniques was revived by a report by Denny et al (1987) of only one patient developing a headache out of 117 in whom 20-gauge intrathecal catheters were inserted through 18-gauge needles. The suggested explanation given for this low incidence of headache was that, as has been shown in animals (Yaksh et al, 1986), some inflammatory reaction and fibrin deposition occurs in relation to the catheter in the dura mater and this may help to seal the hole. However, the mean age of the patients was 63 years, and there were more men than women in the series. This criticism applies to other work claiming a low incidence of headache after continuous spinal anaesthesia (Kallos and Smith, 1972), and it seems very unlikely that obstetric patients would have such a low incidence after the use of such relatively large spinal catheters. Indeed, Giuffrida et al (1972) reported a 16% incidence of headache in 74 obstetric patients in whom a continuous spinal catheter had been inserted for Caesarean section through a 21-gauge needle.

Of more likely application to obstetric patients are the 32-gauge microcatheters (which will pass through some 26-gauge spinal needles) now available in the USA. It remains to be seen whether these tiny catheters, which contain a permanently indwelling steel stylet, will be easy enough to use to be of value in obstetric patients.

Summary of comparison of epidural and spinal anaesthesia

Spinal anaesthesia is quicker in onset, more reliable and non-toxic, although modifications to epidural technique may improve its speed of onset and efficacy. However, anatomical variations make it impossible for epidural local anaesthetic always to gain access in adequate amounts to all the required nerve roots. Provided small-gauge needles are used for spinal blockade, headaches should not be a significant problem with either technique. The greater tendency of spinal anaesthesia to produce hypotension counts against it to some extent, but its main disadvantage is that at present it is regarded as a non-continuous technique, so that if the anaesthesia is not perfect it cannot be modified without repeating the procedure, and there is no possibility of providing postoperative pain relief by local anaesthetic or opioids.

THE COMBINED SPINAL–EPIDURAL TECHNIQUE

As both epidural and spinal anaesthesia have their limitations, it is tempting to combine the two techniques to obtain the advantages of both. This can be done in two ways. Firstly, it is possible to insert the epidural catheter at one lumbar interspace and then perform the spinal block at another (Brownridge, 1981). The second method is to perform a single-space, spinal needle through epidural needle technique, as first described for orthopaedic cases by Coates (1982) and Mumtaz et al (1982). This latter technique was first used in obstetrics by Carrie and O'Sullivan (1984) and is steadily growing in popularity. As well as combining the advantages of spinal and epidural anaesthesia, the needle-through-needle technique has the benefit of using the epidural needle to guide the finer spinal needle almost as far as the dura mater.

Equipment

The important requirement for this technique is a spinal needle with a shaft long enough to protrude about 10 mm beyond the tip of the epidural needle. In obstetrics, because of the high incidence of spinal headache, no needle larger than 26-gauge should ever be used. Such long-shafted needles can be obtained from specialist needle makers. One equipment company already produces packs of matching spinal and epidural needles of appropriate lengths. Finer gauge, long-shafted spinal needles may become available as even 29-gauge needles have proved surprisingly easy to use in preliminary trials (unpublished observations).

Procedure

If a needle-through-needle technique is to be performed with a hyperbaric solution the patient may be placed in the modified lateral position (Figure 1). This involves placing the patient in the left lateral position with an inflatable bag under the dependent shoulder

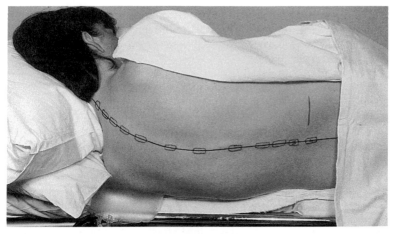

Figure 1. Patient positioned for combined spinal–epidural technique with spinous processes marked. The uphill slope from thoracic to cervical regions can be clearly seen. A slight head-down tilt helps to concentrate the local anaesthetic solution over the mid-thoracic nerve roots.

and three pillows under the head, reproducing the uphill slope from the thoracic to the cervical regions of the vertebral column which is normally present when the patient is supine. This has the advantages not only of minimizing the effects of aortocaval occlusion, but also of 'trapping' the local anaesthetic solution in an appropriate area – the mid to upper thoracic region – while the epidural catheter is being passed and stuck down with adhesive tape. The patient is then turned into the identical position on her right side. A few degrees of head-down tilt helps to ensure a thicker painting of the mid-thoracic nerves, as otherwise the block with 0.5% heavy bupivacaine tends to be of rather short duration. The level of analgesia is tested every 2 minutes, so that the degree of head-down tilt can be increased if analgesia is slow to spread, or reduced if adequate levels are rapidly achieved.

While the main advantages of the combined spinal–epidural technique are the speed of onset and reliability of the spinal block, combined with the ability of the epidural catheter to modify the spinal if it is not perfect and to provide postoperative pain relief, it does additionally provide greater flexibility in the provision of anaesthesia for the Caesarean section itself. The simplest method is to perform the Caesarean section under the spinal alone, using the epidural only if required. Others might use both the spinal and epidural for the Caesarean section, thus producing a reliable but perhaps unnecessarily intense block, which may also spread excessively high. A third method is to perform a spinal that is deliberately low, thus ensuring intense analgesia in the lower segments, and then to extend this cephalad with the epidural block (Rawal et al, 1988). Given good postoperative recovery facilities, some might inject an opioid intrathecally with the local anaesthetic to help provide both peroperative and postoperative analgesia (Abouleish et al, 1988).

CONCLUSION

Increasing numbers of Caesarean sections are being performed with patients awake, presenting anaesthetists with one of the great challenges of regional anaesthesia.

Adequate standards of speed of onset, efficacy and freedom from toxicity may be difficult to provide with epidural anaesthesia using currently available local anaesthetic drugs. Spinal anaesthesia overcomes most of these deficiencies, but has other disadvantages. A combination of spinal and epidural blockade can help to overcome the deficiencies of both.

REFERENCES

Abouleish E, Rawal N, Fallon K & Hernandez D (1988) Combined intrathecal morphine and bupivacaine for Cesarean section. *Anesthesia and Analgesia* **67**: 370–374.

Albright GA (1979) Cardiac arrest following regional anesthesia with etidocaine or bupivacaine (editorial). *Anesthesiology* **51**: 285–287.

Brizgys RV, Dailey PA, Shnider SM, Kotelko DM & Levinson G (1987) The incidence and neonatal effects of maternal hypotension during epidural anesthesia for Cesarean section. *Anesthesiology* **67**: 782–786.

Bromage PR, Burfoot MF, Crowell DE & Truant AP (1967) Quality of epidural blockade. III: Carbonated local anaesthetic solutions. *British Journal of Anaesthesia* **39**: 197–209.

Brown DT, Morison DH, Covino BG & Scott DB (1980) Comparison of carbonated bupivacaine and bupivacaine hydrochloride for extradural anaesthesia. *British Journal of Anaesthesia* **52**: 419–422.

Brownridge P (1981) Epidural and subarachnoid analgesia for elective Caesarean section. *Anaesthesia* **36**: 70.

Carrie LES & O'Sullivan GM (1984) Subarachnoid bupivacaine 0.5% for Caesarean section. *European Journal of Anaesthesiology* **1**: 275–283.

Coates MB (1982) Combined subarachnoid and epidural techniques. *Anaesthesia* **37**: 89–90.

Corke BC, Datta S, Ostheimer GW, Weiss JB & Alper MH (1982) Spinal anaesthesia for Caesarean section. The influence of hypotension on neonatal outcome. *Anaesthesia* **37**: 658–662.

Crawford JS (1972) Lumbar epidural block in labour: a clinical analysis. *British Journal of Anaesthesia* **44**: 66–74.

Datta S, Kitzmiller JL, Naulty JS, Ostheimer GW & Weiss JB (1982) Acid-base status of diabetic mothers and their infants following spinal anesthesia for Cesarean section. *Anesthesia and Analgesia* **61**: 662–665.

Denny N, Masters R, Pearson D et al (1987) Postdural puncture headache after continuous spinal anesthesia. *Anesthesia and Analgesia* **66**: 791–794.

DiFazio CA, Carron H, Grosslight KR et al (1986) Comparison of pH-adjusted lidocaine solutions for epidural anesthesia. *Anesthesia and Analgesia* **65**: 760–764.

Flaatten H, Rodt, SA, Vamnes J et al (1989) Postdural puncture headache. A comparison between 26- and 29-gauge needles in young patients. *Anaesthesia* **44**: 147–149.

Gaffud MP, Bansal P, Lawton C, Velasquez N & Watson WA (1986) Surgical analgesia for Cesarean delivery with epidural bupivacaine and fentanyl. *Anesthesiology* **65**: 331–334.

Galindo A (1983) pH-adjusted local anesthetics: clinical experience. *Regional Anesthesia* **8**: 35–36.

Gibbs CP, Werba JV, Banner TE, James CF & Hill CR (1983) Epidural anesthesia: leg-wrapping prevents hypotension. *Anesthesiology* **59**: A405.

Giuffrida JG, Bizzarri DV, Masi R & Bondoc R (1972) Continuous procaine spinal anesthesia for Cesarean section. *Anesthesia and Analgesia* **51**: 117–124.

Jouppila P, Jouppila R, Barinoff T & Koivula A (1984) Placental blood flow during Caesarean section performed under subarachnoid block. *British Journal of Anaesthesia* **56**: 1379–1382.

Kallos T & Smith TC (1972) Continuous spinal anesthesia with hypobaric tetracaine for hip surgery in lateral decubitus. *Anesthesia and Analgesia* **51**: 766–771.

Kang YG, Abouleish E & Caritis S (1982) Prophylactic intravenous ephedrine infusion during spinal anesthesia for Cesarean section. *Anesthesia and Analgesia* **61**: 839–842.

Knapp RM & Writer WDR (1988) Epidural narcotics in obstetrics. Survey of SOAP members. *Abstracts of the Society for Obstetric Anesthesia and Perinatology Meeting*, San Francisco, p 66.

Laishley RS, Morgan BM & Reynolds F (1988) Effect of adrenaline on extradural anaesthesia and plasma bupivacaine concentrations during Caesarean section. *British Journal of Anaesthesia* **60**: 180–186.

Lee A, McKeown D & Wilson J (1987) Evaluation of the efficacy of elastic compression stockings in prevention of hypotension during epidural anaesthesia for elective caesarean section. *Acta Anaesthesiologica Scandinavica* **31**: 193–195.

Lindblad A, Bernow J, Vernersson E & Marsal K (1987) Effects of extradural anaesthesia on human fetal blood flow in utero. *British Journal of Anaesthesia* **59**: 1265–1272.

Luyendijk W (1963) Canalography. *Journal Belge de Radiologie* **46**: 236–254.

Luyendijk W (1976) The plica mediana dorsalis of the dura mater and its relation to lumbar peridurography (canalography). *Neuroradiology* **11**: 147–149.

Luyendijk W & Van Voorthuisen AE (1966) Contrast examination of the spinal epidural space. *Acta Radiologica* **5**: 1051–1066.

Mehta PM, Theriot E, Mehrotra D, Patel K & Kimball BG (1987) A simple technique to make bupivacaine a rapid-acting epidural anesthetic. *Regional Anesthesia* **12**: 135–138.

Mumtaz MH, Daz M & Kuz M (1982) Another single space technique for orthopaedic surgery. *Anaesthesia* **37**: 90.

Norton AC, Davis AG & Spicer RJ (1988) Lignocaine 2% with adrenaline for epidural Caesarean section. *Anaesthesia* **43**: 844–849.

Parnass SM, Curran MJA & Becker GL (1987) Incidence of hypotension associated with epidural anesthesia using alkalinized and nonalkalinized lidocaine for Cesarean section. *Anesthesia and Analgesia* **66**: 1148–1150.

Rawal N, Schollin J & Wesstrom G (1988) Epidural versus combined spinal epidural block for cesarean section. *Acta Anaesthesiologica Scandinavica* **32**: 61–66.

Reid JA & Thorburn JT (1988) Extradural bupivacaine or lignocaine anaesthesia for elective Caesarean section: the role of maternal posture. *British Journal of Anaesthesia* **61**: 149–153.

Scott DB, McClure JH, Giasi RM, Seo J & Covino BG (1980) Effects of concentration of local anaesthetic drugs in extradural block. *British Journal of Anaesthesia* **52**: 1033–1037.

Thorburn J & Moir DD (1984) Bupivacaine toxicity in association with extradural analgesia for Caesarean section. *British Journal of Anaesthesia* **56**: 551–553.

Yaksh TL, Noueihed RY & Durant PAC (1986) Studies of the pharmacology and pathology of intrathecally administered 4-anilinopiperidine analogues and morphine in the rat and cat. *Anesthesiology* **64**: 54–66.

11

Factors modifying epidural block for Caesarean section

J. THORBURN

In 1979, at the second symposium on epidural analgesia, two papers describing epidural techniques for Caesarean section were presented. Since then a great number of investigators have been refining, developing and improving the technique, with the object of enhancing safety and reducing both the incidence of side-effects and the time required to prepare a patient for theatre.

It was already clear in 1979 that an extensive and profound sensory block from T6 to S5 was necessary to ensure good operating conditions and a high level of patient enthusiasm. Yet to achieve these ideals requires considerable time, and epidural analgesia is slower in onset than either spinal or general anaesthesia. Maternal safety remains of paramount importance, and the provision of block with a rapid onset would at first glance appear to conflict with safety, if speed of onset depended solely on larger injection volumes administered with greater rapidity. There are, however, other factors affecting block onset time. The developments can be conveniently considered under the following headings:

1. The effects of different local anaesthetic agents.
2. The effects of the addition of adrenaline.
3. The advantages of a bolus or incremental technique.
4. The influence of maternal posture.
5. Safety, side-effects and complications.

THE CHOICE OF LOCAL ANAESTHETIC SOLUTION

Bupivacaine has long been recognized as a safe, effective and long-acting local anaesthetic agent; it is often thought to have slower onset time than the other available agents. Early work by Scanlon et al (1974) demonstrated that analgesia in labour provided by epidural lignocaine affected the neurobehavioural scores of the infants, an effect that was not observed with bupivacaine (Scanlon et al, 1976). The babies were described as 'floppy but alert' and this was sufficient to inhibit further work on lignocaine for some years. Abboud et al (1981, 1983a) and Kileff et al (1982) compared the neonatal neurobehavioural effects of bupivacaine and lignocaine for epidural and anaesthesia. Abboud's studies slightly favoured lignocaine, but no conclusions can be drawn from Kileff's study in which 57% of babies were withdrawn from the lignocaine group (see Chapter 14).

Initial studies were principally concerned with neonatal effects and when these proved to be reassuring (Abboud et al, 1983a, 1983b), subsequent studies by Reid and Thorburn (1988) and Norton et al (1988) clearly demonstrated the more rapid (and equally effective) block with lignocaine with a mean onset time of 20 minutes (but see Current Research 3).

Chloroprocaine has an even more rapid onset time than lignocaine and is extremely rapidly metabolized, which ensures minimal fetal transfer. Unfortunately, neurological deficit has followed accidental total spinal block with chloroprocaine in a small number of cases (Reisner et al, 1980; Ravindran et al, 1980; Covino et al, 1980). The use of preservative and antioxidant in the solution, its low pH and the lack of CSF pseudocholinesterase to metabolize the drug are among the theories advanced to explain the phenomenon. It is most unlikely that chloroprocaine will be introduced to British practice in the foreseeable future, despite its undoubted advantages. It is of interest that one report of neurobehavioural testing suggested that infants whose mothers received chloroprocaine did not score as well as those whose mothers had received bupivacaine (Kuhnert et al, 1988) (see Chapter 14). Currently in the UK lignocaine and bupivacaine are the agents of choice.

The introduction of bupivacaine 0.75% offered hope of a more rapid onset. However, a number of maternal deaths were reported in the USA in 1982 following its use, and although precise details were not published, the deaths were ascribed to inadvertent intravenous injection (Albright, 1984). Following a meeting of the Anesthetic and Life Support Drug Advisory Committee of the Department of Health and Human Service, of the Public Health Service, Food and Drug Administration of the US Government in 1982, it was agreed that the recommendation for the use of 0.75% bupivacaine should be withdrawn in obstetrics. Shortly after, the UK followed suit. Fortunately, work had indicated that 0.75% bupivacaine did not offer any advantages over the 0.5% solution; indeed, when the 0.75% solution was used for Caesarean section almost half the patients received more than the manufacturer's recommended maximum dose, the onset time of the two solutions was almost identical and plasma bupivacaine concentrations were within acceptable limits in both groups (Dutton et al, 1984).

THE EFFECT OF ADRENALINE

Bromage (1978) suggested that the addition of adrenaline to local anaesthetic solutions accelerated the onset time of blocks and had the added advantage that the plasma concentration of the drug was reduced. As the mass of drug used to provide an effective epidural block for Caesarean section is close to the maximum recommended by the manufacturers, any reduction in peak plasma concentration might reduce the risk of toxicity. The effect of adding adrenaline to bupivacaine for epidural analgesia for Caesarean section is disappointing, however, and onset time is not consistently reduced (Table 1). Both Wilson et al (1988) and Laishley et al (1988) noted a reduction in the plasma bupivacaine level which in general barely reached statistical significance, and which was ascribed by Laishley to reduced dose requirements rather than to reduced absorption. Abboud and her colleagues did not observe any effect on the plasma concentration when adrenaline was added to bupivacaine (Abboud et al, 1985). However, there is a suggestion that the quality of block is superior.

The same, however, is not true for lignocaine. Work undertaken at the Queen Mother's Hospital, Glasgow (unpublished) and that

Table 1. Effect of adrenaline on onset time of epidural analgesia.

Author(s)	Local anaesthetic		Onset time (min)	
			Plain	Adrenaline $(5 \ \mu g \ ml^{-1})$
Abboud et al (1983a)	lignocaine	2%	15	23
Thorburn (unpublished)	lignocaine	2%	35	29
Laishley & Morgan (1988)	bupivacaine	0.5%	20	20
Wilson et al (1988)	bupivacaine	0.5%	48	47

of Abboud et al (1983a) showed that lignocaine without adrenaline did not produce a satisfactory epidural block for Caesarean section. Moreover the former study demonstrated that lignocaine 2% with 1:200 000 adrenaline produced a quicker onset (Table 1) and significantly lower plasma levels, because both dose requirement and absorption were reduced.

Adrenaline is known to affect uterine blood flow, and its safety when added to epidural solutions is controversial. Rosenfeld et al (1976) and Wallis et al (1976) demonstrated a transient but significant reduction in uterine blood flow in pregnant ewes when adrenaline was added to epidural anaesthetic solutions. However, Albright et al (1981) did not observe any change with human studies using radioactive xenon. Subsequent and less invasive work has not confirmed adverse effects on the baby when adrenaline-containing solutions are used (Abboud et al, 1985). Using Doppler techniques, we have failed to demonstrate any differences in *fetal* umbilical blood vessel velocity when adrenaline is added to the epidural solution. When adrenaline-containing local anaesthetic solution is injected intravenously in experimental animals to simulate inadvertent intravenous injection, a significant, if temporary, reduction in uterine blood flow has been described by both Chestnut et al (1985) and Hood et al (1986).

On balance the clinical effects of adrenaline would appear to be negligible, adverse reports being confined to experimental preparations from which it is difficult to extrapolate to clinical practice. The value of adrenaline in the test dose is discussed in Chapter 3.

VOLUME OF INJECTATE

Both common sense and clinical experience suggest that injection of a single large volume will spread further than multiple injections of small volumes of, say, 3–6 ml. However, an incremental technique using multiple small volumes is widely believed to be safer. If subarachnoid displacement of the catheter occurs, injection of a small volume will be relatively safe. Similarly, intravenous injection is less likely to cause a major toxic reaction. Additionally, Thompson et al (1985) reported that the incremental technique was associated with lower plasma concentrations of bupivacaine.

An important paper by Laishley and Morgan (1988) assessed a 'fractionated' epidural technique in which 100 mg of bupivacaine is injected slowly (over 5 minutes) through the Tuohy needle, additional bupivacaine being administered by the catheter if the block did not extend to T6 at 20 minutes. Supplementation was required by only 10 of 40 patients. Thus the block onset was extremely rapid and plasma concentrations of bupivacaine were within safe limits (Laishley et al, 1988).

The controversy between incremental, bolus or 'fractionated' techniques was highlighted by Laishley et al (1987) who questioned the need for long intervals between supplements as described by Crawford (1986), as the fractionated technique had proved to be safe and effective. Hypotension occurred in the 27% of Laishley's patients who were in the wedged rather than the full lateral position, but only 25% required more than the initial 100 mg of bupivacaine. Crawford (1987) gently took them to task. He had noted in his series an incidence of hypotension of 13%, of which 6% were corrected by repositioning the patient. However, 18% required more than five top-up injections, thus requiring more than 60 minutes to be ready for surgery. Crawford pointed out that in his unit the anaesthetist was neither harassed nor harried by staff and he preferred safety to haste. Dangerously large doses were sometimes necessary, however, using his technique.

This in essence highlights the difference between the two techniques. In Laishley's study, the majority of the patients were ready within 20 minutes. Reid and Thorburn (1988) using an incremental technique with bupivacaine 0.5% observed the mean time required to be ready for surgery was over 40 minutes, a time that was significantly greater than that with lignocaine 2% with adrenaline.

Slow injection of local anaesthetic through the Tuohy needle as described by Laishley and Morgan (1988) may be as safe as incremental injections through a catheter. It eliminates the risk of the catheter penetrating the arachnoid or a blood vessel. The reduction in total dose is also a benefit that can be weighed against the increase in incidence of hypotension (see Chapter 6).

MATERNAL POSITION

A number of investigators have examined the effect of administering epidural block with the patient in the lateral or sitting position. Though Reid and Thorburn (1988) found that there was a tendency for more rapid cephalad spread in the lateral position, Merry et al (1983) demonstrated that there was less caudal spread in the sitting position, while Norris and Dewan (1987) found more rapid cephalad spread in the sitting position. It would appear that in the vertical position the dural sac may plug the vertebral canal below the level of the catheter tip. Though there may be little benefit in the sitting position, the full lateral position is less likely than the wedged position to be associated with maternal circulatory disturbance and increased epidural pressure leading to an unexpectedly high block (Johnston et al, 1989).

HYPOTENSION

Hypotension is undesirable and continues to be the major problem of epidural anaesthesia. If the period of hypotension is brief, it would appear not to have a significant effect. However, if it is prolonged, fetal acidosis occurs and is not eliminated by restoration of the maternal blood pressure (Antoine and Young, 1982). It is therefore best avoided. Thorburn and Moir (1980) reported an incidence of 16%; but a later publication from the same institution (Reid and Thorburn, 1988) noted an overall frequency of 43% with a higher incidence when the epidural was administered with the patient in the sitting position. Moving a patient with extensive sympathetic blockade to theatre was also a factor in the observed increase. The administration of an intravenous preload was popularized by Wollman and Marx (1968) as prophylaxis against hypotension. Many studies have now been published on the prophylactic effects of varying preload volumes, but a large and inconsistent variation in the incidence of hypotension has been reported (Table 2). Lewis et al (1983) administered 1 to 2 litres of preload, and found the larger volume associated with a lower incidence of

Table 2. Incidence of hypotension in patients undergoing epidural Caesarean section. Hypotension is defined as an arterial pressure of less than 90 mmHg or a reduction of 25%.

Author(s)	Drug	Incidence (%)	Preload volume (l)
Norton et al (1988)	Lignocaine	10	1
	Bupivacaine	23	1
Reid and Thorburn (1988)	Lignocaine	30*	1
	Bupivacaine	43*	1
Antoine and Young (1982)	Bupivacaine	43	0.5–1
Thorburn and Moir (1980)	Bupivacaine	16	1
Laishley and Morgan (1988)	Bupivacaine	27.5	1–2
Crawford (1987)	Bupivacaine	13.1	1.4–1.9
Murray et al (1989)	Bupivacaine	33, 63	1–2

* Patients had to be moved to theatre when ready.

hypotension. Murray et al (1989) found no difference in patients given 1 litre of colloid or 2 litres of crystalloid as a preload and concluded, following a review of the literature, that circulating volume expansion was an unreliable method of prophylaxis. Prophylactic ephedrine is ineffective and may produce an unacceptable incidence of hypertension (Rolbin et al, 1982).

Despite the uncertainty, preloading is a simple and safe technique and it is usual to administer 1 litre of crystalloid in the 15 minutes preceding the institution of the block. Prevention of caval occlusion is mandatory and *patients should be placed and remain in the lateral position from the time of the initial epidural injection*. Meticulous monitoring is essential and ephedrine should be administered immediately if hypotension develops.

OTHER SIDE-EFFECTS

Vomiting continues to be a common complication. It is most frequently associated with maternal hypotension but its occurrence after delivery is minimized by avoiding the use of ergometrine (Thorburn and Moir, 1980).

Shivering also continues to be a nuisance, but its frequency is reduced by warming the intravenous preload solution (Aglio, 1988) and the local anaesthetic solution (Walmsley et al, 1986). This may also accelerate the onset of block.

Pain from entry of blood and amniotic fluid into the paracolic gutters may be minimized by breaking the table to a 5° head-up tilt (Thorburn and Moir, 1980), or treated by the administration of epidural opioids. These have proved of value in 'papering over the cracks' of an incomplete block, but the safety of indiscriminate use has been questioned (Morgan, 1989). However, epidural fentanyl has been used for many years and has proved to be safe and effective (see Chapter 13).

CONCLUSION

Refinements of epidural technique have improved the efficacy of epidural anaesthesia for Caesarean section. The use of a slow, single-bolus injection technique ensures a rapid and reliable onset of block if speed is essential. The use of an incremental technique has a lower incidence of hypotension but it is unquestionably slower in onset, and requires larger doses of local anaesthetic. The effect of epidural anaesthesia for Caesarean section on the newborn has been extensively investigated (see Chapter 14). Avoidance of hypotension, with rapid and effective treatment should it occur, is one of the most important elements in the meticulous care required in the provision of a safe and effective epidural block.

REFERENCES

Abboud TK, William V, Miller F et al (1981) Comparative fetal, maternal and neonatal responses following epidural analgesia with bupivacaine, chloroprocaine and lidocaine. *Anesthesiology* (supplement) **55**: A315.

Abboud TK, Kim KC, Nouheid R et al (1983a) Epidural bupivacaine, chloroprocaine or lidocaine for Cesarean section: maternal and neonatal effects. *Anesthesia and Analgesia* **62**: 914–919.

Abboud TK, Sarkis F, Abilikan A et al (1983b) Lack of adverse neonatal neurobehavioral effects of lidocaine. *Anesthesia and Analgesia* **63**: 421–428.

Abboud TK, Sheik-ol-Eslam A, Yanagi T et al (1985) Safety and efficacy of epinephrine added to bupivacaine for lumbar epidural analgesia in obstetrics. *Anesthesia and Analgesia* **64**: 585–591.

Aglio D (1988) Effects of warming intravenous preload. *Anesthesiology* **69**: A701.

Albright GA (1984) Epinephrine should be used with the therapeutic dose of bupivacaine in obstetrics. *Anesthesiology* **61**: 217–218.

Albright GA, Jouppila R, Hollemen AI et al (1981) Epinephrine does not alter intervillous blood flow during epidural anesthesia. *Anesthesiology* **54**: 131–135.

Antoine C & Young BK (1982) Fetal lactic acidosis with epidural anesthesia. *American Journal of Obstetrics and Gynecology* **142**: 55–59.

Bromage PR (1978) *Epidural Analgesia*. Philadelphia: WB Saunders.

Covino BG, Marx GF, Finster M & Zsigmond EV (1980) Prolonged sensory/motor deficits following inadvertent spinal anesthesia. *Anesthesia and Analgesia* **59**: 399–400.

Chestnut DH, Weiner CP, Herrig BS et al (1985) Effects of intravenous epinephrine upon uterine blood flow velocity in the pregnant guinea pig. *Anesthesiology* **63**: A453.

Crawford JS, Davis P & Lewis M (1986) Some aspects of epidural block provided for elective Caesarean. *Anaesthesia* **41**: 1039–1046.

Crawford JS (1987) Epidural anaesthesia for elective Caesarean section (letter). *Anaesthesia* **42**: 555.

Dutton DA, Moir DD, Howie HB et al (1984) Choice of local anaesthetic drug for extradural Caesarean section. *British Journal of Anaesthesia* **56**: 1361–1371.

Hood DD, Dewan DM & James FM (1986) Maternal and fetal effects of epinephrine in gravid ewes. *Anesthesiology* **64**: 610–613.

Johnston GM, Rodgers RC & Tunstall ME (1989) Alteration of maternal posture and its immediate effect on epidural pressure. *Anaesthesia* **44**: 750–752.

Kileff M, James FM & Dewan R (1982) Neonatal neurobehavioral responses after epidural anesthesia for Cesarean section with lidocaine and bupivacaine. *Anesthesiology* **57**: A403.

Kuhnert BR, Kennard MJ & Linn PL (1988) Neonatal neurobehavior after epidural anesthesia for Cesarean section: a comparison of bupivacaine and chloroprocaine. *Anesthesia and Analgesia* **67**: 64–68.

Laishley RS & Morgan B (1988) A single dose epidural technique for Caesarean section. *Anaesthesia* **43**: 100–103.

Laishley RD, Reynolds F & Morgan B (1987) Epidural analgesia for elective Caesarean section (letter). *Anaesthesia* **42**: 554–555.

Laishley RS, Morgan BM & Reynolds F (1988) Effect of adrenaline on extradural anaesthesia and plasma bupivacaine concentration during Caesarean section. *British Journal of Anaesthesia* **60**: 180–186.

Lewis M, Thomas P & Wilkes RG (1983) Hypotension during epidural analgesia for Caesarean section. *Anaesthesia* **38**: 250–253.

Merry AF, Cross JA, Mayadeo SV et al (1983) Posture and spread of extradural analgesia in labour. *British Journal of Anaesthesia* **55**: 303–307.

Morgan M (1989) The rational use of intrathecal and extradural opioids. *British Journal of Anaesthesia* **63**: 165–188.

Murray AM, Morgan M & Whitwam JG (1989) Crystalloid versus colloid for circulatory preload for epidural Caesarean section. *Anaesthesia* **44**: 463–470.

Norris MC & Dewan DM (1987) Effect of gravity on the spread of extradural anaesthesia for Caesarean section. *British Journal of Anaesthesia* **59**: 338–341.

Norton AC, Davis AG & Spicer RJ (1988) Lignocaine 2% with adrenaline for epidural Caesarean section. A comparison with 0.5% bupivacaine. *Anaesthesia* **43**: 844–849.

Ravindran RS, Bond VK, Tasch MD et al (1980) Prolonged neural blockade following regional analgesia with chloroprocaine. *Anesthesia and Analgesia* **59**: 447–451.

Reid J & Thorburn J (1988) Bupivacaine and lignocaine for epidural Caesarean section and the role of maternal posture. *British Journal of Anaesthesia* **61** 149–153.

Reisner LS, Hochman BN & Plumer MH (1980) Persistent neurological deficit and adhesive arachnoiditis following intrathecal 2-chloroprocaine injection, *Anesthesia and Analgesia* **59**: 452–454.

Rolbin SH, Cole AFD, Hew EM et al (1982) Prophylactic IM ephedrine before epidural anaesthesia for Caesarean section, efficacy and actions on fetus and newborn. *Canadian Anesthetists Society Journal* **29**: 148–153.

Rosenfeld CR, Barton MD & Meschia A (1976) Effects of epinephrine on distribution of blood flow in the pregnant ewe. *American Journal of Obstetrics and Gynecology* **124**: 156–163.

Scanlon JW, Brown WU, Weiss JB & Alper MH (1974) Neurobehavioral responses of newborn infants after maternal epidural anesthesia. *Anesthesiology* **40**: 121–128.

Scanlon JW, Ostheimer GW, Lurie AO et al (1976) Neurobehavioral responses and drug concentrations in newborns after maternal epidural analgesia with bupivacaine. *Anesthesiology* **45**: 400–406.

Thompson EM, Wilson CM, Moore J et al (1985) Plasma bupivacaine levels associated with extradural anaesthesia for Caesarean section. *Anaesthesia* **40**: 427–432.

Thorburn J & Moir DD (1980) Epidural analgesia for elective Caesarean section. Technique and its assessment. *Anaesthesia* **35**: 3–6.

Wallis KL, Shnider SM & Hicks JS (1976) Epidural anesthesia in the normotensive pregnant ewe; effects of epinephrine on uterine blood flow and acid base status. *Anesthesiology* **44**: 481–487.

Walmsley AJ, Giesecke AH, Lipton JM (1986) Contribution of extradural temperature to shivering during extradural anaesthesia. *British Journal of Anaesthesia* **58**: 1130–1134.

Wilson CM, Moore J, Ghaly RG et al (1988) Plasma concentrations of bupivacaine during extradural anaesthesia for Caesarean section; the effect of adrenaline. *Anaesthesia* **43**: 12–15.

Wollman SB & Marx GF (1968) Acute hydration for prevention of hypotension of spinal anesthesia in parturients. *Anesthesiology* **29**: 374–376.

Current Research 3

Are two better than one? A preliminary assessment of an epidural mixture of lignocaine and bupivacaine for elective Caesarean section

P. HOWELL, M. WRIGLEY, P. TAN, W. DAVIES and B. MORGAN

Mixtures of bupivacaine and lignocaine used epidurally have been shown in non-obstetric patients to produce a block of rapid onset, good quality and long duration (Magee et al, 1983). This study on elective Caesarean sections was set up to compare the use of such a mixture with three other solutions to establish whether the time to adequacy of block can be reduced, or the quality of anaesthesia improved, if lignocaine and bupivacaine are mixed.

METHOD

In a double-blind randomized study, 80 patients presenting for elective Caesarean section had epidural blockade established using one of four solutions: bupivacaine 0.5% plain (n = 20); bupivacaine 0.5% with 1:200 000 adrenaline (n = 20); lignocaine 2% with adrenaline (n = 20); or a 50:50 mixture of bupivacaine 0.5% and lignocaine 2% with adrenaline (n = 20). Management of all groups followed standard hospital protocol. The volume of solution used was recorded, and the spread of the blockade was assessed, as was pain, and both the patient's and the anaesthetist's satisfaction with the block. Analyses were performed using Kruskal Wallis and chi-squared tests as appropriate, and $P < 0.05$ was considered significant.

RESULTS

Groups were similar with respect to patient age and weight, and duration of surgery. The degree of satisfaction with the analgesia is shown in Table 1.

160

Table 1. Number of women with satisfactory analgesia ($n = 20$) in each group.

	Lignocaine + adrenaline	Mixture	Bupivacaine plain	Bupivacaine + adrenaline
Pain-free surgery without supplementation	7 *	15	13	17
Mother's opinion – very good or excellent	14	18	16	20

* $P = 0.02$

There was no difference between the groups in the time to readiness for surgery (mean 26 ± 7 min), or in the other variables assessed.

CONCLUSION

In spite of reducing the concentration of each drug, the mixture of bupivacaine and lignocaine produced conduction blockade as effectively as both bupivacaine solutions alone. The addition of bupivacaine to lignocaine improves the success of the block, but does not affect the induction time. The lignocaine solution produced blockade inferior to the other three agents.

Bupivacaine with adrenaline produced the most consistent block. This study shows that the mixture provides good epidural blockade for Caesarean section with potentially less risk of bupivacaine-related cardiotoxicity (Albright, 1979).

References

Albright GA (1979) Cardiac arrest following regional anesthesia with etidocaine or bupivacaine. *Anesthesiology* **51**: 285–286.

Magee DA, Sweet PT & Holland AJ (1983) Epidural anaesthesia with mixtures of bupivacaine and lidocaine. *Canadian Anaesthetists Society Journal* **30**: 174–178.

Current Research 4

The effects of warming bupivacaine in patients undergoing elective Caesarean section under epidural anaesthesia

JANE E. HOWIE and DAVID A. DUTTON

The effect of warming epidural bupivacaine on the incidence of shivering, time to block (T6) and anaesthetic volume was studied.

METHOD

Seventy patients having epidural anaesthesia for elective Caesarean section were randomized on a double-blind basis to receive 0.5% bupivacaine at either 20 °C ($n = 35$) or 38 °C ($n = 35$). A standard technique was used: following intravenous preload of 1500 ml of Ringer Lactate at room temperature, epidural catheters were inserted at L2/3 or L3/4 interspace; a test dose of 3 ml 0.5% bupivacaine was followed 5 minutes later by 10 ml with the patient sitting. The level of blockade was assessed after 15 minutes and subsequent top-ups given on the basis of 1.5 ml per segment unblocked below T6. Axillary temperature, pulse and blood pressure were recorded every 5 minutes.

RESULTS

See Table 1. There were no significant differences between the two groups for weight, height or mean axillary temperature.

CONCLUSION

Warm bupivacaine given epidurally in patients undergoing elective Caesarean section significantly reduces the incidence of shivering.

Table 1.

Bupivacaine	Shivering (n)	Time from test dose to block to T6 (min) mean ± SEM	Volume 0.5% bupivacaine to block T6 (ml) mean ± SEM
Room temperature	11	39.5 ± 1.9	25.1 ± 1.1
Warm	2	27.4 ± 1.4	19.2 ± 0.8
P	< 0.02	< 0.01	< 0.01

Smaller doses of warm bupivacaine are required to achieve this block and the speed of onset is significantly increased.

SECTION IV – DISCUSSION

CHAIRMAN: DR A. RUBIN, London

Dr Rubin I am slightly concerned that we may be changing an incidence of awareness with its medicolegal consequences to one of unacceptable pain during conduction anaesthesia with its medicolegal consequences. I have recently heard of four such cases.

Dr O'Sullivan If the block is inadequate at a critical stage in the surgery, then you must be prepared to induce general anaesthesia. Every patient should be warned beforehand that perfect analgesia cannot be guaranteed in every case.

Dr Morison (Ontario) Carbonated local anaesthetics may be useful for epidural anaesthesia because they give a more dense and complete block than hydrochloride salts.

Dr Carrie One of the great benefits of spinal anaesthesia is adequacy of block. Out of 50 patients studied recently, only one required intravenous supplementation for Caesarean section.

Dr Bryson (Liverpool) It worries me that spinals seem to be regarded as *alternatives* to epidurals. I think we should be seeking to identify indications and contraindications for each technique. Those who favour epidurals try to ape spinals by attempting to speed up the onset of epidurals, while those who favour spinals try to minimize headache by making holes in the dura ever smaller. The two techniques are similar only insofar as both involve insertion of a needle into the lumbar spine, just as figure-skating and ice hockey are similar in that both are performed on ice. Figure-skating, like epidural analgesia, is aesthetically pleasing, and at the end the audience throws flowers, whereas with ice hockey people throw coins and beer cans. Occasionally when figure skaters do a triple axel they may fall, but with a smile they are quickly up again; whereas in ice hockey when two players crash into one another, they are out for an hour, and may have headaches for weeks afterwards.

Dr Carrie The analogy is excellent but I am not sure that there is any disadvantage in using smaller and smaller needles for spinals.

[*Editor's note: Many of us find ultra-fine needles very hard to handle.*]
I think the combined spinal and epidural technique may give the
best of both worlds.

Question   What is the incidence of headache with 26-gauge spinal
needles?

Dr Carrie   The figure of 6% in my paper is a composite one from
several sources. At my hospital the overall rate is 3% and in my
personal series 1%. To minimize headache it is important to insert
the spinal needle with the bevel facing laterally.

Dr Rubin   Would any of the panellists like to say why they think
patients shiver with epidurals but not with spinals?

Dr Howie   It is almost certain that shivering in association with
epidural anaesthesia results from the exposure of thermoreceptors
within the epidural space to large volumes of relatively cold local
anaesthetic. These receptors have been demonstrated in small
mammals and circumstantial evidence supports their existence in
man (Sevarino et al, 1989).
   For this reason we use bupivacaine stored in its package in a
warming cabinet similar to that used for intravenous fluids. The
ampoule is dropped from its package, still sterile, on to the epidural
tray immediately prior to administration.

Dr Lynch (Ormskirk)   I work in an underfunded and understaffed
hospital in the north-west of England, and found that we could not
spare the time and the staff required to set up a Caesarean section
under epidural anaesthesia. Our first attempts at spinal anaesthesia
for Caesarean section were abandoned as they did rather resemble
ice hockey. We later adopted Dr Carrie's meticulous technique, with
far better results. With strict attention to detail, even spinal
anaesthesia can resemble figure skating. High block, hence hypotension and nausea, must be prevented by keeping the shoulders raised
at all times and by never letting the uterus press even momentarily
on the vena cava, especially when turning from side to side. Turning
must be swift but gentle. An infusion of dilute ephedrine must be
started as soon as the blood pressure *begins* to drop. If given early
only 5–10 mg may be needed. An epidural catheter, which we insert
into a separate space, is normally only used for postoperative
analgesia or if the surgery is prolonged. It is omitted in emergencies.
Our headache rate was initially unacceptably high but dropped
dramatically when nurses stopped sitting patients upright between
6 a.m. and 8 a.m. on the first day for bedmaking. Gentle laxatives
are prescribed early in the puerperium to ensure that the mothers
do not have to strain at stool.

Spinals are now preferred by the mothers as a method of anaesthesia for Caesarean section. Those with previous experience of section under epidural appreciate the absence of apprehension while the block is taking effect. The technique receives the unanimous approval of obstetricians, midwives and anaesthetists.

Reference

Sevarino FB, Johnson MD, Lema MJ, Datta S, Ostheimer GW & Naulty JS (1989) The effect of epidural sufenantil on shivering and body temperature in the parturient. *Anesthesia and Analgesia* **68**: 530–533.

SECTION V

Spinal Opioids

12

Epidural and spinal opiates in labour

J. STEPHEN NAULTY

Local anaesthetics have been widely used for epidural analgesia in labour, and recently continuous epidural infusions have become popular (see Chapter 4). Their value, however, is limited by the fact that to maintain analgesia it is often necessary to use doses that produce significant motor blockade. A technique that could avoid this complication would be a major improvement. Epidural and subarachnoid opiate administration would appear to offer this possibility.

NEUROPHYSIOLOGY

Peripheral sensory nerves have their cell bodies in the dorsal root ganglion, and the central projections of the Aδ and C fibres that conduct painful stimuli enter the dorsal horn, where many synapse in lamina II (substantia gelatinosa). A series of interneurones convey impulses mostly via the wide dynamic response (WDR) neurones, whose cell bodies are in lamina V, to the anterolateral ascending columns.

Ascending impulses stimulate the reticular formation and tegmental tract in the brain stem, where they evoke the typical 'reflex' responses to pain. These include such phenomena as tachycardia, hyperventilation, increased blood pressure, release of catecholamines and hypothalamic hormones. The nervous impulses then continue upward to the ventral posterolateral nucleus of the thalamus. From there, fibres project to the sensory cortex for localization and discrimination of pain.

Nerve fibres also arise from these areas of the medulla, thalamus and cortex, and project caudad to the dorsal horn of the spinal cord, where they participate in the release of various neurotransmitters which modify pain impulses entering the spinal cord, creating a feedback loop in which afferent (even painful) stimuli are capable of producing analgesia, as is seen with acupuncture, transcutaneous electrical nerve stimulation, biofeedback techniques, etc. This feedback loop system seems to be particularly effective during pregnancy, with measured pain thresholds roughly 2–3 times higher for pregnant than non-pregnant subjects (Gintzler, 1982). This decrease in pain sensitivity is probably due to increased cerebrospinal fluid and plasma concentrations of endogenous opiates (enkephalins, endorphins) and progesterone (or its metabolites), which have a generalized stabilizing effect on neural tissue (Flanagan et al, 1987; Steinbrook et al, 1982).

The direct or indirect application of either inhibitory neuro-transmitters such as opioids which can act on substantia gelatinosa as well as brain, or antagonists of excitatory neurotransmitters such as clonidine, to the spinal cord or elsewhere in the central nervous system (CNS) can diminish the transmission of pain to consciousness (Cousins and Mather, 1984). This forms the basis for the application of narcotics and other drugs to the CNS, and in particular to the spinal cord, in order to produce analgesia.

EPIDURAL OPIATES IN LABOUR

The epidural injection of opiates alone has proved to be of limited value for the relief of labour pain. Intraspinal opiates were first shown to produce profound analgesia in humans in 1979 (Wang et al, 1979). Shortly thereafter, several researchers attempted to apply this technique for the relief of the pain of labour. High doses of morphine (7.5 mg) provided satisfactory analgesia for only the first stage of labour for 6 hours in one study (Booker et al, 1980), whereas doses of 2–5 mg produced satisfactory analgesia in less than 50% of patients (Husemeyer et al, 1980). In fact, the results with even the higher doses of morphine did not differ significantly from those found using natural childbirth techniques (Scott and Rose, 1976). Also, the slow onset (one hour or more) proved to be a significant problem. Studies using epidural fentanyl alone have also yielded indifferent results (Youngstrom et al, 1984; Reynolds and O'Sullivan, 1989). Epidural morphine and fentanyl, however, have been used to produce incomplete but adequate analgesia for labour in patients with diseases in which the use of local anaesthetics was thought to be contraindicated, such as Eisenmenger's syndrome, cystic fibrosis or pulmonary hypertension (Robinson and Leicht, 1988). Generally, however, epidural narcotics used as the sole analgesic drug have proved inferior to dilute concentrations of local anaesthetics, even when rapidly acting lipid-soluble drugs such as pethidine (meperidine) or fentanyl have been employed

(Skjolderbrand et al, 1982). The addition of adrenaline (epinephrine) appears to increase slightly the incidence of satisfactory analgesia, but not sufficiently to make this a reliable technique at present.

The best results that have been achieved with epidural narcotics on their own are excellent analgesia for the first stage, and poor analgesia for second and third stage (Francke and Frahm, 1988). However, if even an extremely dilute concentration of local anaesthetic is added to the opiate, vastly different results are obtained.

Epidural opiate and local anaesthetic combinations

Dilute solutions of local anaesthetics are best able to block Aδ fibres, while opiate drugs work most efficiently on impulses generated by C-fibre stimulation. The analgesia produced by a combination of epidural local anaesthetic and opiate can be profound. In general, patients who receive this combination report rapid onset of analgesia, which is more profound, longer-lasting and with less motor block than in patients receiving either drug alone.

Fentanyl and bupivacaine

Fentanyl was the first narcotic widely employed as an adjunct to local anaesthetics in labour (Justins et al, 1982). The initial idea that spinal synergism existed with bupivacaine and fentanyl was challenged by the contention that the systemic absorption of a large dose of fentanyl (50–100 μg) produced potentiation, rather than a specific spinal effect (Ross and Hughes, 1987). For example, Cohen et al (1987) were unable to demonstrate any superiority of bupivacaine 0.25% with fentanyl 5 μg ml^{-1} over bupivacaine alone, except for a decrease in motor block in the fentanyl group. However, the total dose of local anaesthetic was decreased in the fentanyl group, and the duration of analgesia was longer. This apparent lack of improvement in efficacy was undoubtedly due to the ability of 0.25% bupivacaine to produce satisfactory analgesia by itself in most patients, albeit with significant motor blockade. Indeed, Celleno & Capogna (1988) found that fentanyl (50 or 100 μg) improved the efficacy and duration of bupivacaine 0.125% during labour, roughly doubling its potency.

Reynolds and her colleagues performed a cleverly designed clinical study to elucidate the mechanism of action of epidural fentanyl analgesia when combined with bupivacaine (Vella et al, 1985). They observed that patients who received 80 μg fentanyl with the initial dose of 12 mg of bupivacaine exhibited a faster onset of more complete and long-lasting analgesia (and less need for supplementation) than patients in whom 80 μg of fentanyl was given intravenously at the time of epidural injection of local anaesthetic. They concluded that fentanyl produces regional analgesia in combination with bupivacaine, and not merely systemic analgesia.

Chestnut et al (1988) compared a continuous epidural infusion of a solution contianing 0.0625% bupivacaine with 2 μg ml⁻¹ of fentanyl with an infusion of 0.125% bupivacaine alone. Both groups, however, were given a test dose of bupivacaine 15 mg. There was no significant difference in the quality of analgesia in the first or second stages of labour. However, women who received bupivacaine alone were more likely to have motor block at full cervical dilatation ($P < 0.001$), secondary to a larger overall dose of local anaesthetic. There was no significant difference between groups in duration of the second stage of labour, duration of pushing, position of the vertex before delivery, method of delivery, Apgar scores, or umbilical cord blood gas and acid-base values. Thus the addition of fentanyl roughly doubled the efficacy of bupivacaine.

It appears that satisfactory analgesia in a wide variety of parturients can be achieved with an initial dose of 25 to 50 μg fentanyl combined with 0.25 to 0.125% bupivacaine, followed by a continuous infusion of 0.0625–0.125% bupivacaine with 1–2 μg ml⁻¹ fentanyl at 10–15 ml per hour (Table 1). Further decreases in fentanyl dose or concentration of local anaesthetic do not appear to produce completely reliable analgesia. Using this regimen, many authors have demonstrated that the dose of local anaesthetic required for labour pain relief can be diminished by one-half to two-thirds. These decreased doses of local anaesthetics still provide excellent analgesia for the

Table 1. Continuous infusion protocols.

	Bupivacaine alone	Bupivacaine and fentanyl	Bupivacaine and butorphanol	Bupivacaine and sufentanil
Loading dose:				
Bupivacaine	0.25–0.5%	0.125–0.25%	0.125–0.25%	0.0625–0.125%
Narcotic	none	2.5–5.0 μg ml⁻¹	0.2 mg ml⁻¹	0.1–0.2 μg ml⁻¹
Volume	10–15 ml	10 ml	10 ml	10 ml
Infusion:				
Bupivacaine	0.125–0.25%	0.0625–0.125%	0.0625–0.125%	0.031–0.125%
Narcotic	none	2 μg ml⁻¹	0.1 mg ml⁻¹	0.2–0.3 μg ml⁻¹
Rate	10–20 ml h⁻¹	8–12 ml h⁻¹	8–12 ml h⁻¹	6–10 ml h⁻¹

entirety of labour. No adverse effects on either the mother or baby have been attributed to the technique.

Sufentanil and bupivacaine

Phillips (1987) found that patients in labour given infusions containing 20–30 µg sufentanil combined with 10 ml 0.25% bupivacaine had a faster onset of more profound and long-lasting analgesia than those who received lower doses of sufentanil or bupivacaine alone. More recently this author demonstrated the efficacy of adding 1 µg ml^{-1} of sufentanil to 0.125% bupivacaine for continuous infusion at 10 ml/h^{-1} (Phillips, 1988). Analgesia was found to be significantly better and motor weakness less in patients who received epidural sufentanil. The author concluded that 'the addition of sufentanil to epidural bupivacaine infusions given in labor improves analgesia and reduces top-up requirements'.

Van Steenberge et al (1987) attempted to identify the optimum dosage of sufentanil used with bupivacaine for labour analgesia. In this study 120 patients received a 10 ml injection of 0.125% bupivacaine with adrenaline, either alone or with 7.5 µg or 15 µg of sufentanil. A second injeciton, given on request, was identical to the first. Subsequently, a further 10 ml of bupivacaine with adrenaline was given if required. The addition of sufentanil significantly shortened the onset and increased the duration and intensity of the analgesia; it also reduced the bupivacaine dose requirement, resulting in less motor blockade at delivery. There were no differences between the three groups in regard to Apgar scores, but no neurobehavioural testing was done. Vercauteren et al (1988) subsequently reported one case of neonatal respiratory depression following a 20 µg dose of sufentanil. Caution should be exercised when using large doses of sufentanil for labour analgesia until the neonatal effects are clearly understood.

Naulty et al (1989) showed that 5 µg of sufentanil produced satisfactory analgesia when added to 10 ml of 0.125, 0.0625 or even 0.03125% bupivacaine (0.2–0.3 µg ml^{-1}), and similar low doses are successful by infusion (see Table 1) with no observed adverse neonatal effects. With these concentrations there is no perceptible motor or sensory block and patient ambulation is possible, and it is suggested that larger doses of either agent are unnecessary.

Butorphanol and bupivacaine

With increased knowledge of opiate receptor pharmacology in animals, there has been an increased interest in the use of non-µ receptor agonists to produce spinal analgesia (Carr and Murphy,

1988; Yaksh, 1987). Kappa opiate receptors are found in the dorsal horn of the spinal cord, and epidural administration of κ-receptor agonist has been shown to produce significant analgesia, particularly for visceral pain.

Butorphanol is a narcotic analgesic with significant κ-receptor agonist activity. Hunt and her colleagues showed in a clinical dose-response study (Hunt et al, 1989) that butorphanol will potentiate epidural analgesia produced by 0.25% bupivacaine (see Table 1 for dosing recommendations). They observed that the addition of 0.2–0.3 mg ml^{-1} butorphanol to 10 ml of 0.25% bupivacaine significantly hastened the onset and doubled the duration of analgesia when compared with 0.25% bupivacaine alone. A transient low-amplitude sinusoidal fetal heart-rate pattern occurred in the 0.3 mg ml^{-1} group, but no adverse neonatal effects were observed. However, the study consisted of only 40 patients, and the authors point out that subsequent patients have complained of somnolence and occasional dysphoria, two side-effects of κ-receptor agonism. Further study of this class of drugs is needed to elucidate psychotomimetic side-effects and neonatal outcome.

Alfentanil and bupivacaine

Alfentanil, with its short duration of action and low systemic toxicity, would appear to offer potential advantages over longer-lasting drugs for epidural infusion during labour. However, this may not be the case. In a preliminary report, Heytens et al (1987) described 16 patients in labour who received alfentanil by epidural infusion at a rate of 30 μg kg^{-1} h^{-1}. Supplementary bolus doses of alfentanil were administered when necessary. Excellent pain relief was rapidly obtained in early labour in all patients, but it became inadequate in late labour in 5 of the 16 patients, and bupivacaine had to be administered. No serious maternal side-effects, except nausea, were encountered. Although all neonatal Apgar scores were between 7 and 10, the Amiel-Tison neonatal neurobehavioural assessment indicated the existence of neonatal hypotonia. In addition, Penon et al (1988) demonstrated rostral spread of epidural alfentanil, with significant, albeit short-lived (approximately 100 min), decreases in the ventilatory response to carbon dioxide following the injection of 15 μg kg^{-1} alfentanil. Finally, Golub et al (1988) examined the maternal–fetal disposition and neonatal respiratory depressant effect of pethidine (2 mg kg^{-1} IV) or alfentanil (IV infusion, 0.1 mg kg^{-1} total dose) during labour in rhesus monkeys. Fetal/maternal plasma ratios were lower for alfentanil, the more highly protein-bound drug (fetal/maternal ratio 0.20 versus 0.46 for pethidine). However, they found that elimination of alfentanil was delayed in the neonate. Neonatal plasma concentrations of alfentanil actually increased during the first two postnatal hours, indicating a compartmental shift from tissues to circulation. Six of ten alfentanil-treated monkeys had suboptimal respiratory rates at birth. Further work is necessary to determine the safety of lower-dose alfentanil combined with dilute local anaesthetic.

Local anaesthetic choice

The most satisfactory analgesia appears to be produced when the narcotic analgesics are combined with bupivacaine, rather than other local anaesthetics such as chloroprocaine. Chloroprocaine appears to antagonize some of the analgesic effects of the narcotic agonists and to increase the incidence of side-effects, most notably nausea and pruritus (Naulty et al, 1986). The exact nature of this interaction is unknown, but it appears that the combination of chloroprocaine and epidural narcotics should be avoided.

Advantages and disadvantages of epidural opiates and local anaesthetics

A few papers have attempted to assess the advantages and disadvantages of narcotic and local anaesthetic combinations in labour. The major advantage would appear to be the potential reduction in motor blockade that can be produced by the use of very low doses of local anaesthetic. Chestnut et al (1988), Phillips (1987, 1988), Naulty et al (1989) and Hunt et al (1989) all document decreased motor blockade produced by these combinations of dilute local anaesthetics and narcotics. However, these papers really contain too few patients to be conclusive about the effects of this decreased drug dose and motor blockade on complications of labour, fetal distress, forceps and Caesarean deliveries. Preliminary data (Naulty et al, 1988) from a retrospective study which examined changes in labour outcome following an abrupt change from a high-dose pure local anaesthetic technique to a low-dose bupivacaine-fentanyl technique indicate a decreased incidence of emergency Caesarean sections and forceps deliveries. However, much more work needs to be done in this area.

In an era when the safety of epidural administration of local anaesthetics (particularly bupivacaine) is questioned, a technique that allows the use of smaller doses of this drug would appear to offer significant advantages, even in the absence of a positive effect on labour. If the initial dose of bupivacaine injected is less than 20 mg, and the drug is then given by continuous infusion at less than 10–15 mg per hour, the risk of serious toxicity from an intravenous injection is considerably less than with bolus injections of the larger doses required in the absence of narcotics.

The disadvantages of this technique would appear to be the possible adverse maternal and fetal effects of epidural narcotics. The risks are essentially those of narcotics in general, and the most serious is respiratory depression. Large-scale studies are needed to determine whether the advantages of the technique outweigh the potential risks of introducing narcotics into epidural analgesic solutions. In the USA, however, parturients routinely receive much larger parenteral doses of these same narcotics in labour, without excessive concern on the part of obstetricians and neonatologists. At this time, the benefits of combining local anaesthetics and opiates appear to outweigh the potential risks.

SUBARACHNOID OPIATES

Morphine

The subarachnoid administration of opioids in obstetrics has been somewhat more successful than epidural administration. Brookshire et al (1983) reported excellent analgesia for the entirety of labour using fairly large doses of subarachnoid morphine (5–10 mg). Smaller doses (1–2 mg) produced analgesia that was reliable for the first stage of labour, but not for the second stage or operative deliveries. Unfortunately, these successes were associated with a high incidence of side-effects, most notably nausea, vomiting, pruritus and somnolence, probably due to the large doses used, even in the lower dose groups. Continuous i.v. infusion of naloxone following subarachnoid morphine can diminish the incidence and severity of these side-effects without decreasing the efficacy of the drug, but is at best an awkward solution to the problem. Carton et al (1987) reported the use of subarachnoid morphine (1 mg) in 24 healthy parturients, and found that 83% experienced a reduction in pain score, both in first and second stage. Most complained of severe pruritus and none reported a pain score of 0 (i.e. no pain), as is usually found with epidural opiates plus local anaesthetics. In addition, 4 patients developed spinal headaches (17%), and 10% of the primiparae required supplementary injections of bupivacaine. It appears that this technique cannot be relied on to produce satisfactory analgesia. However, it is useful when local anaesthetics are felt to be contraindicated. Abouleish (1988) reported a case in which the intrathecal administration of 1 mg hyperbaric morphine was followed, 7 hours after injection and 1 hour after delivery, by severe, life-threatening respiratory depression. The apnoea was noted by an alarm from a pulse oximeter. One mg of naloxone i.v. was administered, with complete remission of the respiratory depression. A continuous infusion of naloxone 0.4 mg h^{-1} i.v. was used to prevent recurrence. The total dose of naloxone administered over an 8-hour period was 3.6 mg. Patients who receive these large doses of intrathecal morphine during labour must be observed carefully in the postpartum period for the development of respiratory depression.

It appears that subarachnoid morphine may be quite useful for labour analgesia when local anaesthetics are contraindicated, but is of limited value in other circumstances (Copel et al, 1986; Hyde and Harrison, 1986). Smaller doses (0.1–0.2 mg) of morphine can provide good analgesia, with a lower incidence of side-effects, after Caesarean section, when pain is considerably less than in labour (Abboud et al, 1988). The onset of analgesia is slow (40–60 minutes) with these smaller doses, and combinations of morphine with other analgesics may be necessary to circumvent this problem.

Other subarachnoid opiates

Oyama et al (1980) described the highly successful use of β-endorphin for obstetric analgesia, but its cost ($10 000 per dose) is prohibitive. It is possible that the intrathecal use of more potent drugs such as fentanyl and its congeners, particularly sufentanil (Donadoni et al, 1987), and κ agonists such as butorphanol and nalbuphine, might produce better analgesia with fewer side-effects, but little other than anecdotal data exists at present.

Advantages and disadvantages of subarachnoid opiates

The theoretical advantage of spinal opiate analgesia is the absence of motor and sympathetic blockade. This promise has not yet been fulfilled by subarachnoid opiates alone, at least not without significant side-effects. Apart from side-effects, however, one of the major difficulties with the use of subarachnoid narcotics has been the lack of flexibility in the technique. That is, a patient may have adequate analgesia for labour, but if an instrumental or operative delivery becomes necessary, another form of anaesthetic must be used. The advent of fine-gauge intraspinal catheters may popularize continuous spinal analgesia during labour. This would permit the provision of analgesia for longer periods of time than 'single shot' techniques, and small doses of local anaesthetics, if required, could be added through the catheter before operative or instrumental deliveries.

CONCLUSION

Complete analgesia for labour with epidural and subarachnoid opiates alone, with few side-effects, seems to be an unfulfilled goal.

However, the combination of extremely small doses of local anaesthetic with opiate drugs can provide excellent analgesia with a minimum of side-effects. This concept of a combination of opiate and local anaesthetic is comparable to that of modern 'balanced' general anaesthesia, and holds great promise for the future, especially with the discovery of further drugs that can produce spinal analgesia by a variety of mechanisms. These drugs include catecholamines, clonidine, GABA agonists, substance P antagonists, prostaglandin synthetase inhibitors and many other drugs capable of inhibiting pain transmission. Labour analgesia is an area in which these combinations will be explored extensively.

REFERENCES

Abboud TK, Afrasiabi A, Sarkis F et al (1984) Continuous infusion epidural analgesia in parturients receiving bupivacaine, chloroprocaine, or lidocaine – maternal, fetal, and neonatal effects. *Anesthesia and Analgesia* **63**: 421–428.

Abboud TK, Dror A, Mosaad P et al (1988) Mini-dose intrathecal morphine for the relief of post-cesarean section pain: safety, efficacy, and ventilatory responses to carbon dioxide. *Anesthesia and Analgesia* **67**: 137–143.

Abouleish E (1988) Apnoea associated with the intrathecal administration of morphine in obstetrics. A case report. *British Journal of Anaesthesia* **60**: 592–594.

Booker PD, Wilkes RG, Bryson THL & Beddard J (1980) Obstetric pain relief using epidural morphine. *Anaesthesia* **35**: 377–379.

Brookshire GL, Shnider SM, Abboud TK et al (1983) Effects of naloxone on the mother and neonate after intrathecal morphine for labor analgesia. *Anesthesiology* **59**: A417.

Carr DB & Murphy MT (1988) Operation, anesthesia, and the endorphin system. *International Anesthesiology Clinics* **26**: 199–205.

Carton EG, McDonald N & McCarthy JR (1987) Intrathecal morphine in labor-efficacy and side effects. *Irish Journal of Medical Science* **156**: 323–327.

Celleno D & Capogna G (1988) Epidural fentanyl plus bupivacaine 0.125 per cent for labour: analgesic effects. *Canadian Journal of Anaesthesia* **35**: 375–378.

Chestnut DH, Bates JN & Choi WW (1987) Continuous infusion epidural analgesia with lidocaine: efficacy and influence during the second stage of labor. *Obstetrics and Gynecology* **69**: 323–327.

Chestnut DH, Owen CL, Bates JN, Ostman LG, Choi WW & Geiger MW (1988) Continuous infusion epidural analgesia during labor: a randomized, double-blind comparison of 0.0625% bupivacaine/0.0002% fentanyl versus 0.125% bupivacaine. *Anesthesiology* **68**: 754–757.

Cohen SE, Tan S, Albright GA & Halpern J (1987) Epidural fentanyl/bupivacaine mixtures for obstetric analgesia. *Anesthesiology* **67**: 403–407.

Copel JA, Harrison D, Whittemore R & Hobbins JC (1986) Intrathecal morphine analgesia for vaginal delivery in a woman with a single ventricle. A case report. *Journal of Reproductive Medicine* **31**: 274–276.

Cousins MJ & Mather LE (1984) Intrathecal and epidural opioids. *Anesthesiology* **61**: 276–310.

D'Athis F, Macheboeuf M, Thomas H et al (1988) Epidural analgesia with a bupivacaine-fentanyl mixture in obstetrics: comparison of repeated injections and continuous infusion. *Canadian Journal of Anaesthesia* **35**: 116–122.

Donadoni R, Vermeulen H, Noorduin H & Rolly G (1987) Intrathecal sufentanil as a supplement to subarachnoid anaesthesia with lignocaine. *British Journal of Anaesthesia* **59**: 1523–1527.

Flanagan HL, Datta, S, Lambert DH, Gissen AJ & Covino BG (1987) Effect of pregnancy on bupivacaine-induced conduction blockade in the isolated rabbit vagus nerve. *Anesthesia and Analgesia* **66**: 123–126.

Francke A & Frahm R (1988) Peridural analgesia with fentanyl – an alternative to control of labor pain. *Zentralblatt für Gynakologie* **110**: 215–223.

Gambling DR, Yu P, Cole C, McMorland GH & Palmer L (1988) A comparative study of patient controlled epidural analgesia (PCEA) and continuous infusion epidural analgesia (CIEA) during labour. *Canadian Journal of Anaesthesia* **35**: 249–254.

Gintzler AR (1982) Activation of opioid-containing systems during gestation. *Annals of the NY Academy of Science* **398**: 302–307.

Golub MS, Eisele JH & Kuhnert BR (1988) Disposition of intrapartum narcotic analgesics in monkeys. *Anesthesia and Analgesia* **67**: 637–643.

Hew EM, Rolbin SH, Cole AFD & Virgint S (1981) Obstetrical anaesthesia practice. *Canadian Anaesthetists Society Journal* **28**: 158–166.

Heytens L, Cammu H & Camu F (1987) Extradural analgesia during labour using alfentanil. *British Journal of Anaesthesia* **59**: 331–337.

Hicks JA, Jenkins JG, Newton MC & Findley IL (1988) Continuous epidural infusion of 0.075% bupivacaine for pain relief in labour. A comparison with intermittent top-ups of 0.5% bupivacaine. *Anaesthesia* **43**: 289–292.

Hunt CO, Naulty JS, Malinow AM, Datta S & Ostheimer GW (1989) Epidural butorphanol-bupivacaine for analgesia during labor and delivery. *Anesthesia and Analgesia* **68**: 323–327.

Husemeyer RP, O'Connor MC, Davenport HT, Cummings AJ & Rosankiewicz JR (1980) Failure of epidural morphine to relieve pain in labour. *Anaesthesia* **35**: 161–163.

Hyde NH & Harrison DM (1986) Intrathecal morphine in a parturient with cystic fibrosis. *Anesthesia and Analgesia* **65**: 1357–1358.

Justins DM, Francis D, Houlton PG & Reynolds F (1982) A controlled trial of extradural fentanyl in labour. *British Journal of Anaesthesia* **54**: 409–414.

Li DF, Rees GA & Rosen M (1985) Continuous extradural infusion of 0.0625% or 0.125% bupivacaine for pain relief in primigravid labour. *British Journal of Anaesthesia* **57**: 264–270.

MacLeod DM, Tey HK, Byers GF, Dollery WC & Tunstall ME (1987) The loading dose for continuous infusion epidural analgesia. A technique to reduce the incidence of hypotension. *Anaesthesia* **42**: 377–381.

Naulty JS (1988) Obstetrical analgesia. *Problems in Anesthesia* **2**: 408–422.

Naulty JS, Hertwig L, Hunt CO et al (1986) Duration of analgesia of epidural fentanyl following Cesarean delivery. *Anesthesiology* **65**: A369.

Naulty JS, Ross R & Smith R (1988) Effects of a change in labor analgesic practice on labor outcome. *Anesthesiology* **69**: A660.

Naulty JS, Ross R & Bergen W (1989) Epidural sufentanil-bupivacaine for labor analgesia. *Anesthesiology* **71**: A842.

Oyama T, Matsuki A, Taneichi T, Ling N & Guillemin R (1980) Beta-endorphin in obstetric analgesia. *American Journal of Obstetrics and Gynecology* **137**: 613–616.

Penon C, Negre I, Ecoffey C, Gross JB, Levron JC & Samii K (1988) Analgesia and ventilatory response to carbon dioxide after intramuscular and epidural alfentanil. *Anesthesia and Analgesia* **67**: 313–317.

Phillips GH (1987) Epidural sufentanil/bupivacaine combinations for analgesia during labor: effect of varying sufentanil doses. *Anesthesiology* **67**: 835–838.

Phillips GH (1988) Continuous infusion epidural analgesia in labor: the effect of adding sufentanil to 0.125% bupivacaine. *Anesthesia and Analgesia* **67**: 462–465.

Reynolds F & O'Sullivan G (1989) Epidural fentanyl and perineal pain in labour. *Anaesthesia* **44**: 341–344.

Robinson DE & Leicht CH (1988) Epidural analgesia with low dose bupivacaine and fentanyl for labor and delivery in a parturient with severe pulmonary hypertension. *Anesthesiology* **68**: 285–288.

Rosenblatt R, Wright R, Denson D & Raj P (1983) Continuous epidural infusions for obstetric analgesia. *Regional Anesthesia* **8**: 10–15.

Ross BK & Hughes SC (1987) Epidural and spinal narcotic analgesia. *Clinics in Obstetrics and Gynecology* **30**: 552–565.

Sapsford DJ & Howard C (1988) Epidural infusions – shortage of infusion devices (letter). *Anaesthesia* **43**: 332.

Scott JR & Rose NB (1976) Effect of psychoprophylaxis on labor and delivery in primiparas. *New England Journal of Medicine* **294**: 1205–1207.

Skjolderbrand A, Garle M, Gustaffson LL, Johansson H, Lunnell N-O & Rane A (1982) Extradural pethidine with and without adrenaline during labour: wide variation in effect. *British Journal of Anaesthesia* **54**: 415–420.

Steinbrook RA, Carr, DB, Datta S et al (1982) Dissociation of plasma and cerebrospinal fluid endorphin levels during pregnancy and parturition. *Anesthesia and Analgesia* **61**: 893–897.

Van Steenberge A, Debroux HC & Noorduin H (1987) Extradural bupivacaine with sufentanil for vaginal delivery. A double-blind trial. *British Journal of Anaesthesia* **59**: 1518–1522.

Vella LM, Willatts DG, Knott C, Lintin DJ, Justins DM & Reynolds F (1985) Epidural fentanyl in labour. An evaluation of the systemic contribution to analgesia. *Anaesthesia* **40**: 741–747.

Vercauteren MS, Boeckx E & Noorduin H (1988) Respiratory arrest after sufentanil (letter). *Anaesthesia* **43**: 69–70.

Wang JK, Nauss LE & Thomas JE (1979) Pain relief by intrathecally applied morphine in man. *Anesthesiology* **50**: 149–151.

Watkins DE (1986) Multiple endogenous opiate and non-opiate analgesia systems: evidence of their existence and clinical implications. *Annals of the NY Academy of Science* **467**: 273–299.

Yaksh TL (1987) Opioid receptor systems and the endorphins: a review of their spinal organization. *Journal of Neurosurgery* **67**: 157–176.

Yaksh TL, Wilson PR, Kaiko RF & Inturissi CE (1979 Analgesia produced by a spinal action of morphine and effects on parturition in the rat. *Anesthesiology* **51**: 386–392.

Youngstrom P, Eastwood D, Patel H, Bhatia R, Cowan R and Sutheimer C (1984) Epidural fentanyl and bupivacaine in labor: double-blind study. *Anesthesiology* **61**: A414.

13

Spinal opioids for Caesarean section

GORDON LYONS

Since spinal opioids were first used in the clinical setting in the 1970s, obstetric anaesthetists have been keen to explore their potential, especially for postoperative pain relief. As experience has grown, spinal opioids have been used with increasing success to control pain in labour and to supplement regional anaesthesia for Caesarean section. In this chapter the place of intrathecal and epidural opioids in the intraoperative and postoperative management of Caesarean section is discussed, together with comparisons of their efficacy and the incidences of side-effects when given spinally or by more conventional regimens.

INTRATHECAL ADMINISTRATION

The intrathecal administration of opioids has been associated with an increased incidence of unwanted effects, possibly because inappropriately large doses have been used. Advantages of intrathecal administration include reduced systemic absorption and deposition in epidural fat, and because the dura is bypassed, the drug is delivered closer to the receptors. Consequently intrathecal opioids are rapidly effective and will provide intraoperative analgesia. Hunt et al (1989) gave varying doses of fentanyl combined with intrathecal bupivacaine to 28 women for elective Caesarean section. All doses of fentanyl improved intraoperative analgesia and extended the duration of complete analgesia to more than 100 minutes. The smallest dose was 6.25 μg. Larger doses bestowed no advantage in terms of efficacy, but produced more side-effects. Abouleish et al (1988) evaluated the effects of morphine 0.2 mg in a randomized double-blind study of 34 patients: 82% of the morphine group did not require analgesic supplements during the course of their

Caesarean sections, compared with 41% of the controls, while postoperative analgesia lasted 27 hours. Continuous monitoring of postoperative oxygen saturation showed periods of desaturation that were more frequent, lower and longer-lasting than in the control group who had received conventional narcotic analgesia.

Two other studies of the use of intrathecal morphine only examined postoperative analgesia. Chadwick and Ready (1988) compared the efficacy of morphine 3–5 mg given epidurally with 0.3–0.5 mg given intrathecally in 399 consecutive patients. There was no randomization or selection, and a retrospective analysis allowed the inclusion of some patients who had been through labour. Pain scores for the two groups were similar (Figure 1), but intrathecal morphine lasted longer (Figure 2). Abboud et al (1988) compared morphine (0.25 mg and 0.1 mg) with heavy bupivacaine in 33 patients having spinal anaesthesia for Caesarean section. The two doses of morphine provided equivalent analgesia for 18–28 hours. Depression of the response to carbon dioxide was found only in the

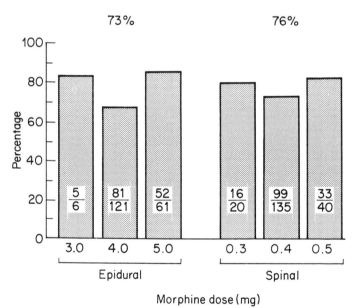

Figure 1. Intrathecal and epidural morphine sulphate for post-Caesarean analgesia. Within each bar is the number of patients who reported an analgesia score of 70 or greater at each dose, divided by the number of patients who received that dose. The height of each bar represents the resulting percentage for each dose. The numbers above the bars indicate the overall percentages for each group. Differences are not statistically different. From Chadwick and Ready (1988) with permission.

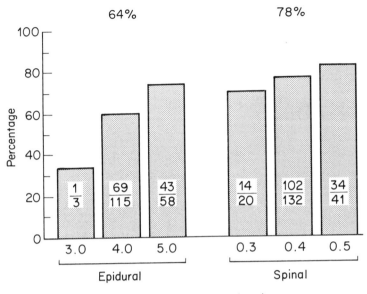

Figure 2. Intrathecal and epidural morphine sulphate for post-Caesarean analgesia. Within each bar is the number of patients who had 20 or more hours of analgesia, divided by the number of patients who received the dose. The height of each bar represents the resulting percentage. The numbers above the bars indicate the overall percentages for each group. The difference between the groups is statistically significant ($P < 0.005$). From Chadwick and Ready (1988) with permission.

control group who had received morphine 8 mg subcutaneously. Abouleish et al (1988) commented on the ease of intrathecal administration, the longer duration of action compared with epidural administration, improved safety – because the risk of subarachnoid migration of excessive opioid is abolished – and the minute doses required for effective analgesia. They also pointed out that reports of respiratory depression associated with intrathecal morphine have all followed doses of 1 mg or more.

EPIDURAL ADMINISTRATION

Intraoperative

In order for an epidurally administered drug to be effective during surgery, rapid dural transfer is required. Fentanyl is a strongly lipophilic drug that meets this requirement. Three studies have examined the influence of epidural fentanyl on anaesthesia for

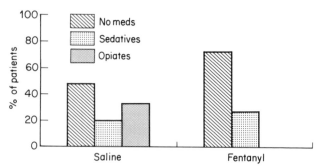

Figure 3. Women received epidural lignocaine 2% plus adrenaline, either alone or with fentanyl 1 μg kg^{-1}, for Caesarean section. The bars represent the percentages of patients requiring additional analgesia during the study period. Patients in the fentanyl group required less opioids ($P < 0.05$). From Preston et al (1988) with permission.

Caesarean section. Preston et al (1988) reported on 30 patients having lignocaine for epidural anaesthesia; epidural fentanyl 1 μg kg^{-1} was given to their study group, who experienced less moderate or severe pain, and required no analgesic supplements (Figure 3). Madej and Strunin (1987) found fentanyl 100 μg more effective than sufentanil 10–50 μg during surgery, although both had rapid onset. Gaffud et al (1986), using bupivacaine anaesthesia, gave 100 μg fentanyl to the ten patients in his study group. Over the 2-hour study period patients in this group experienced less pain and required fewer analgesic supplements. Neonatal outcome was unaffected in both studies.

Postoperative

Comparison with systemic therapy

Advantages of spinal administration are not accepted by all. In a randomized double-blind study, Jacobson et al (1983) compared diamorphine 0.1 mg kg^{-1} given intramuscularly with the same dose given epidurally to 21 patients who had undergone major gynaecological surgery. The only difference in analgesia that they could detect was that epidural diamorphine lasted longer. In their conclusion they stated that epidural diamorphine is safe and effective, but appears to be an exotic way of giving a systemic opioid. Two similar studies (Youngstrom et al, 1982; Thind et al, 1986), however, conducted with morphine after Caesarean section, found lower pain scores, slower onset and longer duration after epidural administration. Plasma concentrations peaked lower and later, and one of the authors commented on the better quality of analgesia.

Most reports are of randomized, double blind studies which have been carried out on women scheduled for elective Caesarean section. When two modes of administration are compared, patients are given both injections, one being a placebo. Conventional analgesia is available to all patients on demand. One difficulty with this is the potential for increasing the likelihood of late onset respiratory depression. First treatments are generally given as regional anaesthesia is waning. Given that it takes epidural morphine 60 minutes to produce analgesia (Cousins and Mather, 1984), this may cause patients unnecessary discomfort. Pain is assessed by linear analogue scores, by the time to first supplementary analgesia and by the total analgesic requirement for the period studied. Respiratory depression is generally monitored by measuring rate, which is not an accurate index of hypoventilation (Etches et al, 1989). This format allows comment on comparative efficacies and durations, but many reports contain words such as 'better', 'superior' and 'quality' when considering analgesia. The inference is that there is an additional facet to the analgesia from the spinal opioid that is picked up by the observer, but not by standard methods of pain assessment.

In a study designed to reveal this elusive attribute, Brownridge and Frewin (1985) gave each of 19 patients who had undergone Caesarean section or lower abdominal gynaecological surgery, four different treatments in a random order (Table 1). Each patient received both vials with each treatment. Epidural pethidine 50 mg was found to be superior to intramuscular pethidine 100 mg, but was not statistically better than epidural bupivacaine 25 mg. There was no significant difference in duration of action, but epidural pethidine was preferred over other treatments. By a chance event, more patients in this study received intramuscular pethidine as an early treatment. As pain declines with time, this may have biased the results in favour of the epidurally administered drugs. Brownridge (1987) stated that epidural pethidine was favoured by his postnatal staff because of speed of onset, better analgesia, fewer side-effects and greater patient mobility.

Table 1. Treatments given to patients in Brownridge and Frewin's study (1985).

Treatment	IM vial 2 ml	Epidural vial 10 ml
1	pethidine 100 mg	saline
2	saline	bupivacaine 25 mg
3	saline	pethidine 50 mg
4	saline	saline

Comparison with systemic therapy

Comparisons also exist between epidurally and intravenously administered opioid. Cohen et al (1988) investigated the analgesic effect of 50 μg epidural sufentanil with 10 μg given intravenously in 40 patients after Caesarean delivery. Both groups were then given sufentanil by patient-controlled analgesia (PCA). There was little difference between the groups, but longer duration of action was seen following epidural sufentanil 50 μg. However, at 12 hours the total doses of sufentanil given were the same for each group. The case for epidural administration was therefore not proven.

These studies are essentially comparisons of single doses of drugs given by different routes. They show that drugs given epidurally can provide analgesia, sometimes more effectively than drugs given by other routes. However, to enable the best choice for postoperative analgesia, a comparison of regimens is needed. Most patients no longer require parenteral narcotics beyond the first 24 postoperative hours (Webster et al, 1986); studies of shorter duration may not be adequate.

Webster et al (1986) examined the outcome after Caesarean section in 58 patients given either a single dose of 2–4 mg epidural morphine following regional anaesthesia, or intramuscular papaveretum as required following general anaesthesia. Both groups had equivalent analgesia, as measured by linear analogue scales, but the epidural morphine group required less opioid in the first 12 hours. The epidural morphine group slept better than the papaveretum group, but the difference was not significant. The presence of an indwelling urinary catheter delayed mobilization in the epidural morphine patients. The reported incidence of urinary retention varies widely. Evron et al (1984) found that 26 out of 30 patients who had received epidural morphine 4 mg following bupivacaine anaesthesia for Caesarean section complained of difficulty with micturition, and 14 required catheterization. In the study group who received phenoxybenzamine 10 mg both before and after the operation, 2 complained of difficulty with micturition, and 3 required catheterization. (See also Current Research 6.)

Harrison et al (1988) and Eisenach et al (1988) both compared 5 mg epidural morphine with PCA and with intramuscular (IM) administration in 60 post-Caesarean section patients. Eisenach found varying use of morphine between the groups (Figure 4), though Harrison found no difference in use between the PCA and IM groups, and no difference in analgesic effect. Eisenach found more sedation with PCA and both found that analgesia was significantly better in the epidural group (Figure 5) for up to 16 hours, but patient satisfaction was higher with PCA. Patients in the epidural and PCA groups, who were having repeat sections, preferred their

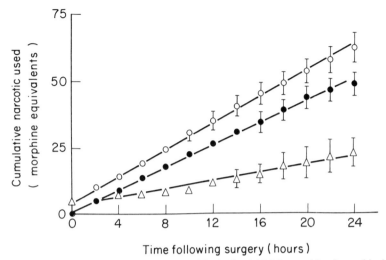

Figure 4. Cumulative narcotic administered (including initial 5 mg epidural morphine) for the first 24 hours following Caesarean section in groups receiving PCA (○), IM (●), and epidural morphine (△) groups ($n = 20$ in each group). From Eisenach et al (1988) with permission.

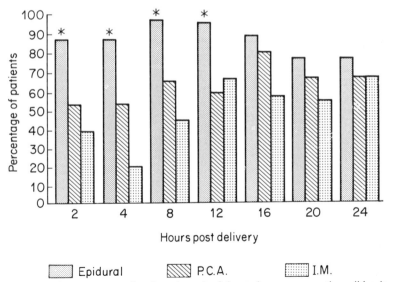

Figure 5. The percentage of patients in each of the study groups reporting mild pain (visual analogue scale 0–3) at each of the observation points. $*P < 0.05$ (epidural versus PCA and IM). All the remaining patients experienced moderate or severe pain. From Harrison et al (1988) with permission.

current therapy to IM administration, but only the epidural group said that they had had better pain relief. The incidence of nausea and vomiting has been reported as 50% after epidural and 30% after intramuscular morphine (Cousins and Mather, 1984), but Eisenach et al (1988) found no difference between epidural, IM or patient-controlled administration.

Where equivalent analgesic regimens have been compared, it appears that analgesia produced by a single epidural dose of morphine lasts for 24 hours, and for the first 12–16 hours pain scores are lower than with conventional narcotic regimens. Side-effects can make epidural morphine unpopular, however. Smaller doses of epidural opioids are capable of producing analgesia of longer duration than is possible with other routes of administration, though this advantage diminishes with the more lipophilic drugs.

ALTERNATIVES TO MORPHINE

Morphine is the most extensively studied of the spinal opioids. However, Crawford (1981) found 2 mg inadequate for postoperative pain relief. Most studies reported here have used 5 mg with good effect, but Douglas et al (1988) found that 3 mg was as effective as 5 mg. Pethidine (Brownridge, 1983), diamorphine (Semple et al, 1988), phenoperidine (Macrae et al, 1987), methadone (Beeby et al, 1984), fentanyl (Madej and Strunin, 1987; Naulty et al, 1985), sufentanil (Madej and Strunin, 1987; Naulty et al, 1986) and buprenorphine (Simpson et al, 1988) have all been used epidurally following Caesarean section.

In one study fentanyl 100 µg was shown to be little more effective than fentanyl 50 µg, both providing 5 hours of pain relief (Naulty et al, 1985). When fentanyl 100 µg was compared with varying doses of sufentanil (Madej and Strunin, 1987), both drugs had rapid onset and lasted for 2–3 hours. Sufentanil 50 µg had an unacceptable incidence of side-effects, but the 20–30 µg doses were equivalent to fentanyl 50–100 µg. In conclusion it was felt that sufentanil had no advantage over fentanyl.

A comparison of epidural diamorphine 5 mg with phenoperidine 2 mg (Macrae et al, 1987) found no difference except in duration, with diamorphine lasting 8.5 hours, and phenoperidine less than 6 hours.

Brownridge (1983) reported favourably on the effects of pethidine 50 mg given epidurally on demand. His patients had no urinary retention or respiratory depression, but some had pruritus. A comparative study with morphine is not available. Beeby et al (1984) reported satisfactory analgesia in 88% of patients following repeated doses of methadone 4 mg. Each patient required an average of 2.2 doses. A comparison with epidural morphine 4 mg was attempted, but patients were not assessed beyond 30 minutes.

Simpson et al (1988) compared epidural buprenorphine 0.09 mg and 0.18 mg with morphine 3 mg for up to 24 hours. Morphine was marginally superior to buprenorphine 0.18 mg, and both were better than buprenorphine 0.09 mg. The incidence of side-effects was similar. More such studies extending over the first 24 postoperative hours with a morphine control group are required.

Adrenaline has been added to epidural opioids to reduce vascular uptake and increase the concentration gradient across the dura. One potential effect of this is to increase the intensity of minor side-effects (Cousins and Mather, 1984). The addition of adrenaline made no difference to the effect of morphine 4 mg (Youngström et al, 1982). However, when adrenaline was added to diamorphine 5 mg, the duration increased from 10 hours to 12.5 hours. The plasma morphine level peaked lower and later in the adrenaline group, but nausea and vomiting occurred more commonly. Pruritus, though, was unaffected (Semple et al, 1988). Adrenaline also increased the duration of small doses of sufentanil (Naulty et al, 1986).

The reported incidence of pruritus varies widely, being 100% after epidural morphine 10 mg (Cousins and Mather, 1984), and in the region of 50% to 72% after 5 mg (Cohen and Woods, 1983; Abboud et al, 1987; Harrison et al, 1988; Rosen et al, 1988); it may be higher in the parturient. Thangthurai et al (1988) found an incidence of 62% after 2.5–3 mg following Caesarean section, compared with 11% after 5–10 mg in patients having major cancer surgery. Most itching is not troublesome. Antihistamines are frequently prescribed (Etches et al, 1989), but many are not convinced of their efficacy. An infusion of naloxone 2 mg over 12 hours after epidural morphine 4 mg did not affect analgesia, but reduced the incidence of itching. However, this was not significant (Thind et al, 1986). Nalbuphine 5 mg given intravenously to a patient itchy after epidural hydromorphone 1 mg was effective in 15–30 minutes, and did not disturb the analgesia (Henderson and Cohen, 1986). Nalbuphine is a partial agonist for the μ receptor and an agonist for the κ receptor, and has a plasma half-life of some hours. Its value as a treatment for pruritus merits investigation.

Recently herpes simplex labialis has been associated with epidural morphine after Caesarean section; the incidence is quoted at 10–29% (Gieraerts et al, 1987; Crane et al, 1988). One of the mechanisms suggested for this is that the response to itching acts as a trigger for the virus.

OTHER EFFECTS OF SPINAL OPIOIDS

Epidural opioids have been advocated as a remedy for the shivering sometimes associated with regional anaesthesia (Brownridge, 1986).

Fentanyl 25 μg was effective in abolishing shaking in 18 out of 25 women in labour, and took 15 minutes to work (Matthews and Corser, 1988). Potential dangers perhaps exist with this therapy, in that shivering may prevent hypothermia (Johnson et al, 1989).

Attempts to reveal hidden advantages of postoperative analgesia with epidural morphine have not been very successful. Cohen and Woods (1983) investigated the effects of 5 mg epidural morphine compared with 5 mg intravenously in 40 patients. While the epidural group had better, longer analgesia and required fewer supplements, there was no difference with regard to first voiding, hours slept, duration of stay or bonding. Stenkamp et al (1989), in a retrospective study, examined the length of hospital stay. The shortest mean stay of 3 days, 21 hours was found in those who had spinal anaesthesia with morphine, compared with 4 days, 8 hours in those who had epidural anaesthesia and conventional narcotic analgesia. Whether an 11-hour difference is an advantage worth pursuing is doubtful.

The spectre of late onset respiratory depression haunts those who use hydrophilic spinal opioids. Many early reports followed what we would now consider to be inappropriately large doses, given to unsuitable patients, who may also have received concurrent narcotic therapy by another route. Depression of the response to carbon dioxide occurs, but the clinical significance of this is uncertain, particularly as the most commonly used alternative to a spinal opioid is a narcotic given by another route, with its own potential for respiratory depression. In a review by Etches et al (1989), epidural morphine was thought by the authors to have a safe record in parturients. Comparisons with conventional analgesia using valid parameters of measurement are few and far between. Choi et al (1986) used a pulse oximeter for up to 16 hours on patients of whom 10 had been given 5 mg epidural morphine, and 10 conventional narcotic analgesia. Half of the patients had episodes of desaturation to 85% or below, and for 1 patient in each group this desaturation persisted for nearly 5 minutes. However, there was no difference between the groups. Intrathecal morphine has perhaps an undeserved reputation; Abboud et al (1988) reported depression of the response to carbon dioxide following subcutaneous morphine 8 mg, but not following intrathecal morphine 0.1 mg and 0.25 mg. Abouleish et al (1988) reported more frequent and longer oxygen desaturation following conventional morphine than following intrathecal morphine 0.2 mg. Only further investigation will establish what the relative risks are from the various modes of administration, but when appropriate doses are used evidence of additional risk is lacking.

Many clinical anaesthetists manage their patients on postnatal wards, but are criticized for doing so. Bromage (1981) wrote, 'the single-bedded hospital room, with all its comfort and privacy, is not a safe place to risk delayed respiratory depression, unless special surveillance is provided'. Hughes (1989), reviewing the same topic, wrote, 'any hospital or nursing staff that is able to administer IV or IM narcotics and feels happy doing so is also capable of using epidural and intrathecal narcotics'. Etches et al (1989) stated that 'no patient given a single dose of spinal morphine should be nursed on a general ward until 18 to 24 hours have passed, with the possible exception of post-Caesarean section patients'; and Morgan (1989) gave the opinion that 'some form of respiratory monitoring is mandatory'. In many units thousands of patients have been managed without special surveillance, without incident. An unwatched oximeter does not amount to surveillance. Perhaps the best form of monitoring is an educated and attentive nurse.

REFERENCES

Abboud TK, Klepper ID, Moore M et al (1987) Epidural butorphanol or morphine for the relief of post Cesarean section pain: ventilatory responses to CO_2. *Anesthesia and Analgesia* **66**: 887–893.

Abboud TK, Drov A, Mosaad P et al (1988) Minidose intrathecal morphine for the relief of post Cesarean section pain: safety, efficacy, and ventilatory responses to CO_2. *Anesthesia and Analgesia* **67**: 137–143.

Abouleish E, Rawal N, Fallon K & Hernandez D (1988) Combined intrathecal morphine and bupivacaine for Cesarean section. *Anesthesia and Analgesia* **67**: 370–374.

Beeby D, MacIntosh KC, Bailey M & Welch DB (1984) Postoperative analgesia for Caesarean section using epidural methadone. *Anaesthesia* **39**: 61–63.

Bromage PR (1981) The price of intraspinal narcotics: basic constraints. *Anesthesia and Analgesia* **60**: 461–463.

Brownridge P (1983) Epidural and intrathecal opiates for postoperative pain relief. *Anaesthesia* **38**: 74–75.

Brownridge P (1986) Shivering related to epidural blockade with bupivacaine in labour, and the influence of epidural pethidine. *Anaesthesia and Intensive Care* **14**: 412–417.

Brownridge P (1987) Epidural opioids. *Anaesthesia and Intensive Care* **15**: 351–353.

Brownridge P & Frewin DB (1985) A comparative study of techniques of postoperative analgesia following Caesarean section and lower abdominal surgery. *Anaesthesia and Intensive Care* **13**: 123–130.

Chadwick HS & Ready LB (1988) Intrathecal and epidural morphine sulphate for post Cesarean analgesia – a clinical comparison. *Anesthesiology* **68**: 925–929.

Choi HJ, Little MS, Fujita RA, Garber SZ & Tremper KK (1986) Pulse oximetry for monitoring during ward analgesia: epidural morphine versus parenteral narcotics. *Anesthesiology* **65**: A371.

Cohen SE & Woods WA (1983) The role of epidural morphine in the post Cesarean patient: efficacy and effects on bonding. *Anesthesiology* 1983 **58**: 500–504.

Cohen SE, Tan S & White PF (1988) Sufentanil analgesia following Cesarean section: epidural versus intravenous administration. *Anesthesiology* **68**: 129–134.

Cousins MJ & Mather LE (1984) Intrathecal and epidural opioids. *Anesthesiology* **61**: 276–310.

Crawford SJ (1981) Experiences with epidural morphine in obstetrics. *Anaesthesia* **36**: 207–209.

Crone L-A, Conly JM, Clark KM et al (1988) Recurrent Herpes Simplex Virus

Labialis and the use of epidural morphine in obstetric patients. *Anesthesia and Analgesia* **67**: 318–323.

Douglas MJ, McMorland GH & Janzen JA (1988) Influence of bupivacaine as an adjuvant to epidural morphine for analgesia after Cesarean section. *Anesthesia and Analgesia* **67**: 1138–1141.

Eisenach JC, Grice SC & Dewan DM (1988) Patient controlled analgesia following Cesarean section: a comparison with epidural and intramuscular narcotics. *Anesthesiology* **68**: 444–448.

Etches R, Sandler A & Daley MD (1989) Respiratory depression and spinal opioids. *Canadian Journal of Anaesthesia* **36**: 165–185.

Evron S, Magora F & Sadovsky E (1984) Prevention of urinary retention with phenoxybenzamine during epidural morphine. *British Medical Journal* **288**: 190.

Gaffud MP, Bansal P, Lawton C, Velasquez N & Watson WA (1986) Surgical analgesia for Cesarean delivery with epidural bupivacaine and fentanyl. *Anesthesiology* **65**: 331–334.

Gieraerts R, Navalgund A, Vaes L, Soetens M, Chang J-L & Jahr J (1987) Increased incidence of itching and herpes simplex in patients given epidural morphine after Cesarean section. *Anesthesia and Analgesia* **66**: 1321–1324.

Harrison DM, Sinatra R, Morgese L & Chung JH (1988) Epidural narcotic and patient controlled analgesia for post Cesarean section pain relief. *Anesthesiology* **68**: 454–457.

Henderson SK & Cohen H (1986) Nalbuphine augmentation of analgesia and reversal of side effects following epidural hydromorphine. *Anesthesiology* **65**: 216–218.

Hughes SC (1989) Intraspinal narcotics after Cesarean section. *Current Opinion in Anesthesiology* **2**: 295–302.

Hunt CO, Naulty JS, Bader AM et al (1989) Perioperative analgesia with subarachnoid fentanyl-bupivacaine for Cesarean delivery. *Anesthesiology* **71**: 535–540.

Jacobson L, Phillips PD, Hull CJ & Conacher ID (1983) Extradural versus intramuscular diamorphine. *Anaesthesia* **38**: 10–18.

Johnson MD, Sevarino FB & Lenia MJ (1989) Cessation of shivering and hypothermia associated with epidural sufentanil. *Anesthesia and Analgesia* **68**: 70–71.

Macrae DJ, Munishankarappa S, Burrow LM, Milne MK & Grant IS (1987) Double blind comparison of the efficacy of extradural phenoperidine, extradural diamorphine and intramuscular diamorphine following Caesarean section. *British Journal of Anaesthesia* **59**: 354–359.

Madej TH & Strunin L (1987) Comparison of epidural fentanyl with sufentanil. Analgesia and side effects after a single dose during elective Caesarean section. *Anaesthesia* **42**: 1156–1161.

Matthews NC & Corser G (1988) Epidural fentanyl for shaking in obstetrics. *Anaesthesia* **43**: 783–785.

Morgan M (1989) The rational use of intrathecal and extradural opioids. *British Journal of Anaesthesia* **63**: 165–188.

Naulty JS, Datta S, Ostheimer GW, Johnson MD & Burger GA (1985) Epidural fentanyl for post Cesarean delivery pain management. *Anesthesiology* **63**: 694–698.

Naulty JS, Sevarino FB, Lema MJ, Hunt CO, Datta S & Ostheimer GW (1986) Epidural sufentanil for post Cesarean delivery pain management. *Anesthesiology* **65**: A396.

Preston PG, Rosen MA, Hughes SC et al (1988) Epidural anesthesia with fentanyl and lidocaine for Cesarean section: maternal effects and neonatal outcome. *Anesthesiology* **68**: 938–943.

Rosen MA, Dailey PA, Hughes SC et al (1988) Epidural sufentanil for postoperative analgesia after Cesarean section. *Anesthesiology* **68**: 448–454.

Semple AJ, Macrae DJ, Munishankarappa S, Burrow LM, Milne MK & Grant IS (1988) Effect of the addition of adrenaline to extradural diamorphine analgesia after Caesarean section. *British Journal of Anaesthesia* **60**: 632–638.

Simpson KH, Madej TH, McDowell JM, Macdonald R & Lyons G (1988) Comparison of extradural buprenorphine and extradural morphine after Caesarean section. *British Journal of Anaesthesia* **60**: 627–631.

Stenkamp SJ, Easterling TR & Chadwick HS (1989) Effect of epidural and intrathecal morphine on length of hospital stay. *Anesthesia and Analgesia* **68**: 66–69.

Thangthurai D, Bowles HF, Allen HW & Mikhail M (1988) The incidence of pruritus after epidural morphine. *Anaesthesia* **43**: 1055–1056.

Thind GS, Wells JCD & Wilkes RG (1986) The effects of continuous intravenous naloxone on epidural morphine analgesia. *Anaesthesia* **41**: 582–585.

Webster NR, Lyons G & Macdonald R (1986) Sleep and comfort after Caesarean section. *Anaesthesia* **41**: 1143–1145.

Youngström PC, Cowan RI, Sutheimer C, Eastwood DW & Yu JC (1982) Pain relief and plasma concentrations from epidural and intramuscular morphine in post Cesarean patients. *Anesthesiology* **57**: 404–409.

Current Research 5

Epidural methadone and bupivacaine in labour

E. M. McGRADY, C. S. MARTIN and J. THORBURN

Epidural bupivacaine can provide excellent analgesia in labour; disadvantages include concomitant motor and sympathetic blockade and the potential for systemic toxicity. Epidural opioids administered with bupivacaine to women in labour improve the quality of analgesia and reduce degree of motor blockade (Justins et al, 1982; McGrady et al, 1989).

Epidural diamorphine and fentanyl are not without side-effects; pruritus is common although usually not troublesome. Methadone, a lipophilic opioid with a mean duration of action of up to 8.7 hours when administered epidurally (Torda and Pybus, 1982) has proved an effective analgesic in the postoperative period and seems to have a lower incidence of associated pruritus (Beeby et al, 1984).

The bupivacaine sparing effects of epidural opioid administration in labour, with their potential to minimize motor blockade, encourages the search for the agent with fewest side-effects. Therefore a double-blind study was undertaken to assess the properties of epidural methadone in labour.

METHOD

Mothers requesting epidural analgesia in early labour were investigated; they were randomly allocated into two groups. Once the epidural space was identified they received either 5 mg methadone in 10 ml sodium chloride (group 1), or 10 ml sodium chloride alone (group 2). Subsequently they received bupivacaine top-ups as required. The rate of bupivacaine administration was calculated and the degree of motor blockade assessed. Associated side-effects of bupivacaine and methadone were noted.

RESULTS

See Table 1.

Table 1.

	Group 1	Group 2	P
	median (range)	median (range)	
n	18	17	
Bupivacaine rate (mg h^{-1})	12.3 (6.3–22)	13.8 (8–38)	NS
Pain during labour (visual analogue score cm)	1.45 (0–4.7)	3.16 (0–7)	<0.01

CONCLUSION

Analysis of data indicates that methadone has little bupivacaine sparing effect but causes significant reductions in visual analogue pain scores. Pruritus was a rare side-effect, and when it occurred it was very mild.

References

Beeby D, Macintosh KC, Bailey M & Welch DB (1984) Postoperative analgesia for Caesarean section using epidural methadone. *Anaesthesia* **39**: 61–63.

Justins DM, Francis D, Houlton PG & Reynolds F (1982) A controlled trial of extradural fentanyl in labour. *British Journal of Anaesthesia* **54**: 409–414.

McGrady EM, Brownhill DK & Davis AG (1989) Epidural diamorphine and bupivacaine in labour. *Anaesthesia* **44**: 400–403.

Torda TA & Pybus DA (1982) Comparison of four narcotic analgesics for extradural analgesia. *British Journal of Anaesthesia* **54**: 291–295.

Current Research 6

Bladder function during intramuscular papaveretum and epidural diamorphine analgesia following Caesarean section

J. A. PATRICK, J. S. L. YOON and F. REYNOLDS

Urinary dysfunction following epidural opioids, particularly morphine, is well documented (Rawal et al, 1987; Dray, 1988). In hospital, epidural diamorphine is extensively used to relieve pain following Caesarean section and it was decided to carry out an open study to investigate the effects of our current analgesic policy on postoperative urinary function.

METHOD

The current hospital practice for post-Caesarean analgesia was not altered. All patients were prescribed intramuscular (IM) papaveretum 10–20 mg as required up to 4-hourly. Patients with an epidural catheter were allowed 2.5–5 mg diamorphine in 10 ml normal saline by the epidural route instead of IM analgesia if requested but only during the day. Two groups were selected from 174 mothers who underwent delivery by Caesarean section consecutively in the four months between November 1988 and February 1989. Group 1 consisted of 112 patients who had some or all of their analgesia given by the epidural route, whereas 62 patients in group 2 had IM analgesia only. After removal of the urinary catheter, usually the day after delivery, the mothers were asked to measure and record, for 48 hours, the volume of urine passed at each voiding and the time. The women were also asked specifically about postoperative urinary problems. Statistical analyses were performed using the unpaired t-test, the Mann Whitney U-test or the chi-squared test as appropriate.

RESULTS

There was no significant difference between the groups in terms of duration of catheterization, mean volume of urine passed on the first and second days after catheter removal, or time interval between epidural or IM analgesia and next spontaneous voiding (Table 1). The incidence of recatheterization, the need for prolonged catheterization and the reported frequency of painful micturition were similar in the two groups. In group 1, 22% of women complained of difficulty starting micturition: although they had the urge to pass urine they were unable initially to do so. This was twice the incidence of hesitancy in group 2, but the difference did not reach statistical significance $(0.05 < P < 0.1)$.

Table 1. Bladder function after urinary removal.

	Group 1 – epidural		Group 2 – IM		P
	Mean ± SD	n	Mean ± SD	n	
Time from delivery to first spontaneous voiding (hours)	31.5 ± 8.8	73	29.8 ± 19.9	43	NS
Mean urinary volume after catheter removal (ml)					
First day	342 ± 134	73	339 ± 184	42	NS
Second day	277 ± 119	56	265 ± 156	29	NS
Mean time from analgesia to next spontaneous voiding (hours)	3.8 ± 2.0	44	3.5 ± 3.0	21	NS

CONCLUSION

Although the women in the 'epidural' group reported a greater frequency of urinary problems, this was not reflected clinically as an increased incidence of bladder complications and there was no evidence of urinary retention with overflow. Those who had difficulty starting micturition were aware that they had to pass urine and required some perseverance to succeed, but the rate of recatheterization was not increased. This is an important feature compared with epidural local anaesthesia where bladder sensation may be lost. Motivation to mobilize rapidly after Caesarean section probably helps to minimize urinary problems during epidural diamorphine analgesia.

References

Dray A (1988) Epidural opiates and urinary retention: new models provide new insights. *Anesthesiology* **68**: 323–324.

Rawal N, Arner S, Gustafsson LL & Allvin R (1987) Present state of extradural and intrathecal opioid analgesia in Sweden. *British Journal of Anaesthesia* **59**: 791–799.

SECTION V – DISCUSSION

CHAIRMAN: DR T. THOMAS, Bristol

Question Dr McGrady, did you look for neurobehavioural changes in the babies of mothers who had had methadone?

Dr McGrady We assessed the Apgar scores at 1 and 5 minutes after birth and there was no difference between the groups; but 5 mg methadone is not a large dose.

Dr Gutsche I have one comment and one question. Dr McGrady, when you and others start giving epidural narcotics before delivery I would urge you to carry out either ENNS (early neonatal neurobehavioural scores) or NACS (neural adaptive capacity scores) on these infants. I doubt very much if 5 mg of methadone would have much effect but if you start giving higher doses then you must prove the safety of these drugs and the observations must be made by a blinded investigator. The NACS, particularly, is simple and should be assessed at 15 minutes, 2 hours and 24 hours. An Apgar score is worthless for assessing the effects of narcotics.

Dr Naulty, why do you prefer using sufentanil to fentanyl? In the USA the cost of sufentanil is $9.84 for 2 ml, compared with $0.42 for 2 ml of fentanyl.

Dr Naulty I can achieve results with sufentanil that I cannot with fentanyl. I cannot obtain reliable analgesia with as little as 0.03125% bupivacaine, even if I use 50–100 µg of fentanyl. With sufentanil, the loading dose is 2 µg in 10 ml of bupivacaine 0.0625%. This is followed by an infusion of 0.03125% bupivacaine containing 0.2 µg ml^{-1} of sufentanil, given at a rate of 6–8 ml per hour. The local anaesthetic block is undetectable by pin-prick, though it may be possible to detect a sensory level to cold stimuli. There is no motor block, the women are able to walk.

I agree with your comment about neurobehavioural testing. Van Steenberge (personal communication) reported neurobehavioural changes following sufentanil given in labour in much larger doses than we use. This was one reason we tried diminishing the dose.

Dr Reynolds Referring to your use of butorphanol, did you not find it produced excessive somnolence?

Dr Naulty   I think κ agonists in general have this potential and we did use fairly large doses of butorphanol. It also occasionally produces dysphoria which is why we did not pursue our use of this drug.

Question   Does methadone have a lower incidence of itch than other opioids? Would it increase with a higher dose?

Dr McGrady   We were only using a single dose of methadone, but the incidence of itching was remarkably low even in other studies involving repeated epidural methadone administration. Itch was more common with epidural diamorphine in labour, and in some it lasted a long time. I have had to give naloxone for itching associated with other epidural opioids, but never with methadone.

Dr Russell   Dr Patrick, how long were the urinary catheters left in after Caesarean section? At my hospital we remove urinary catheters at the end of surgery. Do you think that prolonged catheterization might provoke subsequent urinary retention?

Dr Patrick   We have to encourage midwives to remove urinary catheters the morning after surgery rather than to leave them in even longer, so they may be in for between 12 and 24 hours. We did not think it appropriate to remove catheters just before nightfall. However the policy of one consultant obstetrician in our hospital is to remove catheters immediately after surgery, and need for recatheterization arose principally in his patients.

SECTION VI

The Recipient

14

Effects on the baby of conduction blockade in obstetrics

FELICITY REYNOLDS

Epidural and spinal blockade for labour and delivery may affect the baby in a number of ways: because the drugs used cross the placenta, because they affect intervillous blood flow or respiratory gas exchange, or because they alter the course of labour or affect the bonding of mother and child. If there is an effect it is not easy to know how to measure it, or how to assess its importance to the newborn baby.

Fetal welfare may be assessed using cardiotocography, acid-base status measurement or – more fashionably – by using Doppler ultrasound to measure flow-velocity wave forms in the fetal arteries. Neonatal effects are measured using the Apgar score, acid-base status, a neurobehavioural scoring system or, with large numbers, by examining the perinatal mortality rate. Only the latter can be regarded as of unequivocal importance. Long-term outcome can be measured in terms of child development, but the number of environmental variables contributing to this would be likely to conceal any small effect of analgesia.

A direct pharmacological effect on the fetus and newborn is more likely to occur with epidural than with spinal administration, since the dose used by the latter route is small. Moreover, although a direct effect may occur with the more cumulative lignocaine, it appears unlikely with bupivacaine. The techniques may, however, affect placental exchange of respiratory gases, which in turn affects fetal well-being. This may occur because of altered maternal respiration. Hyperventilation in labour is reduced once pain is relieved, hence maternal $P\text{co}_2$ rises. Though this reduces the transplacental carbon dioxide gradient, it also has the effect of reducing the affinity of maternal haemoglobin for oxygen, thereby potentially enhancing oxygen transfer to the fetus. Swanström and

Bratteby (1981) showed that Po_2 values in newborns whose mothers had received epidural lignocaine during labour were higher than in controls, though unlike earlier workers (Thalme et al, 1974) they found no difference in acid-base status between the groups.

HAEMODYNAMIC CHANGES

A more important means whereby conduction blockade may affect respiratory gas exchange is by altering placental blood supply, since respiratory gases are flow-dependent in their placental transfer rate (Reynolds, 1987). Maternal placental (intervillous) flow is largely determined by maternal cardiac output and blood pressure, though it will also be reduced by uterine vasoconstriction. Both spinal and epidural blockade may reduce maternal blood pressure, while evidence of fetal detriment, in the form of a deterioration in fetal heart tracing, may be seen during a dramatic fall in maternal arterial pressure. Because spinal anaesthesia is quicker in onset and therefore likely to cause greater maternal hypotension, it is more likely than epidural blockade to affect the fetus by this means.

Using the radio-xenon technique to measure intervillous blood flow, Finnish workers have shown that following generous preload and the liberal use of ephedrine, subarachnoid block with bupivacaine is not associated with any significant changes in maternal placental flow (Jouppila et al, 1984a). Moreover, provided the mother's circulation is preloaded and she is maintained in the lateral position, epidural blockade for analgesia usually *improves* intervillous blood flow (Hollmen et al, 1982), particularly in the presence of pre-eclampsia (Jouppila et al, 1982), in which the haemodynamic changes are definitely favourable (Newsome et al, 1986). During epidural anaesthesia for Caesarean section, changes in intervillous blood flow are inconsistent, a reduced flow usually coinciding with a fall in maternal arterial pressure (Jouppila et al, 1978) while the protective effects of preload (Huovinen et al, 1979) and ephedrine (Hollmen et al, 1984) have been well demonstrated. Other workers have demonstrated the detrimental effect, in terms of fetal acidosis, of 'significant' hypotension following epidural blockade for Caesarean section (Antoine and Young, 1982; Brizgys et al, 1987), while in a retrospective study of cord pH and blood gas measurements, mild to moderate hypotension during spinal anaesthesia was found to be apparently harmless (Norris, 1987).

Doppler ultrasound has been used to measure flow-velocity wave forms in both maternal and fetal circulations. Giles et al (1987) and Long et al (1988) both used continuous-wave Doppler ultrasound systems to record uteroplacental wave forms. The former team demonstrated a fall in the systolic/diastolic ratio following infusion of Hartmann's solution and epidural plain bupivacaine, which they suggested was related to a reduced resistance to blood flow and therefore beneficial. Long et al however detected no significant changes in the uteroplacental pulsatility index following fluid loading or epidural blockade for Caesarean section, and suggested that the findings of Giles et al could simply have reflected hypotension. More accurate estimates of maternal flow can be made from the dorsalis pedis artery using pulsed Doppler, and following positional changes and epidural blockade, changes in this artery are likely to reflect those in the uterine vessels. Janbu (1989) measured changes in dorsalis pedis blood velocity that occurred in response to pain in labour, in the presence and absence of epidural analgesia. In the non-epidural group, there were marked fluctuations in velocity, while with epidural blockade flow was consistent and well maintained.

Fetal flow

Using real-time ultrasound and a pulsed Doppler technique, Lindblad et al (1984) found that preloading and epidural blockade with etidocaine or bupivacaine for Caesarean section had no significant effect on fetal aortic or umbilical blood flow. Giles et al (1987) using continuous-wave Doppler suggested that umbilical resistance was reduced by epidural plain bupivacaine, while Veille et al (1988) recorded negative findings with chloroprocaine and adrenaline. Lindblad et al (1987a) found that fetal aortic flow increased following epidural bupivacaine with adrenaline or plain bupivacaine, but not following etidocaine with adrenaline, prior to Caesarean section. The same team (Lindblad et al, 1988) found insignificant changes in fetal flow following spinal anaesthesia during which maternal blood pressure was well maintained with an infusion of ephedrine. Fetal heart rate increased slightly, and there was evidence of a reduction in placental vascular resistance. Lindblad et al (1987b) also found that epidural analgesia in labour was associated with a small increase in fetal aortic flow. A similar increase was seen in the control group, but not in the group whose mothers had pethidine.

The only possible deduction from all these data is that provided there is no serious maternal hypotension (and this is the crux), epidural and spinal block do not appear to have any detrimental effect on uteroplacental or fetal blood flow and are if anything beneficial.

CARDIOTOCOGRAPHY

Fetal heart-rate changes, though now rather discredited, have in the past been used as an index of fetal well-being, and are often observed following epidural analgesia in labour. Lavin et al (1981) followed changes in 34 low-risk women receiving bupivacaine or chloroprocaine epidurally, and reported some *increased* beat-to-beat variation following bupivacaine, though lignocaine (Lavin, 1982) was associated with tachycardia or loss of variability. Rickford and Reynolds (1983) studied the fetal heart tracings in a series of 70 women before and for 30 minutes after epidural bupivacaine administration; they found no change or improvement in 63, and deterioration (loss of variability, advent of decelerations, dips deepening) in 7, in only 2 of whom was there associated maternal hypotension. All changes were short-lived. Abboud et al (1984) reported occasional decelerations in the fetuses of 61 women receiving bupivacaine, chloroprocaine or lignocaine, most frequently with the former. Nel (1985) reported abnormalities, usually loss of variability in the fetal heart tracing, in 13 out of 58 women given epidural bupivacaine. With the exception of the occasional dip apparently provoked by the initial epidural dose, changes with bupivacaine are probably random and unimportant.

SYMPATHOADRENAL ACTIVITY

The stress response has recently been the subject of interest, and it is currently believed that this response is best suppressed in the mother (particularly in pre-eclampsia) but preserved in the baby, in whom catecholamines may help withstand hypoxia, improve lung function, adapt to extrauterine life and promote imprinting and bonding (Irestedt, 1989).

Both painful labour (Falconer and Powles, 1982; Jouppila et al, 1984b) and Caesarean section under light general anaesthesia (Loughran et al, 1986) can provoke the maternal stress response, which is associated with a rise in maternal catecholamines, particularly noradrenaline, and results in reduced uteroplacental perfusion (Barrier and Sureau, 1982). Epidural analgesia will suppress these adverse changes.

Until term approaches, sympathoadrenal activity is low in the fetus, in the absence of asphyxia. During labour, fetal catecholamine levels may rise higher than with a phaeochromocytoma (Irestedt, 1989). Neonatal catecholamine levels are, however, higher following Caesarean section under epidural anaesthesia than under general or spinal anaesthesia (Haberer and Monteillard, 1986; Hagnevik et al, 1988), although cardiac function is unaffected by bupivacaine dose.

All these findings would therefore appear to favour epidural analgesia for labour and Caesarean section.

THE NEWBORN

In the bad old days of heavy maternal medication, and the use of short-acting local anaesthetics for continuous epidural analgesia, neonatal depression could be detected by the crudest of methods. Nowadays with less maternal sedation, naloxone to reverse depression by pethidine, and the use of bupivacaine in normal labour, the status of the newborn is generally good. Old methods of neonatal assessment such as the Apgar score are insufficiently sensitive to measure the well-being of such a baby delivered vaginally, and most interest has therefore focused on Caesarean section.

Abboud and her colleagues reported one-minute Apgar scores of 7 or more in all of 52 babies born by Caesarean section whether under spinal, epidural or general anaesthesia (Abboud et al, 1985). This confirms the lack of effect also reported by Hollmen et al (1978) in another small series. However, in a retrospective study of 3940 Caesarean sections, Ong et al (1989) reported that babies born with general anaesthesia did less well in terms of Apgar score, need for oxygen and artificial ventilation, than with regional blockade. Evans et al (1989) in a study of 610 Caesarean sections, reported no babies in the epidural group – compared to 6% in the general anaesthesia group – with Apgar scores less than 4 at one minute and less than 7 at five minutes. There was no difference in umbilical artery pH between the groups, suggesting that the difference was indeed anaesthesia-related and not due to any pre-existing asphyxia in the fetuses whose mothers received general anaesthesia. In a study of 126 babies born by emergency Caesarean section for fetal distress, Apgar scores were significantly better with regional than with general anaesthesia (Marx et al, 1984).

High-risk labour has also been the focus of attention in the last ten years. Osbourne et al (1984) reported that epidural analgesia was to be preferred to narcotic analgesia with infants of low birthweight, because it avoided traumatic delivery and was associated with an increase in Apgar score and a reduction in hyaline membrane disease. Twins, particularly the second twin, have also been shown to benefit from epidural analgesia in labour. Crawford (1987) in a prospective study of 200 consecutive twin deliveries, showed that epidural analgesia was associated with reduced metabolic acidosis and less frequent respiratory distress syndrome in the second twin, in whom the detrimental effect of delayed delivery was removed. Babies born to pre-eclamptic women also profit from maternal epidural blockade (Abboud et al, 1982).

Neonatal retinal haemorrhage

Retinal haemorrhage has been used as an index of traumatic delivery, and a greater incidence of more serious haemorrhage is seen in the newborn following instrumental delivery (Van Zundert et al, 1986). Maltau and Egge (1980) found that epidural analgesia reduced the incidence of serious retinal haemorrhage in infants delivered spontaneously, and attributed this to reduced maternal bearing-down effort. Van Zundert et al (1986), on the other hand, found that epidurals only had a significant beneficial effect with instrumental delivery.

Neurobehavioural assessment

Numerous attempts have been made to develop sophisticated indices of neonatal welfare, in order to detect any minor changes that methods of analgesia may have. The Brazelton neonatal behavioural assessment scale (BNBAS) consists of 49 items, and can record progress. It has been claimed (Kuhnert et al, 1985) to be more sensitive to possible drug effects than the early neonatal neurobehavioural scale (ENNS) and the neurological and adaptive capacity score (NACS), which are both shorter; the latter tests however, are designed to detect most drug effects, and are generally popular. The large number of variables in all the tests necessitates a large number of subjects, and can make statistical handling fraught with pitfalls. However, the unwieldy number of items in the BNBAS can be grouped together into five or six 'clusters' (Lester et al, 1982), so improving the power of the test.

Labour

In the early days, continuous epidural analgesia with lignocaine and mepivacaine was shown to produce detectable decrement in the ENNS, but following bupivacaine ENNS scores were no different from those of unmedicated control babies (Kuhnert et al, 1985). However, using a modified BNBAS, Wiener et al (1979) showed that bupivacaine babies had reduced muscle tone up to 48 hours after birth, and performed less well than those who had had naloxone following maternal pethidine. On the other hand Rosenblatt et al (1981), using large doses of epidural bupivacaine *without preload*, demonstrated rather variable and inconsistent decrement in attention and responsiveness scores, but an *increase* in muscle tone a few days after birth. These workers also claimed no difference between mean scores of epidural babies and unmedicated controls, but a dose-related effect of bupivacaine, and suggested that low-dose bupivacaine must have some protective effect on the babies. It is hard to escape the conclusion that the 'dose-related' changes were associated with the length and stressfulness of labour. Kangas-Saarela et al (1987) studied neonatal effects over 4–5 days following epidural bupivacaine or no medication. They found that the only significant differences were on day 1, when epidural babies habituated better and oriented better than controls. Capogna et al (1987) found that the addition of fentanyl to bupivacaine did not affect neurobehavioural performance.

Elective Caesarean section

Hollmen and his colleagues examined infants of mothers who had received either standard general anaesthesia or epidural lignocaine with adrenaline after colloid preload (Hollmen et al, 1978). They found that where there had been maternal hypotension following epidural blockade, infants had impaired rooting and sucking responses, muscle tone and reflexes, as had all high-risk infants. Abboud et al (1985), comparing epidural lignocaine or chloroprocaine, intrathecal amethocaine and general anaesthesia, found that adaptive capacity, tone, primary reflexes and total NACS were worse after general anaesthesia than after regional anaesthesia at 15 minutes and at 2 hours, but by 24 hours there was no difference between the groups.

Other workers have looked at the effect of different local anaesthetics for epidural blockade. Kileff et al (1984) compared plain lignocaine with bupivacaine; despite the use of toxic doses of lignocaine (several mothers reported dizziness and dyspnoea), analgesia was inadequate in 6 out of 23 patients given lignocaine, but hypotension was more frequent. They reported that there was no difference in neurobehavioural score between the two groups, but this was after excluding 13 babies in the lignocaine group because of low Apgar scores and need for special care, as well as inadequate block. It is therefore hard to be confident of their results.

Kuhnert and her colleagues argued that the use of chloroprocaine provided the nearest thing to a drug-free control group (chloroprocaine being generally unmeasurable in the newborn), and using the BNBAS clusters compared this agent with lignocaine for both vaginal delivery and Caesarean section (Kuhnert et al, 1984). The changes they recorded (Figure 1) were variable and lacked consistency and they concluded that prenatal factors were more important than the choice of local anaesthetic. Later, however, the same team (Kuhnert et al, 1988) compared bupivacaine for Caesarean section with the chloroprocaine historical controls and found that the bupivacaine babies performed *better* or improved their performances more rapidly than the controls (Figure 2). Scores were not related to bupivacaine cord levels and were lower with prolonged

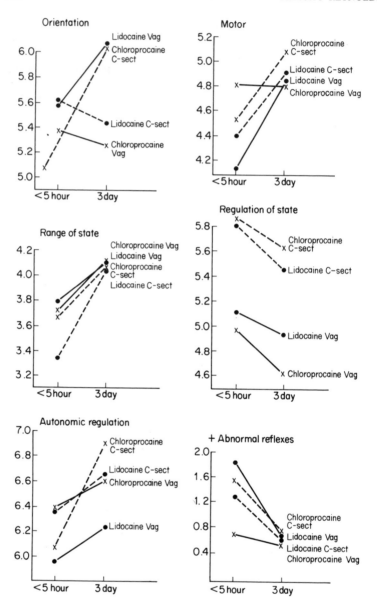

Figure 1. Neurobehavioural scores (BNBAS clusters) of babies born by vaginal delivery (continuous line) or Caesarean section (dotted line) to mothers given epidural chloroprocaine (x) or lignocaine (●). Babies usually improved with age, except in regulation of state. There is no consistent difference between the drugs. Reprinted with permission from the International Anesthesia Research Society from Kuhnert et al (1984).

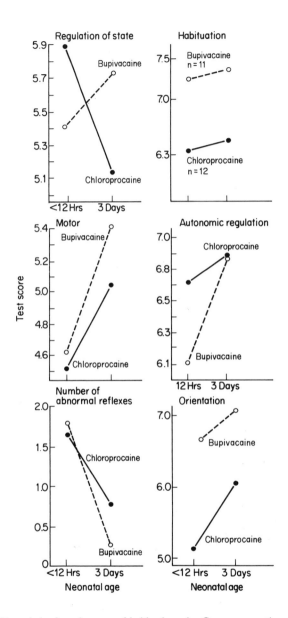

Figure 2. Neurobehavioural scores of babies born by Caesarean section to mothers given epidural bupivacaine (open symbols), compared with chloroprocaine historical controls (closed symbols). Babies performed better and/or recovered faster, and regulation of state improved, following bupivacaine. Reprinted with permission from the International Anesthesia Research Society from Kuhnert et al (1984).

dose–delivery intervals, confirming the extreme unlikelihood that these scores relate to any pharmacological effect of the drugs in the newborn. This is also confirmed by the findings of Jani et al (1989) (summarized on Page 229) that there is no difference in responses between babies born under spinal and epidural bupivacaine. It must be acknowledged, however, that although local anaesthetic doses for Caesarean section are large, there is less time for full fetal drug equilibration than there is following continuous epidural analgesia in labour, as studied by Rosenblatt et al (1981). That bupivacaine babies actually performed *better* than chloroprocaine babies may be related to the better obtunding of maternal stress with the former agent.

Emergency Caesarean section

Nowadays it is becoming increasingly popular to perform emergency Caesarean section under a pre-existing epidural block which can be rapidly extended for the purpose. In these circumstances mothers and babies receive the highest dose of local anaesthetic (Reynolds et al, 1989), and it would perhaps be of interest to compare the effects of general and epidural anaesthesia in these at-risk babies. However, because of the confounding risk factors usually associated with emergency Caesarean section, neurobehavioural studies of such babies have hitherto been few.

Breast-feeding

Breast-feeding after Caesarean section has been shown to be established more quickly (Morgan et al, 1984) and to last longer (Lie and Juul, 1988) following epidural anaesthesia than following general anaesthesia.

Perinatal mortality

Intrapartum and early neonatal death rates are really the only unequivocal measure of outcome in the use of regional analgesia for labour and delivery. An early survey of 6442 births in Cardiff (David and Rosen, 1976) showed that epidural analgesia, though presumably used more in high-risk cases, was associated with a marked reduction in neonatal mortality in low birthweight babies. In two small series of twin deliveries, epidural analgesia was associated with a non-significant halving of the perinatal mortality (Weekes et al, 1977) or no significant difference from historical controls (Jaschevatzky et al, 1977). Osbourne and Patel (1985) associated a marked reduction in the perinatal mortality of low birthweight twins in Dundee around 1976 with, among other things, the increased use of epidural analgesia, although a full statistical analysis was not presented. I have found no more recent comprehensive report on perinatal mortality and regional blocks. Ong et al (1989) studied outcome in 3940 Caesarean sections and found that neonatal mortality under general anaesthesia was double that under regional anaesthesia in elective *and* emergency Caesarean sections, both those performed for fetal distress and in those for failure to progress. Numbers in the treatment groups were not given, but these differences were said not to be significant.

CONCLUSION

Whatever may be the risk/benefit ratio to the mother, all the evidence suggests that, provided the maternal circulation is well maintained, both epidural analgesia in labour and regional block for Caesarean section are, if anything, actually beneficial to the baby, and that of the local anaesthetics in current use bupivacaine would appear the most favourable. It is a pity that women are not told more often of the benefits to the baby of epidural analgesia.

REFERENCES

Abboud T, Artal R, Sarkis F, Henriksen EH & Kammula RK (1982) Sympathoadrenal activity, maternal, fetal and neonatal responses after epidural anesthesia in the pre-eclamptic patient. *American Journal of Obstetrics and Gynecology* **144**: 915–918.

Abboud TK, Afrasiabi A, Sarkis F et al (1984) Continuous infusion epidural analgesia in parturients receiving bupivacaine, chloroprocaine or lidocaine – maternal, fetal and neonatal effects. *Anesthesia and Analgesia* **63**: 421–428.

Abboud TK, Naggappala S, Murakawa K et al (1985) Comparison of the effects of general and regional anesthesia for Cesarean section on neonatal neurologic and adaptive capacity scores. *Anesthesia and Analgesia* **64**: 996–1000.

Antoine C & Young BK (1982) Fetal lactic acidosis with epidural anesthesia. *American Journal of Obstetrics and Gynecology* **142**: 55–59.

Barrier G & Sureau C (1982) Effects of anaesthetic and analgesic drugs on labour fetus and neonate. *Clinics in Obstetrics and Gynaecology* **9**: 351–367.

Brizgys RV, Dailey PA, Shnider SM, Kotelko DM & Levinson G (1987) The incidence of neonatal effects of maternal hypotension during epidural anesthesia for Cesarean section. *Anesthesiology* **67**: 782–786.

Capogna G, Celleno D, McGannon P, Richardson G & Kennedy RL (1987) Neonatal neurobehavioral effects following maternal administration of epidural fentanyl during labor. *Anesthesiology* **67**: A461.

Crawford JS (1987) A prospective study of 200 consecutive twin deliveries. *Anaesthesia* **42**: 33–43.

David H & Rosen M (1976) Perinatal mortality after epidural analgesia. *Anaesthesia* **31**: 1054–1059.

Evans CM, Murphy JF, Gray OP & Rosen M (1989) Epidural versus general anaesthesia for elective Caesarean section. Effect on Apgar score and acid-base status of the newborn. *Anaesthesia* **44**: 778–782.

Falconer AD & Powles AB (1982) Plasma noradrenaline levels during labour. Influence of elective lumbar epidural blockade. *Anaesthesia* **37**: 416–420.

Giles WB, Lah FX & Trudinger BJ (1987) The effect of epidural anaesthesia for Caesarean section on maternal uterine and fetal umbilical artery blood flow velocity waveforms. *British Journal of Obstetrics and Gynaecology* **94**: 55–59.

Haberer JP & Monteillard C (1986) Effets de l'anesthésie peridurale obstétricale sur le foetus et le nouveau né. *Annales Françaises d'Anesthésie et Réanimation* **5**: 381–414.

Hagnevik K, Irestedt L, Lundell B & Skolderfors E (1988) Cardiac function and sympathoadrenal activity in the newborn after Caesarean section under spinal and epidural anaesthesia. *Acta Anaesthesiologica Scandinavica* **32**: 234–238.

Hollmen AI, Jouppila R, Koivisto M et al (1978) Neurologic activity of infants following anesthesia for Cesarean section. *Anesthesiology* **48**: 350–356.

Hollmen AI, Jouppila R, Jouppila P, Koivula A & Vierola H (1982) Effect of extradural analgesia using bupivacaine and 2-chloroprocaine on intervillous blood flow during normal labour. *British Journal of Anaesthesia* **54**: 837–842.

Hollmen AI, Jouppila R, Albright GA et al (1984) Intervillous blood flow during Caesarean section with prophylactic ephedrine and epidural anaesthesia. *Acta Anaesthesiologica Scandinavica* **28**: 396–400.

Huovinen K, Lehtovirta P, Forss M, Kivalo I & Teramo K (1979) Changes in placental intervillous blood flow measured by the ^{133}xenon method during lumbar epidural block for elective Caesarean section. *Acta Anaesthesiologica Scandinavica* **23**: 529–533.

Irestedt L (1989) How does anaesthesia influence fetal and neonatal stress? *Abstracts of the European Society of Regional Anaesthesia*, Oulu, Finland, p 27.

Janbu T (1989) Blood velocities in the dorsal pedis and radial arteries during labour. *British Journal of Obstetrics and Gynaecology* **96**: 70–79.

Jani K, McEvedy B, Harris S & Samaan A (1989) Maternal and neonatal bupivacaine concentrations after spinal and extradural anaesthesia for Caesarean section. *British Journal of Anaesthesia* **62**: 226P–227P.

Jaschevatzky OE, Shalit A, Levy Y & Grunstein S (1977) Epidural analgesia during labour in twin pregnancy. *British Journal of Obstetrics and Gynaecology* **84**: 327–331.

Jouppila R, Jouppila P, Kuikka J & Hollmen A (1978) Placental blood flow during Caesarean section under lumbar extradural analgesia. *British Journal of Anaesthesia* **50**: 275–278.

Jouppila P, Jouppila R, Hollmen A & Koivula A (1982) Lumbar epidural analgesia to improve intervillous blood flow during labor in severe preeclampsia. *Obstetrics and Gynecology* **59**: 158–161.

Jouppila P, Jouppila R, Barinoff T & Koivula A (1984a) Placental blood flow during Caesarean section performed under subarachnoid blockade. *British Journal of Anaesthesia* **56**: 1379–1383.

Jouppila R, Puolakka J, Kauppila A & Vuori J (1984b) Maternal and umbilical cord plasma noradrenaline concentrations during labour with and without segmental extradural analgesia, and during Caesarean section. *British Journal of Anaesthesia* **56**: 251–255.

Kangas-Saarela T, Jouppila R, Jouppila P et al (1987) The effect of segmental epidural analgesia on the neurobehavioural responses of newborn infants. *Acta Anaesthesiologica Scandinavica* **31**: 347–351.

Kileff ME, James FM, Dewan DM & Floyd HM (1984) Neonatal neurobehavioral responses after epidural anesthesia for Cesarean section using lidocaine and bupivacaine. *Anesthesia and Analgesia* **63**: 413–417.

Kuhnert BR, Harrison MJ, Linn PL & Kuhnert PM (1984) Effects of maternal epidural anesthesia on neonatal behavior. *Anesthesia and Analgesia* **63**: 301–308.

Kuhnert BR, Linn PL & Kuhnert PM (1985) Obstetric medical and neonatal behavior. Current controversies. *Clinics in Perinatology* **12**: 423–440.

Kuhnert BR, Kennard MJ & Linn PL (1988) Neonatal neurobehavior after epidural anesthesia for Caesarean section: a comparison of bupivacaine and chloroprocaine. *Anesthesia and Analgesia* **67**: 64–68.

Lavin JP (1982) The effects of epidural anesthesia on electronic fetal heart rate monitoring. *Clinics in Perinatology* **9**: 55–62.

Lavin JP, Samuels SV, Miodovnik M et al (1981) The effects of bupivacaine and chloroprocaine as local anesthetics for epidural anesthesia on fetal heart rate monitoring parameters. *American Journal of Obstetrics and Gynecology* **141**: 717–722.

Lester BM, Als H & Brazelton TB (1982) Regional obstetric anesthesia and newborn behavior: a reanalysis towards synergistic effects. *Child Development* **53**: 687–692.

Lie B & Juul J (1988) Effect of epidural vs general anaesthesia on breast feeding. *Acta Obstetrica Gynaecologica Scandinavica* **67**: 207–209.

Lindblad A, Marsal K, Vernersson E & Renck H (1984) Fetal circulation during epidural analgesia for Caesarean section. *British Medical Journal* **288**: 1329–1330.

Lindblad A, Bernow J & Marsal K (1987a) Obstetric analgesia and fetal aortic blood flow during labour. *British Journal of Obstetrics and Gynaecology* **94**: 306–311.

Lindblad A, Bernow J, Vernersson E & Marsal K (1987b) Effects of extradural anaesthesia on human fetal blood flow *in utero*. Comparison of three local anaesthetic solutions. *British Journal of Anaesthesia* **59**: 1265–1272.

Lindblad A, Bernow J & Marsal K (1988) Fetal blood flow during intrathecal anaesthesia for elective Caesarean section. *British Journal of Anaesthesia* **61**: 376–381.

Long MG, Price M & Spencer JAD (1988) Uteroplacental perfusion after epidural analgesia for elective Caesarean section. *British Journal of Obstetrics and Gynaecology* **95**: 1081–1082.

Loughran PG, Moore J & Dundee JW (1986) Maternal stress response associated with Caesarean delivery under general and epidural anaesthesia. *British Journal of Obstetrics and Gynaecology* **93**: 943–949.

Maltau JM & Egge K (1980) Epidural analgesia and perinatal retinal haemorrhages. *Acta Anaesthesiologica Scandinavica* **24**: 99–101.

Marx GF, Luykx WM & Cohen S (1984) Fetal-neonatal status following Caesarean section for fetal distress. *British Journal of Anaesthesia* **56**: 1009–1013.

Morgan BM, Aulakh JM, Barker JP et al (1984) Anaesthetic morbidity following Caesarean section under epidural or general anaesthesia. *Lancet* **i**: 328–330.

Nel JT (1985) Clinical effects of epidural block during labour. A prospective study. *South African Medical Journal* **63**: 371–374.

Newsome LR, Bramwell RS & Curling PE (1986) Severe preeclampsia: hemodynamic effects of lumbar epidural anesthesia. *Anesthesia and Analgesia* **65**: 31–36.

Norris MC (1987) Hypotension during spinal anesthesia for Cesarean section: does it affect neonatal outcome? *Regional Anesthesia* **12**: 191–194.

Ong BY, Cohen MM & Palahniuk RJ (1989) Anesthesia for Cesarean section – effects on neonates. *Anesthesia and Analgesia* **68**: 270–275.

Osbourne GK & Patel NB (1985) An assessment of perinatal mortality in twin pregnancies in Dundee. *Acta Geneticae Medicae et Gemollogiae* **34**: 193–199.

Osbourne GK, Patel NB & Howat RCL (1984) A comparison of the outcome of low birthweight pregnancy in Glasgow and Dundee. *Health Bulletin* (Edinburgh) **42**: 68–77.

Reynolds F (1987) Placental transfer. In Morgan BM (ed.) *Foundations of Obstetric Anaesthesia*, pp 137–157. London: Farrand Press.

Reynolds F, Laishley R, Morgan B & Lee A (1989) The effect of time and adrenaline on the transplacental distribution of bupivacaine. *British Journal of Anaesthesia* **62**: 509–514.

Rickford WJK & Reynolds F (1983) Epidural analgesia in labour and maternal posture. *Anaesthesia* **38**: 1169–1174.

Rosenblatt B, Belsey EM, Lieberman BA et al (1981) The influence of maternal analgesia on neonatal behaviour. II Epidural bupivacaine. *British Journal of Obstetrics and Gynaecology* **88**: 407–413.

Swanstrom S & Bratteby LE (1981) Metabolic effects of obstetric regional analgesia and of asphyxia in the newborn infant during the first 2 hours after birth. III Adjustment of arterial blood gases and acid-base balance. *Acta Paediatrica Scandinavica* **70**: 811–818.

Thalme B, Belfrage P & Raabe N (1974) Lumbar epidural analgesia in labour. I Acid-base balance and clinical condition of mother, fetus and newborn child. *Acta Obstetrica Gynaecologica Scandinavica* **53**: 27–35.

Van Zundert A, Jansen J, Vaes L et al (1986) Extradural analgesia and retinal haemorrhage in the newborn. *British Journal of Anaesthesia* **58**: 1017–1021.

Veille JC, Youngstrom P, Kanaan C & Wilson B (1988) Human umbilical artery flow velocity waveforms before and after regional anesthesia for Cesarean section. *Obstetrics and Gynecology* **72**: 890–893.

Weekes AR, Cheridjian VE & Mwanje DK (1977) Lumbar epidural analgesia in labour in twin pregnancy. *British Medical Journal* **2**: 730–732.

Wiener PC, Hogg MI & Rosen M (1979) Neonatal respiration, feeding and neurobehavioural state. Effects of intrapartum bupivacaine, pethidine and pethidine reversed by naloxone. *Anaesthesia* **34**: 996–1004.

15

Mothers' views of epidural practices

B. M. MORGAN

Epidural analgesia was once seen by women as heralding a new era of painless labour for all mothers. Over the years the reality has become somewhat different. Women have gained a deeper understanding of the advantages and disadvantages of epidural analgesia and thereby, I believe, gained a better insight into labour itself. Their views will eventually determine many aspects of epidural practice.

Consumer views do influence medical practice; Purdy and Lasnover (1986), in a postal questionnaire of 500 American obstetricians, reported aspects of obstetric practice that seemed to be influenced by the childbirth lobbies. These practices were especially prevalent among younger specialists, and women obstetricians were even more lenient. The move seems to be away from treating the mother as a surgical patient who must be shaved, prepped, placed on an operating table in lithotomy stirrups with an anaesthetized pelvis, and delivered. The approach is towards family-centred obstetrics, encouraging ambulation in labour, with diminished use of conduction and intramuscular analgesia. The presence of the father throughout is permitted or encouraged by 90% of obstetricians and 38% even allow siblings at delivery. These are the sorts of demands mothers have made for many years.

How the mother feels about childbirth is fundamental to our understanding of how she feels about epidural analgesia for labour. 'Control' is the buzzword. The mother's control of the birth event means that she can continue to influence the decisions made, not surrendering responsibility to care providers but rather maintaining a working alliance with midwives and doctors. Maintaining this control leads to a more positive birth experience (Willmuth et al, 1978; Applebaum et al, 1975; Doering et al, 1980; Humenick, 1981). Any treatment or procedure used routinely on all mothers gives the woman the least possible control over her environment (Gillespie, 1981), and this leads to a less satisfactory experience.

The woman's need to maintain control has led to the widespread use of 'birth plans'. The mother can express her wishes in writing before she may be overwhelmed by labour. Usually these birth plans only indicate that she wants nothing done to her that is not essential, and then only with her agreement after adequate explanation – what an indictment of obstetric practice in the past!

Control of the situation is so important because delivery is a major life event with intense personal significance (Kitzinger, 1987). Even greater than the need for analgesia is the need for emotional and psychological support (Farman, 1987), and mothers often consider the midwife more important than the analgesia (Morgan et al, 1984). Women who want, and are given, an active participating role in childbirth are reported as having a more satisfying experience than those who rely on doctors and drugs (Huttle et al, 1972). A more satisfying experience of childbirth leads to greater self-esteem, more self-control and independence (Humenick, 1981). These qualities are beneficial for motherhood and are related to positive mental health.

Factors that are seen to increase the chance of a satisfactory experience are preparation classes (Doering and Entwisle, 1975; Davenport-Slack and Boylan, 1974), partners' involvement and social support by the family (Doering et al, 1980; Felton and Segelman, 1978). Classes do not produce a painless labour (Beck et al, 1980; Melzack et al, 1981) but improve the mother's view of the experience. Social factors are thought to diminish pain and add to enjoyment of labour (Norr et al, 1977). Social support during labour not only improves the mother's experience but also decreases the number of fetal and other labour complications (Sosa et al, 1980).

It is difficult for midwives, let alone doctors, to perceive the mother's experience of labour. Midwives view the pleasantness of labour as more rosy than the mothers do (Bradley et al, 1983a), and I fancy that men rate it worse. An unsatisfactory experience of childbirth may produce long-term psychological morbidity, with increased rates of depression and problems over relationships with the infant and the whole family (Oakley, 1983; Plotsky and Sherenshefsky, 1973).

All mothers are concerned with pain relief in labour, but an increasing number prefer active coping techniques, a tranquil atmosphere and a supportive person. It is believed by mothers and midwives that these techniques in normal labour result in minimal interference and encourage the mother to take responsibility for the progress and outcome of the birth process (Jennings, 1982; Milner,

1986; Crafter, 1987). The addition of minimal analgesia that is patient-controlled, such as Entonox or TENS, is felt to be satisfactory by an increasing number of mothers. At Queen Charlotte's Hospital in 1988 31% of primiparae and 73% of multiparae had no analgesia, not even TENS or Entonox. Walking, and an upright position in the first stage of labour, have been shown by some to improve the outcome of labour (Liu, 1974; Stewart and Calder, 1984; Mendez-Bauer et al, 1975; Flynn et al, 1978), but others have found no benefit (McManus and Calder, 1978). The upright position in the second stage and its effects on the outcome of labour are less clearly beneficial (Gardosi et al, 1989; Stewart and Spiby, 1989).

Epidurals are seen to be the most interventionist form of analgesia (Oakley, 1983), but even worse they are seen to lead to a 'cascade of intervention' (Varney Burst, 1983; Avard and Nimrod, 1985) with augmentation, forceps delivery and episiotomy all at increased rates. Nevertheless, many mothers prefer epidural analgesia in labour to a more active approach. Poore and Cameron Foster (1989) in a study of 90 women, half of whom had epidural analgesia for labour and vaginal delivery, found that mothers with epidurals were more likely to believe in 'powerful others' and show 'passive compliance' rather than active participation in childbirth. These mothers are said to have an 'external locus of control', that is they believe that their life events are mainly controlled by others rather than themselves.

In Kitzinger's review (Kitzinger, 1987), epidural analgesia was seen as a means of gaining or regaining control by some women who found themselves no longer able to cope with labour pain, and by others as producing a loss of control, especially because of the additional interventions and the increased number of professionals involved.

In a study of the opinions of mothers antenatally, their fears about epidurals were of permanent paralysis, and a general fear of injection, but most commonly fear of the effects of epidurals on the labour (Brown, 1988). Many mothers feared the long-term consequences on the baby that might result from the alteration of the labour (Williams, 1985). In Kitzinger's study (1987), 18% of a group of highly self-selected mothers associated with the National Childbirth Trust who volunteered information, thought that they themselves had suffered long-term consequences from epidural analgesia, mostly backache. Williams et al (1985) in a study of 85 mothers found that they believed that effective analgesia is frequently bought at the price of longer labours, obstetric interventions, painful perineums and problems with the bladder postpartum. He suggested that the use of epidurals in normal labour may be ill-advised. Newson (1984) asked the question, 'If women were fully informed, would so many still agree so willingly?'

The causal relationship between epidural analgesia and forceps delivery is accepted as proven by mothers. Anaesthetists often remain in doubt.

Only 18% of women regretted having epidural anaesthesia in Kitzinger's study; this was because there was pressure to consent to it, a poor epidural block, side-effects or forceps delivery. Only 5% felt they had cheated, or were a failure. Fifty per cent found birth a completely positive experience with epidural analgesia. However, it has repeatedly been refuted that painless labour will give a satisfying experience of childbirth to all mothers. A small number of primiparae feel that painless labour has deprived them of part of the experience of childbirth (Billevicz-Driemel and Milne, 1976; Morgan et al, 1982). Slavazza et al (1985) found no difference in self-esteem in a group of 77 primiparae who had received epidural, intramuscular or no analgesia. The epidural group had better analgesia but a less positive feeling about childbirth experience when interviewed 48 hours postpartum. They did, however, describe the infant at birth more positively than the other groups.

It is important that the mother be free to choose her method of analgesia. Many could hardly contemplate labour without epidural analgesia, and others would never consider it. Most do accept that when there is a real threat to the life of mother or child all the necessary technology must be used, including epidural analgesia, which has been shown to improve the fetal state (Sangoul et al, 1975; Levinson et al, 1974; Miller et al, 1974; Gutsche, 1982; Shnider et al, 1983). It must not be forgotten, however, that the psychological impact of this technology is similar to that experienced in intensive care units (Oakley, 1983; Varney Burst, 1983).

The means of identifying the child at risk are poor. Mothers believe that in the diagnosis of possible pathology, modern obstetric practice focuses on the fetus at the expense of the mother to the point that obstetricians believe that they have control over the woman's body, and the emphasis is laid completely on outcome of birth rather than on the birth process. The conflict is about 'who has the right to dictate what the birth experience will be?' (Varney Burst, 1983). The mother needs information at all times to distinguish interference dictated by hospital policy from intervention that is essential for her or her baby.

Mothers believe that much of the 'interference' in labour results from the attitude of their obstetric care-givers, who see labour and delivery as a dangerous rather than a physiological event. An important paper much quoted by authors writing from the mothers' point of view is the retrospective survey of low-risk mothers published by Klein et al (1983). Two comparable groups of 63 primigravidae delivered in the same hospital were studied; one group delivered in a general practitioner unit and the other in a consultant unit, after having shared antenatal care with their general practitioners. The results show that mothers delivered in the general practitioner unit arrived in labour at a more advanced state of cervical dilatation, fewer had analgesia, augmentation or electronic fetal monitoring and the neonatal outcome was better; fewer babies had low Apgar scores and fewer needed intubation. 'There is a strong case to be made to identify women at low risk and to tailor their management so that it is based primarily on supportive care by midwives' (Klein et al, 1983.)

Caesarean section

The literature exposes some ambivalence about epidural analgesia for normal labour and vaginal delivery, but there is no such doubt expressed about epidural anaesthesia for Caesarean section. I have not found a single paper extolling the virtues of general anaesthesia for Caesarean section from the mother's point of view, or one that has cast doubts on the value of conduction anaesthesia to the mother and her emotional acceptance of abdominal delivery. Almost all papers express the view that the psychological problems caused to the mother by Caesarean birth are mitigated by her being conscious during the delivery. Mothers have reported it as a positive experience (Hardwick, 1983), and 'almost as good as natural birth' (Kitzinger, 1987).

Emergency Caesarean section is perceived by mothers to be the most negative birth experience, especially if general anaesthesia is used. These mothers commonly exhibit profound physiological and psychological effects, they display significantly greater hesitancy in naming the infant and more postpartum depression. The effects of the emergency Caesarean section experience can be mitigated by the presence of the father throughout, the use of regional anaesthesia, and being able to see and touch the baby immediately and maintain continuous contact for at least the first hour (Marut and Mercer, 1979; Cranley et al, 1983).

The ill-effects of general anaesthesia for emergency Caesarean section can be diminished by more intensive postpartum nursing (Bradley, 1983b). Overall, the impact of emergency section can be lessened with adequate preparation classes (Fawcett and Henklein, 1987) and postpartum support groups (Cohen, 1977). Poor, inner-city women with few expectations of the childbirth experience exhibited little disappointment at emergency Caesarean section whether under regional or general anaesthesia (Sandelowski and Bustamente, 1988).

One important benefit of the mother's maintaining consciousness is early mother–child contact, which reassures the mother that the infant is hers. Identification and claiming the infant are important

factors in the attachment process (Marut and Mercer, 1979). More
women abuse their children after abnormal delivery, with the rate
of Caesarean sections among abusing mothers almost twice that
among similar non-abusers (Lynch and Roberts, 1977). Early and
continuous contact between mother and newborn is linked with
increased maternal self-confidence, ability to care for the newborn
and success in breastfeeding. Greater maternal interaction is shown
by increased tendency to hold the infant. Fondling, kissing, soothing
and eye-to-eye contact were more commonly observed in mothers
who had contact with the child in the first 12 hours of its life than
in those who did not (Klaus et al, 1972; Ringler et al, 1975;
McClennan and Cabianca, 1980; Hales et al, 1977; Ileifer et al,
1973).

The presence of the father at the birth is one of the most
astonishing changes in obstetric practice over the last twenty years.
From being an 'unnecessary source of infection he has become a
necessary source of affection' (Shearer, 1984). There is no proof of
the beneficial effects of the father's presence nor was there any
proof in the past that it was beneficial to exclude him (Shearer,
1984). He is a source of emotional support to the mother which
makes his presence particularly important in operative deliveries,
especially Caesarean section. Anecdotal reports of mothers' views
regarding the father's presence at Caesarean section under general
anaesthesia have been reported by Marut and Mercer (1979): 'It
reassured the mother that someone would be there to welcome the
baby as she had wanted to – he would note special characteristics
of the infant when it was first born'. Cranley et al (1983) reported
further statements: 'Good to know he was in the delivery room
after I went to sleep and could stay with the baby!' 'It's a special
moment for them [fathers] as well and I feel my husband should
have been there even if I was under anaesthetic. He could have
told me of his feelings about it after I was awake!'

Evidence of an improved father–child relationship has not been
clearly shown to result from the father's presence at the birth or
from early contact with the infant (Palkovitz, 1985; Rodholm and
Larrson, 1979; Cain et al, 1984; Greenberg and Morris, 1974). There
has been surprisingly little interest in the effect on the father himself
of his presence at the birth.

The evidence elucidating mothers' opinions must be viewed with
caution. Much is anecdotal; the studies, when they have been done,
are of small numbers with few controls and often highly selected
populations. The outcomes are often vague or contradictory, the
interpretations at times fanciful. However, people's emotional and
psychological responses are difficult to quantify and are extremely
various, but are no less important because they cannot easily stand
up to scientific scrutiny.

We must listen to what mothers are saying, thinking and feeling. We must believe them and try to understand them; after all, mothers do spend many hours discussing labour and childbirth (Colman and Colman, 1973). Their views are formed by their cultural norms and their peers. We can use their views to improve our practice. We can encourage the mother to make her own decisions about analgesia; we can advise her, and involve her in active participation and discussion. She may need advice on alternatives to epidural analgesia such as patient-controlled analgesia, Entonox and TENS.

There is no doubt that we are in a unique position to improve women's experience of childbirth at Caesarean section. The father should never be expelled if he wishes to stay for any part of the process; this requires us to develop greater confidence in our anaesthetic skills and abilities. We should encourage the use of conduction anaesthesia whenever possible, especially for emergency Caesarean section, for the mother's psychological well-being as well as for her safety (DHSS, 1989).

More important benefits will follow from our efforts to increase facilities and improve the organization of obstetric anaesthetic services. Kitzinger's survey (1987) offers a serious indictment of obstetric anaesthetic skills; epidurals were much delayed or took a long time to be inserted, fathers were often expelled for the procedure, the anaesthetist was in the mother's view often still learning, and 15% of epidurals failed to function adequately. Hypotensive episodes, dural puncture and four cases of accidental total spinal anaesthesia requiring ventilation were reported in her survey. This may not reveal the incidence, but does reveal poor anaesthetic teaching.

Mothers' perceptions of the importance of anaesthetic services for obstetrics are such that 44% of women in a three-city survey would wish to change their booking to a unit where epidural analgesia was available (Macdonald et al, 1988).

Only when mothers' attitudes to childbirth are understood and treated sympathetically by medical and midwifery staff can we hope to regain their trust.

REFERENCES

Applebaum AS, Tuma JM & Johnson JH (1975) Internal–external control and assertiveness of subjects high and low in social desirability. *Psychology Reports* 37: 319–321.

Avard DM & Nimrod CM (1985) Risks and benefits of obstetric epidural analgesia. A review. *Birth* 12: 215–225.

Beck NC, Siegel LZ, Davidson NP et al (1980) The prediction of pregnancy outcome:

maternal preparation, anxiety and attitudinal sets. *Journal of Psychosomatic Research* **24**: 343–351.

Billevicz-Driemel AM & Milne MD (1976) Long-term assessment of extradural analgesia for the relief of pain in labour. II Sense of deprivation after extradural analgesia in labour: relevant or not? *British Journal of Anaesthesia* **48**: 139–144.

Bradley C, Brewin CR & Duncan SLB (1983a) Perceptions of labour: discrepancies between midwives' and patients' ratings. *British Journal of Obstetrics and Gynaecology* **90**: 1176–1179.

Bradley CF, Ross SE & Warnyca J (1983b) A prospective study of mothers' attitudes and feelings following Caesarean and vaginal births. *Birth* **10**: 79–83.

Brown JS (1988) Epidurals: a survey into women's knowledge and attitudes. *Midwife, Health Visitor and Community Nurse* **72**: 24–25.

Cain RL, Pedersen FS, Zaslow MJ & Kramer E (1984) Effects of the father's presence or absence during a Caesarean delivery. *Birth* **11**: 10–15.

Caldeyro-Barcia R (1979) The influence of maternal position on time of spontaneous rupture of membranes, progress of labour and foetal head compression. *Birth and the Family* **61**: 10–18.

Cohen M (1977) Minimising emotional sequelae of Caesarean birth. *Birth* **4**: 114–119.

Colman A & Colman L (1973) *Pregnancy and Psychological Experience*. New York: Seabury Press.

Crafter HR (1987) Study of a couples' planned labour. *Midwives' Chronicle and Nursing Notes* **100**: 302–303.

Cranley MS, Hedahl KJ & Pegg SH (1983) Women's perceptions of vaginal and Caesarean deliveries. *Nursing Research* **32**: 10–15.

Davenport-Slack B & Boylan C (1974) Psychological correlates of childbirth pain. *Psychosomatic Medicine* **36**: 215–223.

DHSS (1989) *Report on Confidential Enquiries into Maternal Deaths in England and Wales 1982–84*, p 95. London: HMSO.

Doering SG & Entwisle D (1975) Preparation during pregnancy and ability to cope with labour and delivery. *American Journal of Orthopsychiatry* **45**: 825–837.

Doering SG, Entwisle DR & Quinlan D (1980) Modelling the quality of women's birth experience. *J Health Soc Behav* **21**: 12–21.

Farman M (1987) A midwife's experience of active birth. *Midwives' Chronicle and Nursing Notes* **100**: 312–316.

Fawcett J & Henklein JC (1987) Antenatal education for Caesarean births: extension of a field test. *Journal of Obstetric Gynecological and Neonatal Nursing* **16**: 61–65.

Felton GS & Segelman FB (1978) Lamaze childbirth training and changes in belief about personal control. *Birth* **3**: 5.

Flynn M, Kelly J, Hollins G & Lynch PF (1978) Ambulation in labour. *British Medical Journal* **2**: 591–593.

Gardosi J, Sylvester S & Lynch CB (1989) Alternative positions in the second stage of labour: a randomised controlled trial. *British Journal of Obstetrics and Gynaecology* **66**: 1290–1296.

Gillespie SA (1981) Childbirth in the 1980s: What are the options? *Issues in Health Care of Women* **3**: 101–128.

Greenberg M & Morris N (1974) Engrossment, the newborn's impact upon the father. *American Journal of Orthopsychiatry* **44(4)**: 520–521.

Gutsche B (1982) Obstetric anaesthesia: Why? *Clinical Perinatology* **9**: 215–224.

Hales DJ, Lozoff B, Soso P et al. (1977) Defining the limits of the maternal sensitive period. *Developmental Medicine and Child Neurology* **19**: 454–456.

Hardwick M (1983) Caesarean section under epidural. A personal account. *British Medical Journal* **287**: 35–36.

Hoffman K, Lorkovic M, Rayburn W & Goodlin R (1987) Alternative birth centres. A few years experience at the University of Nebraska Medical Centres. *Nebraska Medical Journal* 286–288.

Humenick JS (1981) Mastery: the key to childbirth satisfaction? A review. *Birth* **6**: 79–83.

Huttle FA, Mitchell-Fisher MZ & Meyer AE (1972) A quantitative evaluation of psychoprophylaxis in childbirth. *Journal of Psychosomatic Research* **16**: 81–85.

Ileifer AD, Leiderman PH, Barnet CR et al (1979) Effect of mother-infant separation on maternal attachment behaviour. *Child Development* **43**: 1203–1205.

Jennings B (1982) Childbirth choices: are there safe options? *Nurse Practitioner* **7**: 26–37.

Kirchmeier R (1986) Caesarean section: psychological problems. *Nursing* **3**: 52–53.

Kitzinger S (1987) *Some Women's Experiences of Epidurals – a Descriptive Study.* London: National Childbirth Trust.

Klaus MH, Jerrauld R, Kleger NC et al (1972) Maternal attachment – importance of the first postpartum days. *New England Journal of Medicine* **286**: 460–463.

Klein M, Lloyd I, Redman C et al (1983) A comparison of low-risk women booked for delivery in two systems of care. *British Journal of Obstetrics and Gynaecology* **90**: 118–122.

Levinson C, Shnider SM & de Lorrimer AA (1974) Effect of maternal hyperventilation on uterine blood flow and fetal oxygenation and acid-base status. *Anesthesiology* **40**: 340–347.

Liu YC (1974) Effects of an upright position during labour. *Am J Mat Child Nursing* **74**: 2202–2205.

Lynch MA & Roberts J (1977) Predicting child abuse. Signs of bonding failure in the maternity hospital. *British Medical Journal* **1**: 624–626.

McClellan M & Cabianca W (1980) Effects of early mother–infant contact following Caesarean birth. *Obstetrics and Gynecology* **56**: 52–55.

Macdonald R, Owen B & Wilson J (1988) Patients' perceptions of obstetric anaesthetic services. *Anaesthesia* **43**: 601.

McKay S (1982) Maternal position during labour and birth – a reassessment. *Journal of Obstetric Gynecological and Neonatal Nursing* **9**: 288–291.

McManus TJ & Calder AA (1978). Upright posture and the efficiency of labour. *Lancet* i: 72–74.

Marut J & Mercer R (1979) Comparison of primiparas' perception of vaginal and Caesarean births. *Nursing Research* **28**: 260–266.

Melzack R, Raenzer P, Feldman P & Kinch RA (1981) Labour is still painful after prepared childbirth traiing. *Canadian Medical Association Journal* **125**: 357–363.

Mendez-Bauer C, Arroyo J, Garcia Ramos A et al (1975) Effect of standing position on spontaneous uterine contractility and other aspects of labour. *Journal of Perinatal Medicine* **3**: 39–100.

Miller FC, Petrie RH & Acre JJ (1974) Hyperventilation during labour. *American Journal of Obstetrics and Gynecology* **120**: 489–495.

Milner I (1986) Choosing a natural or an active childbirth. *Nursing* **3**: 39–45.

Morgan BM, Bulpitt CJ, Clifton P & Lewis PJ (1982) Analgesia and satisfaction in childbirth. *Lancet* ii: 808–810.

Morgan BM, Bulpitt CJ, Clifton P & Lewis PJ (1984) The consumer's attitude to obstetric care. *British Journal of Obstetrics and Gynaecology* **90**: 624–628.

Newson K (1984) Care during labour. *British Journal of Obstetrics and Gynaecology* **91**: 609–610.

Norr KL, Block CR & Charles A (1977) Explaining pain and enjoyment in childbirth. *Journal of Health and Social Behaviour* **18**: 260–275.

Oakley A (1983) Social consequences of obstetric technology: the importance of measuring 'soft' outcomes. *Birth* **10**: 96–108.

Palkovitz R (1985) Fathers' birth attendance, early contact, and extended contact with the newborn: a critical review. *Child Development* **56**: 392–406.

Plotsky H & Sherenshefsky P (1973) Psychological meaning of labour delivery experience. In Yarrow L & Sherenshefsky P (eds) *Psychological Aspects of a First*

Pregnancy and Early Postnatal Adaptation. New York: Raven Press.

Poore M & Cameron Foster J (1989) Epidural and no epidural anaesthesia: differences between mothers and their experience of birth. *Birth* **12**: 205–213.

Purdy RJ & Lasnover AL (1986) Alternative birth practices and settings – indications of prevalence and use among California obstetricians. *Western Journal of Medicine* **145**: 124–127.

Ringler MM, Kennel JH, Jarvella R et al (1975) Mother-to-child speech at 2 years – effects of early postnatal contact. *Behaviour Paediatric* **86**: 141–144.

Rodholm M (1981) Effects of father–infant postpartum contact on their interaction – 3 months after birth. *Early Human Development* **5**: 79–85.

Rodholm M & Larrson K (1979) Father–infant interaction at the first contact after delivery. *Early Human Development* **3**: 21–27.

Sandelowski M & Bustamante R (1986) Caesarean birth outside the natural childbirth culture. *Research in Nursing and Health* **9**: 81–88.

Sangoul F, Fox GS & Houle CL (1975) Effect of regional anaesthesia on maternal oxygen consumption during the first stage of labour. *American Journal of Obstetrics an Gynecology* **121**: 1080–1083.

Shearer EC (1984) Some limits on small studies of fathers' attendance at Caesarean birth. *Birth* **11**: 15.

Shnider SM, Abboud TK, Artal R, Henrikson S, et al (1983) Maternal catecholamines decrease during labour after lumbar epidural. *American Journal of Obstetrics and Gynecology* **147**: 13–15.

Slavazza K, Mercer RT & Marut JS (1985) Anaesthesia, analgesia for vaginal childbirth: differences in maternal perception. *Journal of Obstetric Gynecological and Neonatal Nursing* **14**: 321–329.

Stewart P & Calder AA (1984) Posture in labour: patients' choice and its effects on performance. *British Journal of Obstetrics and Gynaecology* **91**: 1091–1095.

Stewart P & Spiby H (1989) Posture in labour. *British Journal of Obstetrics and Gynaecology* **66**: 1258–1260.

Sosa R, Kennell J, Klaus M, Robertson S & Urrutia J (1980) The effect of a supportive companion on parental problems, length of labour, and mother–infant interaction. *New England Journal of Medicine* **309**: 597–600.

Varney Burst H (1983) The influence of consumers in the birthing movement. *Topics in Clinical Nursing* **5**: 42–54.

Williams S, Hepburn M & McIlwaine G (1985) Consumers' view of epidural anaesthesia. *Midwifery* **1**: 32–36.

Willmuth LR, Weaver L & Berenstein J (1978). Satisfaction with prepared childbirth and locus of control. *Journal of the Obstetric, Gynecology and Neonatal Nurse* **7**: 33–41.

Current Research 7

Neonatal outcome after spinal or epidural bupivacaine 0.5% for elective Caesarean section

K. JANI, B. McEVEDY, S. HARRIS and S. MILLER

Spinal and epidural blockade are both accepted methods of regional anaesthesia for Caesarean section. Abboud et al (1985) showed that neonates delivered by Caesarean section after spinal anaesthesia scored higher for motor activity at 2 h of age than those delivered after epidural anaesthesia. They used 1% amethocaine for the spinal group, and either 3% 2-chloroprocaine or 2% lignocaine for their epidural group. The smaller amounts of local anaesthetic agent used for spinal anaesthesia could have accounted for higher motor scores; but the use of different local anaesthetic agents in the two groups may be a confounding variable. Our study compared the effects of spinal and epidural anaesthesia, using the same local anaesthetic agent (bupivacaine), on neonatal outcome.

METHOD

After informed consent, 41 healthy parturients scheduled for elective Caesarean section were randomly assigned to receive either spinal ($n = 19$) or epidural ($n = 22$) anaesthesia. The spinal group received a bolus dose of 0.5% plain bupivacaine, and the epidural group received incremental doses of plain bupivacaine 0.5%. At delivery, blood samples were collected from a maternal vein and a double clamped segment of umbilical cord. Bupivacaine concentrations were measured using high-pressure liquid chromatography (detection limit 50 ng ml^{-1}; CV ± 5%). Amiel-Tison's neurological and adaptive capacity scores (NACS) were assessed at 2 h and 24 h of age. Comparisons were made using the Mann Whitney U-test.

RESULTS

See Table 1. The two groups were comparable with regard to maternal and gestational age. The incidence of hypotension (systolic < 100 mmHg) was higher in the spinal group (65%) compared to the epidural group (38%) and required more ephedrine ($P < 0.05$). Maternal and umbilical bupivacaine concentrations were higher in the epidural group ($P < 0.001$). All neonates weighed > 2.5 kg; none had 1-min or 5-min Apgar scores < 7, or a cord vein pH < 7.25. The neonates from both groups had comparable scores for adaptive capacity and for the four groups of neurological assessment of the NACS at 2 and 24 h after delivery ($P < 0.1$) (Table 2).

Table 1.

	Spinal group		Epidural group	
	n	median (range)	n	median (range)
Maternal weight (kg)	19	72 (62–92)	22	67 (48–90)
Bupivacaine dose (mg kg^{-1})	19	0.14 (0.12–0.19)	22	1.7 (1.17–3.03)
Maternal bupivacaine concentration (ng/ml^{-1})	7	61 (50–90)	22	770 (390–1310)
Umbilical bupivacaine concentration (ng/mg^{-1})	18	< 50	22	155 (50–400)

Table 2. Total NACS (mean ± SEM).

	Spinal group ($n = 11$)	Epidural group ($n = 17$)
NACS at 2 h	34.5 ± 0.9	33.5 ± 0.8
NACS at 24 h	36.3 ± 0.7	35.2 ± 0.5

CONCLUSION

The bupivacaine concentrations in this study are comparable to data reported using more sensitive measurement techniques (Kuhnert et al, 1987). Although the NACS may have missed subtle differences in neurobehaviour, neither the higher umbilical blood concentration of bupivacaine in the epidural group nor the higher incidence of hypotension in the spinal group produced an adverse neonatal outcome.

References

Abboud TK, Nagapalla S, Murakawa et al (1985) Comparison of the effects of general and regional anesthesia for Cesarean section on neonatal neurological and adaptive capacity scores. *Anesthesia and Analgesia* **64**: 996–1000.

Kuhnert BR, Zuspan KJ, Kuhnert PM et al (1987) Bupivacaine disposition in mother, fetus, and neonate after spinal anesthesia for Cesarean section. *Anesthesia and Analgesia* **66**: 407–412.

SECTION VI – DISCUSSION

CHAIRMAN: DR. ANDREW DOUGHTY

Dr Gutsche In response to Dr Morgan, I would deny that epidural analgesia necessarily detracts from the mother's joy in the experience of labour and delivery. In the cities of the United States, hospitals which provide an epidural service virtually on demand succeed in attracting many more patients. As a result, other hospitals are forced into providing similar facilities.

As a man, I cannot presume to tell a woman anything of what she feels in labour; but I do believe that the obstetric anaesthesiologist can help her, not only by giving instruction classes in the antenatal period but also by his presence as soon as she is admitted to hospital in labour.

I believe that we have the twofold function of preserving life and alleviating pain and I agree with Crawford when he said 'Pain of labour serves no useful function, it is an abomination, it is of no more value than the appendix. If the appendix offends us, we remove it, if pain is a feature of labour we should abolish it' (Crawford, 1983). As an anaesthesiologist I would like to help those women who want the pain abolished and I make no apologies for doing so.

Dr Morgan No mother wants to be in a situation where she cannot be helped when necessary, any more than she wants to be in a hospital where there is no intensive care unit. She knows that she may need one, but that does not mean that she wants to be *in* one. Much has been written recommending what I regard as poor anaesthetic practice, of which Dr Gutsche's quotation from Crawford is a prime example. It is based on a lack of understanding of what mothers feel about the very nature of childbirth. Certainly no one wants a mother to suffer unnecessary pain but labour must never be regarded in the same light as appendicitis.

Dr Thomas From recent personal experience I have found that pain due to exercising is no fun. I can also tell you that TENS is effective only if it is turned up so high that it hurts more than the pain. Back-rubbing is quite nice but it doesn't provide much pain relief. But then I didn't realize that mastery over my pain without any sort of help was supposed to increase my self-confidence.

Obviously I had not been appropriately brainwashed, so I suspect that you, Dr Morgan, have been presenting us with a Saatchi and Saatchi exercise that was launched years ago by a number of women's organizations. Should we not be launching our own Saatchi and Saatchi campaign in order to introduce a little sanity into the situation? I do not wish to match the stance of Dr Gutsche, but there must be a way for us to provide support for patients without deceiving them or ourselves.

Dr Macdonald Anaesthetists would do well to consider the whole concept of their work in the matenity unit. Let us not forget that we are there to contribute to the care of the sick obstetric patient. While we provide analgesia for the mother who wants it, our task is primarily to provide epidural or spinal analgesia for those with an obstetric indication. At the same time, an obstetric anaesthetist must always consider the patient's wishes. She may not want to have a painless labour, she may just wish to be comfortable. At my hospital we make every effort to discuss the management of the epidural and the second stage with the patient. It is the younger (male) anaesthetists who feel that they have failed if they do not confer on the mother a pain-free labour. In normal labour the mother's feelings are of paramount importance.

Dr Lyons For some time I have been teaching my juniors that the purpose of our service to patients is not necessarily to give them a totally pain-free labour. As soon as the mother expresses satisfaction, *that* is the point of success even though the quality of the block may be objectively incomplete.

Dr Morgan I agree with you. Actually, epidurals too often provide anaesthesia rather than just analgesia. We should now be trying to refine our techniques so that we can provide analgesia alone. In reply to Dr Thomas I would say that I think our Saatchi and Saatchi story ought to be that, as doctors, we are here to treat pathology. We know that we run into trouble when we try and treat physiology as if it were pathology. Half our difficulty is that we are often unable to distinguish one from the other.

Dr Naulty The issue of the patient's 'locus of control' – that is, who the patient perceives is in charge of her analgesic management – is an interesting one that is noted throughout the nursing literature. As an example of this, we have been using a patient-controlled analgesia device to infuse epidural local anaesthetics and narcotics in labour in one of our rersearch protocols. Some patients receive continuous infusions, and others continuous infusions at a lower rate with the ability to deliver top-up doses via the PCA button. It is interesting that even those patients whose PCA button is programmed to be non-functional, uniformly report better analgesia than do those who do not have the PCA button at all. More importantly, they also report a much higher level of satisfaction with the analgesia if they feel they, rather than the anaesthesiologist or obstetrician, are in some sort of control of their analgesia.

Dr Reynolds Dr Macdonald rightly recommended that we should strive to make an epidural service available to every parturient (Chapter 2). One thing is certain, that we cannot rely on a consumer groundswell to help us in our efforts to expand the service nationwide. Labour can be like knocking your head against a brick wall: it is so nice when you leave off. This fact, and having a live baby at the end generate a great sense of euphoria, and this coupled with natural amnesia for extreme pain with an unmodified delivery, generate a strong sense of satisfaction when the event is viewed in retrospect. If delivery is not quick and straightforwad, and epidural analgesia and other intervention become necessary, the event will be viewed as less satisfying (Morgan et al, 1982). Cause and effect are then transposed, and epidural analgesia is coupled with other interventions as undesirable interference in what would otherwise be a trouble-free natural event. Only a minority of primiparas believe they would like epidural analgesia before the event, though many more find they need it once they experience labour, but afterwards cannot remember why they wanted it when they did. We are there, however, to treat pain and distress with compassion at the time, as well as to bring both mother and baby the greater safety that well-conducted regional analgesia can provide. Antenatal preparation should not be geared to making women feel guilt and failure when they find that they, like the majority, experience considerable pain in labour. They should feel that in choosing epidural analgesia they are making a wise decision.

References

Crawford JS (1984) From an address to the Royal College of Obstetricians and Gynaecologists.

Morgan BM, Pulpitt CJ, Clifton P & Lewis PJ (1982) Analgesia and satisfaction in childbirth (The Queen Charlotte's 1000 mother survey) *Lancet* **ii**: 808–810.

Postscript

It is indeed a unique experience for one long retired from active practice to be asked to make some personal comments on this third Symposium held under the auspices of the Obstetric Anaesthetists' Association. Reviewing the events of the past 20 years in Britain, one might say that the battle against unreasonable prejudice towards obstetric epidurals was fought and won in the 1970's to be replaced by the bid to curb unbridled enthusiasm in the 1980's. Epidural anaesthesia has matured in 1990 to become a recognised integrated part of modern obstetric management. The field has been broadened by the acquisition of new partners; subarachnoid block, introduced in 1900 by Kreis and superseded by the sacral epidural approach by Stoeckel in 1909, is now fully reinstated; opioids as well as local anaesthetics may be injected into the epidural space and the synergism of the two groups of compounds is being explored and exploited.

What lessons have I learned from attending the symposium and from reading its published proceedings? In the hypothetical circumstances of my accepting another appointment as an obstetric anaesthetist, I would certainly modify the practices that seemed the best available to me six years ago. First of all, I would like to work at a hospital where my senior obstetric colleagues are closely involved in labour ward activities (Chapter 5). I am now convinced that I must always insert the Tuohy needle by the paramedian approach instead of reserving it for the occasions when midline insertion appears to be impracticable (Chapter 1). For labour pain relief I would give dilute bupivacaine solution by continuous infusion (Chapter 4) possibly adding sufentanil (Chapter 12). I cannot forget that it was compassion that first motivated me to give epidurals, so I would continue to feel justified in offering them to mothers who appear to be in pain, braving the retrospective ingratitude of some (Chapter 15) for the sake, at least, of the unspoken approval of their infants (Chapter 14).

For Caesarean section I would set up the epidural by giving 20 ml of *warmed* 0.5% bupivacaine (Current Research 4) in the left lateral position, adding adrenaline to improve the onset and efficacy of the block (Current Research 3) and then insert the catheter for the injection of the incremental doses. I now learn that it is neither necessary nor desirable to give some portion of the dose in the vertical posture to ensure sacral root blockade (Chapter 11). An opioid, possibly methadone, would be given via the catheter for post-operative pain relief (Current Research 5).

I confess to a long-held prejudice against puncturing the dura mater either deliberately or inadvertently, but Chapter 10 and Discussion IV have taught me that there are situations in which subarachnoid block may be the right choice. However, I am still waiting to learn an easy way to persuade a mother with an intractable headache to accept, with confidence, another spinal injection for its cure with a blood patch. Perhaps the headache itself is the most potent persuader!

Andrew Doughty

REFERENCES

Kreis O (1900) Über Medullanarkosen bei Gebärenden. Zentralblatt für Gynäkologie **28**: 724–729.
Stoeckel W (1909) Über sakrale Anästhesie. Zentralblatt für Gynäkologie **33**: 1–15.

INDEX

Abdominal binder, spinal headache management with, 99
Abdominal cavity, pain pathways from (relating to Caesarean section), 140
Accidental total spinal block, 107–118
management, 110–112
α_1-acid glycoprotein binding of local anaesthetics, 86–7
Acid pulmonary aspiration, 128–9
ACTH in the management of dural puncture headache, 121–2
Adrenaline (epinephrine), 143, 153–4
bupivacaine with, 85–6, 153, 161
in Caesarean section, 143, 153–4, 161
epidural opiates with, 173, 191
in epidural test doses, 44, 45, 46
lignocaine with, 153–4
safety, 154
Adrenocorticotrophic hormone (ACTH) in the management of dural puncture headache, 121–2
Air, loss of resistance to injection of, 11–12
Air embolism, chest pain and dyspnoea associated with, 136
Alfentanil, epidural
bupivacaine and, 176–7
continuous infusion, 56
Alkalinization of anaesthetic, in spinal vs. epidural blockade, 141
Anaesthesia
general, see General anaesthesia

local/regional, see Local anaesthesia
Anaesthetics, local, see Local anaesthetics
Anatomy of epidural region, see Epidural region
Antacids in acid pulmonary aspiration management, 129
Anticoagulant therapy, epidural blockade contraindicated in, 22
Antidiuretic therapy, in the management of spinal headache, 99
Anxiety of mother about epidurals, 221
Apgar score of neonate born by Caesarean section, 209
under epidural methadone, 201
under regional vs. general anaesthesia, 133–4, 209
Arteries, spinal/epidural, anatomy, 6
Aspiration, acid pulmonary, 128–9
Aspiration test for catheter placement, 43, 46, 76, 77
Aspirin, epidural blockade contraindicated in patients ingesting, 22
Asthma, epidural analgesia in patients with, 23
Awareness, unplanned, in general anaesthesia, 130–1

Babies, see Newborn
Birth
mothers' views, 210–25
multiple, epidural blockade indicated with, 29

239